HOW THE
Brain Learns
to Read

David A. Sousa

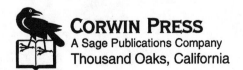

CORWIN PRESS
A Sage Publications Company
Thousand Oaks, California

For information:

 Corwin Press
A Sage Publications Company
2455 Teller Road
Thousand Oaks, California 91320
www.corwinpress.com

Sage Publications Ltd.
1 Oliver's Yard
55 City Road
London EC1Y 1SP
United Kingdom

Sage Publications India Pvt. Ltd.
B-42 Panchsheel Enclave
Post Box 4109
New Delhi 110 017 India

Printed in the United States of America

Library of Congress Cataloging-in-Publication Data

Sousa, David A.
How the brain learns to read / David A. Sousa.
    p. cm.
Includes bibliographical references and index.
ISBN 978-1-4129-0600-5 (cloth) – ISBN 978-1-4129-0601-2 (pbk.)
  1. Reading. 2. Reading disability—Physiological aspects.
3. Brain. I. Title.
LB1573.S7845 2005
418'.4'019—dc22   2004052713

This book is printed on acid-free paper.

07 08 09 10 11 12   10 9 8 7 6 5

Acquisitions Editor:	Robert D. Clouse
Editorial Assistant:	Jingle Vea
Production Editor:	Diane S. Foster
Typesetter:	C&M Digitals (P) Ltd.
Proofreader:	Kristen Bergstad
Cover Designer:	Tracy E. Miller
Graphic Designer:	Anthony Paular

Contents

Acknowledgments

Corwin Press gratefully acknowledges the contributions of the following people:

Sandra Anderson
Educational Consultant
Exemplary Education, L.L.C.
Newcastle, VA

Lori Benton
Reading Specialist
Oakshire Elementary School
Orlando, FL

Diane Barone
Professor, Literacy Studies
Department of Educational Studies
University of Nevada, Reno
Reno, NV

Aileen Carew
Reading Specialist
Bel Aire School
Tiburon, CA

Robin Fogarty
Professional Development Consultant
Robin Fogarty & Associates, Ltd.
Chicago, IL

Jeanine Heil
Professional Development Coordinator
Office of Reading First
N. J. Department of Education
Trenton, NJ

Natalie McAvoy
Reading Specialist
Tibbets Elementary School
Elkhorn, WI

Harvey F. Silver & Richard Strong
Educational Consultants
Silver Strong Associates
Ho-Ho-Kus, NJ

Marilee Sprenger
Educational Consultant
Peoria, IL

Barbara Townsend
Reading Specialist
West Side Elementary School
Elkhorn, WI

Pat Wolfe
Educational Consultant
Napa, CA

About the Author

David A. Sousa, Ed.D., is an international educational consultant. He has made presentations at national conventions of educational organizations and has conducted workshops on brain research and science education in hundreds of school districts and at several colleges and universities across the United States, Canada, Europe, and Asia.

Dr. Sousa has a bachelor of science degree in chemistry from Massachusetts State College at Bridgewater, a master of arts in teaching degree in science from Harvard University, and a doctorate from Rutgers University. His teaching experience covers all levels. He has taught junior and senior high school science, served as a K–12 director of science, and was Supervisor of Instruction for the West Orange, New Jersey, schools. He then became superintendent of the New Providence, New Jersey, public schools. He has been an adjunct professor of education at Seton Hall University, and a visiting lecturer at Rutgers University. He was president of the National Staff Development Council in 1992.

Dr. Sousa has edited science books and published numerous articles in leading educational journals on staff development, science education, and brain research. He has received awards from professional associations and school districts for his commitment and contributions to research, staff development, and science education. He recently received the Distinguished Alumni Award and an honorary doctorate in education from Bridgewater (Mass.) State College.

He has appeared on the NBC *Today* show and on National Public Radio to discuss his work with schools using brain research. He makes his home in south Florida.

Reading is to the mind what exercise is to the body.

— Sir Richard Steele

Introduction

~~~~~~

Most of us don't recall much about learning to talk. It just seemed to come naturally. We probably don't remember much about how we learned to read either. As adults, reading seems so effortless and automatic that we often assume it should be an easy skill for almost any child to acquire. But that is not the case. Learning to speak is an innate ability supported by specialized areas of the brain, and is automatic for almost all children raised in normal circumstances. But for many children, learning to read is a long, complicated task requiring years of conscious effort.

Have you ever thought about what your brain goes through when you read? First, your eyes have to scan those squiggly lines and curves called the alphabet and group them into the words as indicated on the page. Then, certain areas of the brain work to associate the written symbols with the sounds of language already stored in your head. As this association occurs, other neural networks decode the writing into a mental message that you understand. Incredibly, your brain can process and comprehend an entire sentence in a few seconds. It almost seems like magic. But it isn't magic. Reading is the result of an elaborate process that involves decoding abstract symbols into sounds, then into words that generate meaning. Can you remember the first time you encountered printed text and saw those letters? Just turn this page upside down and you get an idea of how alien those squiggles must have looked at first and what a struggle it was to make sense of them.

THE BAD NEWS AND THE GOOD NEWS

The Bad News

Educators have been well aware of the difficulties involved in learning to read and have long debated the best ways to teach beginning reading. No one method or program has triumphed, as evidenced by the lack of substantial progress in improving reading achievement scores. Despite all the time and resources devoted to reading programs, nearly two-thirds of low-income fourth graders cannot read at the proficient level. Grade 8 students have made no gains in reading achievement in the past decade, and the reading scores of grade 12 students have actually declined in that same time period (NAEP, 2003). The number of students identified with reading problems, including dyslexia, is growing rapidly. No one is sure if this is because more students are developing difficulties in reading or whether school districts are getting better at diagnosing previously unidentified students. One thing seems certain: Students who are poor readers in their early years remain poor readers in their later years.

A decades-long battle over the best way to help children learn to read has only polarized the educational community. Critics argue that reading instruction has been out of touch with research in that too many programs minimize the teaching of phoneme-grapheme relationships. The selection of reading programs has often been fueled by debates of philosophical stances and advocacies that have little to do with what research is uncovering about how children learn to read.

The Good News

Scientific methods are now available to study how the brain acquires reading skills. In the last two decades, brain researchers have developed new technologies for looking inside the living brain. These technologies fall into two major categories: those that look at brain *structure* and those that look at brain *function*. When aimed at the brain, computerized axial tomography (CAT) and magnetic resonance imaging (MRI) are very useful diagnostic tools that produce computer images of the brain's internal structure. For example, they can detect tumors, malformations, and the damage caused by cerebral hemorrhages.

Different technologies, however, are required to look at how the brain works. An alphabet soup describes the five most common procedures that can be used to isolate and identify the areas of the brain where distinct levels of activity are occurring. The technologies are the following:

- Electroencephalography (EEG)
- Magnetoencephalography (MEG)
- Positron Emission Tomography (PET)
- Functional Magnetic Resonance Imaging (fMRI)
- Functional Magnetic Resonance Spectroscopy (fMRS)

Here is a brief explanation of how each one works. A summary chart follows.

- ***Electroencephalography (EEG) and Magnetoencephalography (MEG).*** These two techniques are helpful in determining how quickly something occurs in the brain. To do that, they measure electrical and magnetic activity occurring in the brain during mental processing. In an EEG, anywhere from 19 to 128 electrodes are attached to various positions on the scalp with a conductive gel so electrical signals can be recorded in a computer. In a MEG, about 100 magnetic detectors are placed around the head to record magnetic activity. EEGs and MEGs can record changes in brain activity that occur as rapidly as one millisecond (one-thousandth of a second), typical times when the brain is processing language. When a group of neurons responds to a specific event (like a word), they activate and their electrical and magnetic activity can be detected above the noise of the nonactivated neurons. This response is called an *Event-Related Potential* or ERP. ERP evidence has provided information about the time needed for the brain to process reading, including times associated with recognizing the letters and hearing the sounds in one's head. EEG and MEG do not expose the subject to radiation and are not considered hazardous.

- *Positron Emission Tomography (PET).* The first technology to observe brain functions, it involves injecting the subject with a radioactive solution that circulates to the brain. Brain regions of higher activity accumulate more of the radiation, which is picked up by a ring of detectors around the subject's head. A computer displays the concentration of radiation as a picture of blood flow in a cross-sectional slice of the brain regions that are aligned with the detectors. The picture is in color, with the more active areas in reds and yellows, the quieter areas in blues and greens. Two major drawbacks to PET scans are the invasive nature of the injection and the use of radioactive materials. Consequently, this technique is not used with normal children because the radioactive risk is too high.

- *Functional Magnetic Resonance Imaging (fMRI).* This newer technology is rapidly replacing PET scans because it is painless, noninvasive, and does not use radiation. The technology helps to pinpoint the brain areas of greater and lesser activity. Its operation is based on the fact that when any part of the brain is used for thinking, the need for oxygen and nutrients increases. Oxygen is carried to the brain cells by hemoglobin. Hemoglobin contains iron, which is magnetic. The fMRI uses a large magnet to compare the amount of oxygenated hemoglobin entering brain cells with the amount of deoxygenated hemoglobin leaving the cells. The computer colors in the brain regions receiving more oxygenated blood and can locate the activated brain region to within one centimeter (less than a half-inch).

- *Functional Magnetic Resonance Spectroscopy (fMRS).* This technology involves the same equipment as fMRI but uses different computer software to record levels of various chemicals in the brain while the subject is thinking. Like the fMRI, fMRS can precisely pinpoint the area of activity, but it can also identify whether certain key chemicals are also present at the activation site. fMRS has been used to study language function in the brain by mapping the change in specific chemicals, such as lactate, that respond to brain activation during tasks involving language.

Techniques for Mapping Brain Functions		
Technique	**What It Measures**	**How It Works**
Electroencephalography (EEG) Magnetoencephalography (MEG)	The electrical and magnetic activity occurring in the brain during mental processing. The spikes of activity are called Event-Related Potentials (ERP).	In EEG, multiple electrodes are attached to the scalp to record electrical signals in a computer. In MEG, magnetic detectors are placed around the head to record magnetic activity. EEGs and MEGs record changes in brain activity that occur as rapidly as one millisecond. When a group of neurons responds to a specific event, they activate and their electrical and magnetic activity can be detected. This response is called an Event-Related Potential or ERP.
Positron Emission Tomography (PET)	Amount of radiation present in brain regions	The subject is injected with a radioactive solution that circulates to the brain. Brain regions of higher activity accumulate more radiation, which is picked up by a ring of detectors. A computer displays the concentration of radiation in a cross-sectional slice of the brain regions aligned with the detectors. The picture shows the more active areas in reds and yellows, the quieter areas in blues and greens.
Functional Magnetic Resonance Imaging (fMRI)	Levels of deoxygenated hemoglobin in brain cells	Any part of the brain that is thinking requires more oxygen, which is carried to the brain cells by hemoglobin. The fMRI uses a large magnet to compare the amount of oxygenated hemoglobin entering brain cells with the amount of deoxygenated hemoglobin leaving the cells. The computer colors in the brain regions receiving more oxygenated blood and locates the activated brain region to within one centimeter (half-inch).
Functional Magnetic Resonance Spectroscopy (fMRS)	Levels of specific chemicals present during brain activity	This technology involves the same equipment as fMRI but uses different computer software to record levels of various chemicals in the brain while the subject is thinking. fMRS can precisely pinpoint the area of activity, but it can also identify whether certain key chemicals are also present at the activation site.

Using these technologies, researchers have been able to explore how different brains function when carrying out certain tasks, including reading. Here are just a few of the fascinating things that have been uncovered:

- Novice readers use different cerebral pathways while reading than skilled readers
- People with reading difficulties use different brain regions to decode written text than do typical readers
- The brains of people with reading problems are working harder during reading than those of skilled readers
- Even though dyslexia is a brain disorder, it is treatable
- With proper instructional intervention, the brains of young struggling and dyslexic readers can actually be rewired to use cerebral areas that more closely resemble those used by typical readers

As a result of these discoveries, it is now possible to identify with a high degree of accuracy those children who are at greatest risk of reading problems, even before the problems develop, to diagnose the problems accurately, and to manage the problems with effective and proven treatment programs (Shaywitz, 2003). It is not exaggerating to say that reading is very likely the one area of school curriculum to date where neuroscience and cognitive psychology have made their greatest impact. The brain imaging studies have opened a new field in neuroscience that some call developmental cognitive neurology (Habib, 2003). Here one observes how the developing brain reacts to various kinds of environmental constraints. Future studies will enable scientists and educators to work together to better understand both the typical brain as well as the causes and possible treatments for learning deficiencies, including dyslexia.

> It is not exaggerating to say that reading is very likely the one area of school curriculum where neuroscience has made its greatest impact.

ABOUT THIS BOOK

I have been asked on many occasions to give specific examples of how the fruits of scientific research can have an impact on educational practice. That question is a lot easier to answer now than it was 15 years ago because recent discoveries in cognitive neuroscience have given us a deeper understanding of the brain. We now have more knowledge of our short-term and long-term memory systems, the impact of emotions on learning, and how we acquire language and motor skills. But the greatest contribution to date, in my opinion, is the growing body of research on how the brain learns to read.

Because reading is essential for success in our society, teaching all children to read is every school district's highest curriculum priority. Although many children learn to read well, too large a number encounter difficulties. Numerous reasons are cited for this unfortunate situation, such as poor home environment, physical and psychological deficits, and inadequate reading instruction. Regardless of the reasons, teachers of reading are still faced with the awesome responsibility of getting each child to learn the difficult task of reading. The more these teachers know about how the brain learns to read, the more likely they are to choose instructional strategies that will result in successful learning. The purpose of this book is to present what scientists currently believe about how young humans acquire spoken language and then use that capability when learning to read.

Questions This Book Will Answer

This book will answer questions such as these:

- *How do we learn spoken language?*
- *Does a family's socioeconomic status affect a child's vocabulary development?*
- *What must the brain be able to do in order to learn to read effectively?*
- *What has research found out about the effectiveness of the phonics and whole-language approaches to reading instruction?*
- *What are the implications of the current research in reading on everyday classroom practice?*
- *How important is spelling and invented spelling in learning to read?*
- *What strategies are effective in teaching students with limited English proficiency to read?*
- *Why is reading so difficult for so many children?*
- *What do we mean by reading problems?*
- *What have brain imaging scans revealed about the nature of dyslexia?*
- *How can elementary and secondary school classroom teachers successfully detect reading problems?*
- *What are the basic ingredients of successful early intervention programs?*
- *How have some intervention programs actually rewired the brains of struggling readers?*
- *What can secondary school content area teachers do to help their poor readers be more successful in comprehending the course material?*
- *What are the basics of a successful reading program?*
- *What do beginning readers need to learn and what do teachers need to know about teaching reading?*

Chapter Contents

Chapter 1. Learning Spoken Language. Children's competence in spoken language greatly influences how quickly and successfully they learn to read. This chapter examines how the young brain detects language sounds from the background noise and begins to recognize the words, pitch, and tempo of a native language. It looks at the specialized regions of the brain that work together and manipulate sounds to build words, phrases, and sentences, and at how the brain cleverly groups words and phrases to increase the speed of spoken language comprehension.

Chapter 2. Learning to Read. This chapter explores the various stages that the brain must go through while learning to read, including the process of building sounds into words, words into phrases, and phrases into sentences. The alphabetic principle is introduced here as well as the roles that short-term and long-term memories play in reading. Also discussed here are the fascinating discoveries that brain imaging scans have revealed about the cerebral mechanisms responsible for decoding written text and the different neural pathways used by novice and skilled readers.

Chapter 3. Teaching Reading. This chapter reviews the history of the debate over whether phonics or whole-language is the better method for beginning reading instruction. It cites the scientific studies that have gained a deeper understanding of how the brain learns to read. From these studies come valuable implications that educators can consider when deciding on the components of a reading program and on selecting instructional strategies in beginning reading that are likely to be more successful with more students.

Chapter 4. Recognizing Reading Problems. Because early detection of reading problems is essential for early intervention, this chapter focuses on the potential causes of reading difficulties, including what brain imaging scans have revealed about the nature of struggling readers and dyslexia. Also discussed here are the clues that teachers should look for at various grade levels to determine whether a student is having persistent difficulties with reading.

Chapter 5. Overcoming Reading Problems. Numerous suggestions are offered in this chapter for teachers and parents to help students overcome their reading problems. The components of early intervention programs are discussed in some detail as well as successful strategies for older students. Featured here is a discovery of great interest that came from imaging studies: certain reading interventions can actually rewire the brains of struggling readers so that they more closely resemble the neural mechanisms used for reading in the brains of skilled readers.

Chapter 6. Reading in the Content Areas. This chapter discusses the major differences between developmental reading (learning to read) and content area reading (reading to learn). It presents some tested strategies that secondary school content area teachers can use with students who are poor readers to help them understand vocabulary and gain a more accurate and deeper understanding of the content material they are reading. It highlights the value of graphic organizers and suggests some reading patterns that are unique to different subject areas.

       Chapter 7. Putting It All Together. Finally, this chapter examines the essential pieces that are needed to develop, select, implement, and support an effective reading program, based on our current scientific understandings of how the brain learns to read. It suggests what beginning readers need to learn, what teachers need to know about teaching reading, and what kind of professional development needs to be implemented to support the reading program. Some suggestions for closing the reading achievement gap are proposed.

       Most of the chapters contain suggestions for translating the research on reading into instructional practice. These suggestions are indicated with a checkmark (✓).

       The information presented here was current at the time of publication. However, as scientists continue to explore the inner workings of the brain, they will likely discover more about the cerebral mechanisms involved in learning to read. These discoveries should help parents and educators understand more about reading, reading problems, and effective reading instruction.

ASSESSING YOUR CURRENT KNOWLEDGE OF READING

The value of this book can be measured in part by how much it enhances your knowledge about reading . This might be a good time for you to take the following true-false test and assess your current understanding of some concepts related to language, learning to read, reading difficulties, and reading instruction. Decide whether the statements are generally true or false and circle T or F. Explanations for the answers are identified throughout the book in special boxes.

1. T   F   The brain's ability to learn spoken language improves for most people during their early 20s.

2. T   F   Learning to read, like learning spoken language, is a natural ability.

3. T   F   There are about 200 ways to spell the sounds of the 44 phonemes in English.

4. T   F   Research studies have concluded that neither the phonological approach nor the whole-language approach is more effective in teaching most children how to read.

5. T   F   Non-English-speaking children can be taught to read English even if their spoken English vocabulary is weak.

6. T   F   Most children with attention-deficit hyperactivity disorder (ADHD) are also dyslexic.

7. T   F   Dyslexic students often have problems in other cognitive areas.

8. T   F   Many poor readers have attention problems that schools are not equipped to handle.

9. T   F   There is little that secondary school content area teachers can do to improve the comprehension skills of their students who are poor readers.

Children must learn to speak before they can learn to read. How we acquire spoken language is the subject of the first chapter.

CHAPTER 1
Learning
Spoken Language

This chapter addresses several basic questions about how the human brain learns spoken language. They include:

- *Why does spoken language come so easily?*
- *How does a child's brain detect language sounds from background noise?*
- *Does a family's socioeconomic status really affect a child's vocabulary growth?*
- *How does a child learn the irregular forms of verbs?*
- *Can children tell the difference between explicit and inferred comprehension?*

How quickly and successfully the brain learns to read is greatly influenced by the spoken language competence the child has developed. How broad is the child's vocabulary? How many grammatical errors appear in speech? How sophisticated is the sentence structure? How well does the child comprehend variations in sentence structure? The answers to these questions help in determining the breadth and depth of the child's spoken language networks and become the starting points for assessing how well the child will learn to read. Therefore, it is important to understand what cognitive neuroscience has revealed about how the brain acquires and processes spoken words. Figure 1.1 presents a general timeline for spoken language development during the first three years of growth. The chart is a rough approximation. Obviously, some children will progress faster or slower than the chart indicates. Nonetheless, it is a useful guide to show the progression of skills acquired during the process of learning language.

Spoken Language Development

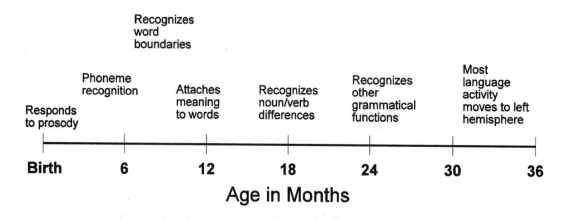

Figure 1.1 An average timeline of spoken language development during the child's first three years. There is considerable variation among individual children.

SPOKEN LANGUAGE COMES NATURALLY

One of the most extraordinary features of the human brain is its ability to acquire spoken language quickly and accurately. We are born with an innate capacity to distinguish the distinct sounds (phonemes) of all the languages on this planet. Eventually, we are able to associate those sounds with arbitrary written symbols to express our thoughts and emotions to others.

Other animals have developed ways to communicate with members of their species. Birds and apes bow and wave appendages; honeybees dance to map out the location of food; and even one-celled animals can signal neighbors by emitting an array of different chemicals. By contrast, human beings have developed an elaborate and complex means of spoken communication that many say is largely responsible for our place as the dominant species on this planet. Spoken language is truly a marvelous accomplishment for many reasons. At the very least, it gives form to our memories and words to express our thoughts. A single human voice can pronounce all the hundreds of vowel and consonant sounds that allow it to speak any of the estimated 6,500 languages that exist today. With practice, the voice becomes so fine-tuned that it makes only about one sound error per million sounds and one word error per million words (Pinker, 1994).

Before the advent of scanning technologies, we explained how the brain produced spoken language on the basis of evidence from injured brains. In 1861, French physician Paul Broca noticed that patients with brain damage to an area near the left temple understood

Figure 1.2 The language system in the left hemisphere is comprised mainly of Broca's area and Wernicke's area. The four lobes of the brain are also identified.

language but had difficulty speaking, a condition known as *aphasia*. About the size of a quarter, this region of the brain is commonly referred to as Broca's area (Figure 1.2).

In 1881, German neurologist Carl Wernicke described a different type of aphasia—one in which patients could not make sense out of words they spoke or heard. These patients had damage in the left temporal lobe. Now called Wernicke's area, it is located above the left ear and is about the size of a silver dollar. Those with damage to Wernicke's area could speak fluently, but what they said was quite meaningless. Ever since Broca discovered that the left hemisphere of the brain was specialized for language, researchers have attempted to understand the way in which normal human beings acquire and process their native language.

Processing Spoken Language

Recent research, using scanners, indicates that spoken language production is a far more complex process than previously thought. When preparing to produce a spoken sentence, the brain uses not only Broca's and Wernicke's areas, but also calls on several other neural networks scattered throughout the left hemisphere. Nouns are processed through one set of patterns; verbs are processed by separate neural networks. The more complex the sentence structure, the more areas that are activated, including the right hemisphere.

In most people, the left hemisphere is home to the major components of the language processing system. Broca's area is a region of the left frontal lobe that is believed to be responsible for processing vocabulary, syntax (how word order affects meaning), and rules of grammar. Wernicke's area is part of the left temporal lobe and is thought to process the sense and meaning of language. However, the emotional content of language is governed by areas in the right hemisphere.

Brain imaging studies of infants as young as four months of age confirm that the brain possesses neural networks that specialize in responding to the auditory components of language. Dehaene-Lambertz (2000) used EEG recordings to measure the brain activity of 16 four-month-old infants as they listened to language syllables and acoustic tones. After numerous trials, the data showed that syllables and tones were processed primarily in different areas of the left hemisphere, although there was also some right hemisphere activity. For language input, various features, such as the voice and the phonetic category of a syllable, were encoded by separate neural networks into sensory memory. These remarkable findings suggest that, even at this early age, the brain is already organized into functional networks that can distinguish between language fragments and other sounds. Another recent study of families with severe speech and language disorders has isolated a mutated gene believed to be responsible for their deficits. This discovery lends further credence to the notion that the ability to acquire spoken language is encoded in our genes (Lai, Fisher, Hurst, Vargha-Khadem, and Monaco, 2001).

The apparent genetic predisposition of the brain to the sounds of language explains why normal young children respond to and acquire spoken language quickly. After the first year in a language environment, the child becomes increasingly able to differentiate those sounds heard in the native language and begins to lose the ability to perceive other sounds. How long the brain retains this responsiveness to the sounds of language is still open to question. However, there does seem to be general agreement among researchers that the window of opportunity for acquiring language within the language-specific areas of the brain begins to diminish for most people around 10 to 12 years of age. Obviously, one can still acquire a new language after that age, but it takes more effort because the new language will be spatially separated in the brain from the native language areas (Gazzaniga, 1998). PET scans show that when children grow up learning two languages, all language activity is found in the same areas of the brain; those who learn a second language at a later age show that the two language areas are spatially separated (Kim, Relkin, Lee, and Hirsch, 1997).

> Most researchers agree that acquiring language within the language-specific areas of the brain diminishes for most people around 10 to 12 years of age.

Gender Differences in Language Processing

One of the earliest and most interesting discoveries neuroscientists made with functional imaging was that there were differences in the way male and female brains process language. Male brains tend to process language in the left hemisphere, while most female brains process language in both hemispheres. Figure 1.3 shows representational fMRIs with the solid white areas indicating areas of the brain that were activated during language processing. Of even greater interest was that these same cerebral areas in both genders were also activated during reading.

Figure 1.3 These are combined representational fMRIs showing the solid white areas of the male and female brains that were activated during language processing (Shaywitz et al., 1995).

Another interesting gender difference is the observation that the large bundle of neurons that connects the two hemispheres and allows them to communicate (called the *corpus callosum*) is proportionately larger and thicker in the female than in the male. Assuming function follows form, this difference implies that information travels between the two cerebral hemispheres more efficiently in females than in males. The combination of dual-hemisphere language processing and more efficient between-hemisphere communications may account for why young girls generally acquire spoken language easier and more quickly than young boys.

Answer to Test Question # 1

Question: The brain's ability to learn spoken language improves for most people during their early 20s.

Answer: *False.* Numerous studies show that the brain's ability to acquire spoken language is best during the first 10 years. Of course, people can learn a new language any time during their lives. It will just take more effort.

STRUCTURE OF LANGUAGE

Learning Phonemes

Languages consist of distinct units of sound called *phonemes*. Although each language has its own unique set of phonemes, only about 150 phonemes comprise all the world's languages. These phonemes consist of all the speech sounds that can be made by the human voice apparatus. Phonemes combine to form syllables. For example, in English, the consonant sound "t" and the vowel sound "o" are both phonemes that combine to form the syllable *to-*, as in *tomato*. Although the infant's brain can perceive the entire range of phonemes, only those that are repeated get attention, as the neurons reacting to the unique sound patterns are continually stimulated and reinforced.

At birth (some say even before birth) babies respond first to the prosody—the rhythm, cadence, and pitch—of their mothers' voice, not the words. Around the age of six months or so, infants start babbling, an early sign of language acquisition. The production of phonemes by infants is the result of genetically determined neural programs; however, language exposure is environmental. These two components interact to produce an individual's language system and, assuming no abnormal conditions, sufficient competence to communicate clearly with others. Their babbling consists of all those phonemes, even ones they have never heard. Within a few months, however, pruning of the phonemes begins, and by about one year of age, the neural networks focus on the sounds of the language being spoken in the infant's environment (Beatty, 2001).

Learning Words and Morphemes

The next step for the brain is to detect words from the stream of sounds it is processing. This is not an easy task because people don't pause between words when speaking. Yet the brain has to recognize differences between, say, *green house* and *greenhouse*. Studies show that parents help this process along by slipping automatically into a different speech pattern when talking to their babies than when speaking to adults. Mothers tend to go into a teaching mode with the vowels elongated and emphasized. They speak to their babies in a higher pitch, with a special intonation, rhythm, and feeling. The researchers suggested that mothers are instinctively attempting to help their babies recognize the sounds of language. Researchers found this pattern in other languages as well, such as Russian, Swedish, and Japanese (Burnham, Kitamura, and Vollmer-Conna, 2002).

Remarkably, babies begin to distinguish word boundaries by the age of 8 months even though they don't know what the words mean (Van Petten and Bloom, 1999). They now begin to acquire new vocabulary words at the rate of about seven to 10 a day. By the age of 10 to 12 months, the toddler's brain has begun to distinguish and remember phonemes of the native language and to ignore foreign sounds. For example, one study showed that at the age of 6 months, American and Japanese babies are equally good at discriminating between the "l" and "r" sounds, even though Japanese has no "l" sound. However, by age 10 months, Japanese babies have a tougher time making the distinction, while American babies have become much better at it. During this and subsequent periods of growth, one's ability to distinguish native sounds improves, while the ability to distinguish nonnative speech sounds diminishes (Cheour et al., 1998). Soon, *morphemes,* such as *-s, -ed,* and *-ing,* are added to their speaking vocabulary. At the same time, working memory and Wernicke's areas are becoming fully functional so the child can now attach meaning to words. Of course, learning words is one skill; putting them together to make sense is another, more complex skill.

Verbal- and Image-Based Words

How quickly a child understands words may be closely related to whether the word can generate a clear mental image. A word like *elephant* generates a picture in the mind's eye and thus can be more easily understood than an abstract word like *justice*. Could it be that the brain maintains two distinct systems to process image-loaded words and abstract words?

To further investigate this point, Swaab and her colleagues used numerous electroencephalographs (EEGs) to measure the brain's response to concrete and abstract words in a dozen young adults (Swaab, Baynes, and Knight, 2002). EEGs measure

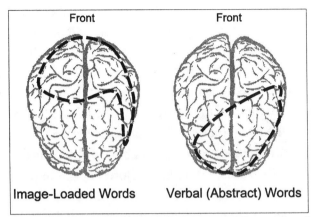

Figure 1.4 The dotted regions represent the areas of highest event-related potentials when subjects processed image-loaded words or verbal (abstract) words (Swaab, et al., 2002).

changes in brain wave activity, called *event-related potentials (ERPs)*, when the brain experiences a stimulus. The researchers found that image-loaded words produced more ERPs in the front area (frontal lobe–the part thought to be associated with imagery) while abstract words produced more ERPs in the top central (the parietal lobe) and rear (the occipital lobe) areas. Furthermore, there was little interaction between these disparate areas when processing any of the words (Figure 1.4). The results support the idea that the brain may hold two separate stores for *semantics* (meaning), one for verbal-based information and the other for image-based information. This discovery has implications for language instruction. Teachers should use concrete images when presenting an abstract concept. For example, teaching the idea of justice could be accompanied by pictures of a judge in robes, the scales of justice, and a courtroom scene.

> Teachers should use concrete images when presenting an abstract concept.

Vocabulary Gaps in Toddlers

In the early years, toddlers acquire most of their vocabulary words from their parents. Consequently, children who experience frequent adult-to-toddler conversations that contain a wide variety of words will build much larger vocabularies than those who experience infrequent conversations that contain fewer words. The incremental effect of this vocabulary difference grows exponentially and can lead to an enormous word gap during the child's first three years.

A particularly significant two-part longitudinal study (Hart and Risley, 2003) documented the vocabulary growth of 42 toddlers from the age of 7 to 9 months until they turned 3 years old. Because parental vocabulary is closely associated with their socio-economic status (SES), part one of this study looked at toddlers in families from three different groups. On the basis of occupation, 13 of the families were upper SES, 23 were middle-lower SES, and 6 were on welfare. By the time the children were 3 years old, the researchers had recorded and analyzed over 1,300 hours of casual conversations between the children and their parents. To their surprise, the analysis showed a wide gap in the number of words present in the vocabularies of the children based on their SES. Children from the welfare families had an average recorded vocabulary size of just 525 words. Those from the middle-low SES had 749 words, while the children in the upper SES had average vocabularies of 1,116 words. Furthermore, the children from welfare families were adding words to their vocabulary more slowly than the other children throughout the length of the study.

Part two of the study was conducted six years later. The researchers were able to test the language skills of 29 of these children who were then in third grade. Test results showed that the rate of early vocabulary growth was a strong predictor of scores at ages 9 to 10 on tests of vocabulary, listening, speaking, syntax, and semantics. This study points out how important the early years are in developing a child's literacy and how difficult it is to equalize children's preschool experiences with language.

Early literacy problems can be addressed successfully through the publically-funded birth-to-school programs now available in just a few states. In these programs, school district personnel meet regularly with parents of infants in low SES households and provide them with inexpensive, age-appropriate resources to use with their children during the preschool years. The idea is to build the child's vocabulary and exposure to enriched language before entering school. Missouri began its Parents as Teachers (PAT) program in 1985, and has since provided preschool resources for more than 164,000 high-needs families. Independent evaluations have shown that PAT children were significantly more advanced in language development, problem solving, and social development at age 3 than comparison children. Furthermore, the program provides significant cost savings to local school districts by having fewer placements in special education, fewer grade retentions, and less remedial education (MDESE, 2003).

Syntax and Semantics

Language Hierarchy

With more exposure to speech, the brain begins to recognize the beginnings of a hierarchy of language (Figure 1.5). Phonemes, the basic sounds, can be combined into morphemes, which are the smallest units of language that have meaning. Morphemes can then be combined into words, and words can be put together according to the rules of syntax (word order) to form phrases and sentences with meaning. The difference in meaning (semantics) between the sentences "The woman chased the dog" and "The dog chased the woman" results from a different word order, or syntax. Toddlers show evidence of their progression through the syntactic and semantic levels when simple statements, such as "Candy," evolve to more complex ones, "Give me candy." They also begin to recognize that shifting the words in sentences can change their meaning.

The Syntactic Network

The rules of syntax in English prohibit the random arrangement of words in a sentence. The simplest sentences follow a sequence common to many languages, that of subject-

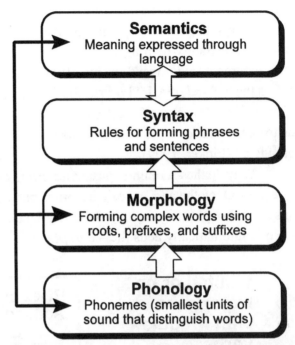

Figure 1.5 The diagram represents the levels of hierarchy in language and in language acquisition. Although the process usually flows from the bottom to the top, recycling from the top to lower levels can also occur, as indicated by the arrows to the left.

verb-object (or SVO) format, as in "He hit the ball." In more complex sentences, syntax imposes a stringent structure on word order to provide clarity and reduce ambiguity. Just look at what happens to meaning when writers neglect to follow the rules of syntax. The following examples are taken from actual headlines that appeared in the nation's newspapers (Cooper, 1987).

- "Defendant's speech ends in a long sentence"
- "Sisters reunited after 18 years in checkout line at supermarket"
- "Dr. Ruth talks about sex with newspaper editors"

Over time, the child hears more patterns of word combinations, phrase constructions, and variations in the pronunciation of words. Toddlers detect patterns of word order—person, action, object—so they can soon say, "I want cookie." They also note statistical regularities heard in the flow of the native tongue. They discern that some words describe objects while others describe actions. Other features of grammar emerge, such as tense. By the age of 3, over 90 percent of sentences uttered are grammatically correct because the child has constructed a syntactic network that stores perceived rules of grammar. For example, the child hears variations in the pronunciation of *walk* and *walked, play* and *played,* and *fold* and *folded.* The child isolates the *-ed* and eventually recognizes it as representing the past tense. At that point, the child's syntactic network is modified to include the rule: "add *-ed* to make the past tense." The rule is certainly helpful, but causes errors when the child applies it to some common verbs. Errors are seldom random, but usually result from following perceived rules of grammar such as the add *-ed* rule. If "I *batted* the ball" makes sense, why shouldn't "I *holded* the bat"? After all, if *fold* becomes *folded,* shouldn't *hold* become *holded*? Regrettably, the toddler has yet to learn that over 150 of the most commonly used verbs in English are irregularly conjugated (Pinker, 1999).

Why do these common past tense errors occur in a child's speech and how do they get corrected? Once the add *-ed* rule becomes part of the syntactic network, it operates without conscious thought (Figure 1.6). So when the child wants to use the past tense, the syntactic network automatically adds the *-ed* to *play* and *look* so that the child can say, "I *played* with

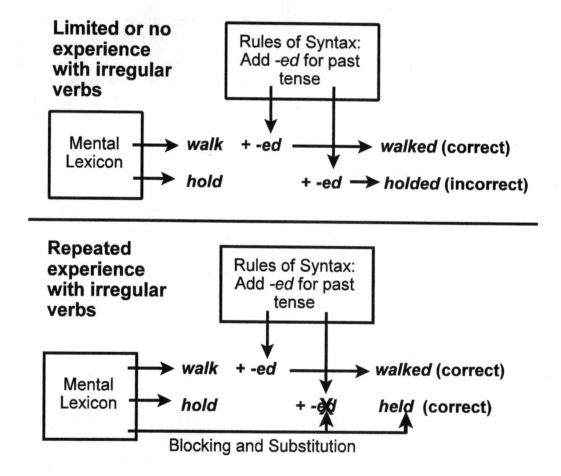

Figure 1.6 The diagrams illustrate how blocking becomes part of the syntactic network. Before a child encounters an irregular verb, the add *-ed* rule applies. Thus *walk* becomes *walked* and *hold* becomes *holded*. After several instances of adult correction and other environmental exposures (repetition is important to memory), the syntactic network is modified to block the rule for the past tense of *hold* and to substitute *held,* a word that now becomes part of the child's lexicon (Pinker, 1999).

Susan and we *looked* at some books." If, however, the child says "I *holded* the bat," repeated adult corrections, repetition, and other environmental encounters will inform the syntactic network that the add -*ed* rule is not appropriate in this case and should be blocked, and that a new word *held* should be substituted and added to the child's lexicon. This principle of *blocking* is an important component of accurate language fluency and, eventually, of reading fluency.

So how does the child eventually learn the irregular forms of common verbs? Long-term memory plays an important role in helping the child learn the correct past tense forms of irregular verbs. The more frequently the irregular verb is used, the more likely the child will remember it. Take a look at Table 1.1, which shows the ten most common verbs in English as computed by Brown University. The verbs are drawn from a million-word database of text used in magazines, newspapers, textbooks, popular books, and other sources (Francis and Kucera, 1982). Note all of these most common verbs are irregular. Interestingly enough, this tends to be true in many other languages. Pinker (1999) explains that irregular forms have to be repeatedly memorized to survive in a language from generation to generation, otherwise the verbs will be lost. He cites several infrequently used irregular verbs whose past tenses have slipped from common usage: *cleave–clove, stave–stove,* and *chide–chid.*

> Most common verbs in English and many other languages are irregular.

Table 1.1 Frequency of Common Verbs in English in a Million Words of Text	
Verb	**Number of Occurrences**
1. *be*	39,175
2. *have*	12,458
3. *do*	4,367
4. *say*	2,765
5. *make*	2,312
6. *go*	1,844
7. *take*	1,575
8. *come*	1,561
9. *see*	1,513
10. *get*	1,486

Source: Francis and Kucera, 1982

The ability of children to remember corrections to grammatical errors—including blocking—would be impossible without some innate mechanism that is genetically guided. No one knows how much grammar a child learns just by listening, or how much is pre-wired. What is certain is that the more children are exposed to spoken language in the early years, the more quickly they can discriminate between phonemes, recognize word boundaries, and detect the emerging rules of grammar that result in meaning.

Syntax and English Language Learners. Each language has its own rules of syntax. Consequently, children learning English as an additional language often have problems with English syntax. For example, unlike English, adjectives in Spanish, French, and other similar languages, are typically placed *after* the noun they modify. *Blue sky* is spoken in French as *ciel bleu.* German verbs usually are placed at the end of a clause and rarely follow the subject-verb-object (or SVO) sequence so common in English. For these beginning English language learners, special attention has to be paid to understanding how English rules of syntax differ from those of their native tongue.

> Beginning English language learners need to understand how English rules of syntax differ from those of their native tongue.

The Semantic Network

As phonemes combine into morphemes, and morphemes into words, and words into phrases, the mind needs to arrange and compose these pieces into sentences that express what the speaker wants to say. Meanwhile, the listener's language areas must recognize speech sounds from other background noise and interpret the speaker's meaning. This interaction between the components of language and the mind in search of meaning is referred to as *semantics.* Meaning occurs at three different levels of language: the morphology level, the vocabulary level, and the sentence level.

Morphology-Level Semantics. Meaning can come through word parts, or morphology. The word *biggest* has two morphemes, *big* and *-est.* When children can successfully examine the morphology of words, their mental lexicons are greatly enriched. They learn that words with common roots often have common meaning, such as *nation* and *national,* and that prefixes and suffixes alter the meaning of words in certain ways. Morphology also helps children learn and create new words, and can help them spell and pronounce words correctly.

Vocabulary-Level Semantics. A listener who does not understand many of the vocabulary words in a conversation will have trouble comprehending meaning. Of course, the listener may infer meaning based on context, but this is unreliable unless the listener understands most of the vocabulary. Children face this dilemma every day as adults around them use words they do not understand.

Sentence-Level Semantics. The sentence "Boiling cool dreams walk quickly to the goodness" illustrates that morphology and syntax can be preserved even in a sentence that lacks semantics. The words are all correct English words in the proper syntactic sequence, but the sentence does not make sense. Adults recognize this lack of sense immediately. But children often encounter spoken language that does not make sense to them. To understand language, the listener has to detect meaning at several different levels. Because adults do not normally speak sentences that have no meaning, a child's difficulty in finding meaning may result from a sentence having meaning for one person but not another. At this level, too, the listener's background knowledge or experience with the topic being discussed will influence meaning.

The cerebral processes involved in producing and interpreting meaning must occur at incredible speed during the flow of ordinary conversation. How it is that we can access words from our enormous storehouse (the mental lexicon) and interpret the meaning of conversation so quickly? What types of neural networks can allow for such speed and accuracy? Although linguistic researchers differ on the exact nature of these networks, most agree that the mental lexicon is organized according to meaningful relationships between words. Experimental evidence for this notion comes form numerous studies that involve word priming. In these studies, the subjects are presented with pairs of words. The first word is called the prime and the second word is the target. The target can be a real word or a nonword (like *spretz*). A real word target may or may not be related in meaning to the prime. After being shown the prime, the subject must decide as quickly as possible if the target is a word. The results invariably show that subjects are faster and more accurate in making decisions about target words that are related in meaning to the prime (e.g., *swan–goose*) than to an unrelated prime (e.g., *tulip–goose*). Researchers suspect that the reduced time for identifying related pairs results from these words being physically closer to each other among the neurons that make up the semantic network, and that related words may be stored together in specific cerebral regions (Gazzaniga, Ivry, and Mangun, 2002).

Additional evidence for this idea that the brain stores related words together has come from imaging studies using PET scans. Subjects in PET scanners were asked to name persons, animals, and tools. The results (Figure 1.7) showed that naming items in the same category activated the same area of the brain (Damasio, Grabowski, Tranel, Hichwa, and Damasio, 1996). It seems that the brain stores clusters of closely associated words in a tightly packed network so that words *within* the

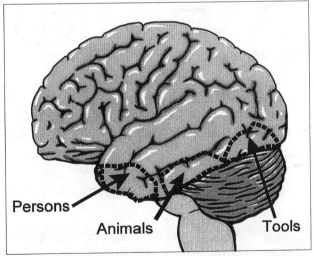

Figure 1.7 The diagram is a representation of the combined PET scan results showing that naming persons, animals, and tools mostly activated different parts of the brain's temporal lobe (Damasio et al., 1996).

network can activate each other in minimal time. Activating words *between* networks, however, takes longer.

How can we best represent these networks? Several different models have been proposed. One that seems to garner substantial support from contemporary neuroscientists is based on an earlier model first proposed by Collins and Loftus (1975) in the mid 1970s. In this model, words that are related are connected to each other. The distance between the connection is determined by the semantic relationship between the words. Figure 1.8 is an example of a semantic network. Note that the word *lemon* is close to—and would have a strong connection to—the word *grapefruit,* but is distant from the word *bird.* If we hear the word *lemon,* then the neural area that represents *lemon* will be activated in the semantic network. Other words in the network such as *lime* and *grapefruit,* would also be activated and, therefore, accessed very quickly. The word *bird* would not come to mind.

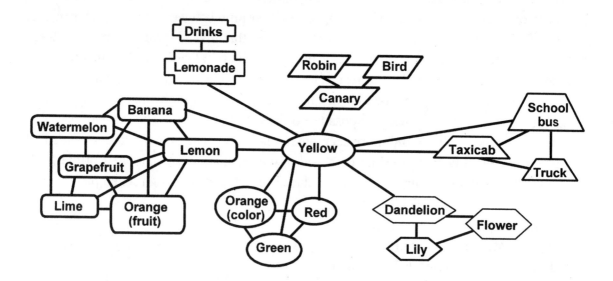

Figure 1.8 This is a representation of a semantic network. Words that are semantically related are closer together in the network, such as *lemon–yellow,* than words that have no close relationship, such as *lemon–bird.* Similar geometric figures identify semantically related words. The lines connect words from different networks that are associated, such as *lemon–yellow.*

From Words to Sentences

We have just discussed how the brain acquires, stores, and recognizes words. But to communicate effectively, the words must be arranged in a sequence that makes sense. Languages have developed certain rules—called grammar—that govern the order of words so that speakers of the language can understand each other. In some languages, such as English, different arrangements of words in a sentence can result in the same meaning. "The girl ate the candy" has the same meaning as "The candy was eaten by the girl." Of course, different word

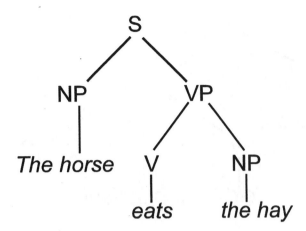

Figure 1.9 This model illustrates how the brain may process sentences to establish meaning. By grouping, or chunking, individual words into phrases, processing time is increased.

arrangements (syntax) can lead to different meanings, as in "The boat is in the water" and "The water is in the boat."

As a child's syntactic and semantic networks develop, context plays an important role in determining meaning. When hearing the sentence "The man bought a hot dog at the fair," the youngster is very likely to picture the man eating a frankfurter rather than a steaming, furry animal that barks. That's because the rest of the sentence establishes a context that is compatible with the first interpretation but not the second.

How does the young brain learn to process the structure of sentences? One prominent model suggests that words in a sentence are assigned syntactic roles and grouped into syntactic phrases (Pinker, 1999). For example, the sentence "The horse eats the hay" consists of a noun phrase (*the horse*), a verb (*eats*), and another noun phrase (*the hay*). A rule of grammar is that a verb (V) can be combined with its direct object to form a verb phrase (VP). In the preceding example, the verb phase would be *eats the hay*. The combination of the noun phrase (NP) and the verb phrase comprises the sentence (S), which can be represented by the syntactic model shown in Figure 1.9.

As sentences become more complicated, each module can contain another module within it. For example, the sentence "The parent told the principal her son is ill" contains a verb phrase that is also a sentence (*her son is ill*). To ensure rapid processing and accurate comprehension, the brain groups the phrases into the hierarchy as represented by the diagram shown in Figure 1.10.

How Can We Speak So Rapidly?

This module-within-a-module pattern (Figure 1.10) has two major advantages. First, by rearranging and including different phrase packets, the brain can generate and understand

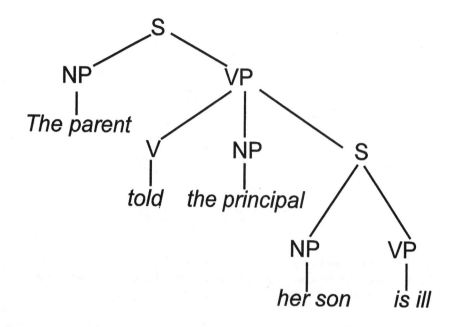

Figure 1.10 This illustrates how the brain proceeds to make additional chunks into phrases to ensure rapid processing and accurate interpretation.

an enormous number of sentences without having to memorize every imaginable sentence verbatim. Second, this pattern allows the brain to process syntactic information quickly so that it can meet the demanding comprehension time required for normal conversation. The efficiency of the system is amazing! The young adult brain can determine the meaning of a spoken word in about one-fifth of a second. The brain needs just one-fourth of a second to name an object and about the same amount of time to pronounce it. For readers, the meaning of a printed word is registered in an astounding one-eighth of a second (Pinker, 1999).

Recognizing Meaning

The brain's ability to recognize different meanings in sentence structure is possible because Broca's and Wernicke's areas establish linked networks that can understand the difference between "The dog chased the cat" and "The cat chased the dog." In an fMRI study, Dapretto and Bookheimer (1999) found that Broca's and Wernicke's areas work together to determine whether changes in syntax or semantics result in changes in meaning. For example, "The policeman arrested the thief" and "The thief was arrested by the policeman" have different syntax but the same meaning. The fMRI showed that Broca's area was highly activated when subjects were processing these two sentences. Wernicke's area, on the other hand, was more activated when processing sentences that were semantically—but not syntactically—different, such as "The car is in the garage" and "The automobile is in the garage."

How is it that Wernicke's area can so quickly and accurately decide that two semantically different sentences have the same meaning? The answer may lie in two other recently discovered characteristics of Wernicke's area. One is that the neurons in Wernicke's area are spaced about 20 percent farther apart and are cabled together with longer interconnecting axons than the corresponding area in the right hemisphere of the brain (Galuske, Schlote, Bratzke, and Singer, 2000). The implication is that the practice of language during early human development results in longer and more intricately connected neurons in the Wernicke region, allowing for greater sensitivity to meaning.

The second recent discovery regarding Wernicke's area is its ability to recognize predictable events. An MRI study found that Wernicke's area was activated when subjects were shown differently colored symbols in various patterns, whether the individuals were aware of the pattern sequence or not (Bischoff-Grethe, Proper, Mao, Daniels, and Berns, 2000). This capacity of Wernicke's area to detect predictability suggests that our ability to make sense of language is rooted in our ability to recognize syntax. The researchers noted that language itself is very predicable because it is constrained by the rules of grammar and syntax.

The Components of Speaking and Understanding Language

Any model for speaking and understanding language has to address the various stages of sound interpretation, beginning with the auditory input and ending with the formation of a mental concept represented by the word or words. Figure 1.11 shows the various neural components that linguistic researchers and neuroscientists believe are required for spoken language comprehension. It is a complex process, but the efficient organization of the linguistic networks that was built up through practice allows it to occur very quickly.

To understand the different components, let's take the word *dog* through the model. After the spoken word *dog* enters the ear canal, the listener has to decode the sound pattern. In the word form area of the brain, acoustic analysis separates the relevant word sounds from background noise, decodes the phonemes of the word (*duh-awh-guh*), and translates them into a phonological code that can be recognized by the mental lexicon. The lexicon

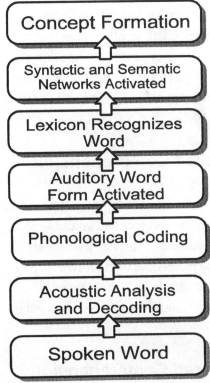

Figure 1.11 This schematic representation shows the major neural components required for spoken language processing. Feedback from higher to lower levels is possible. (Adapted from Gazzaniga et al., 2002).

selects the best representation it has in store and then activates the syntactic and semantic networks, which work together to form the mental image of a furry animal that barks (concept formation). All this occurs in just a fraction of a second thanks to the extensive network of neural pathways that were established during the early years of speaking and listening.

Notice that the flow of information in this model is from the bottom up and, thus, appears linear. However, feedback from higher to lower levels is possible. For example, if the lexicon does not recognize the first set of signals, it could reactivate the phonological coding component to produce another set before they decay. It is important to understand how this spoken language processing works because, as we shall see in the next chapter, the process of reading words shares several steps with this model of spoken language processing.

LEVELS OF LANGUAGE COMPREHENSION

Parents speak differently to their children than to other adults. Elementary teachers use different language with their students than with their principal. Speech can be formal, as in the classroom, or informal, as around the dinner table. When young children use informal language, it is often context-dependent, that is, the conversation focuses on the immediate situation or activities at hand. On the other hand, formal speech may be more context independent or abstract in that the child may be relating different possible endings to a story. Sometimes people say one thing but really mean something else, and they hope that the listener will catch on to the subtler meaning. These different language forms are a recognition that there are several types and levels of spoken language and of language comprehension.

Explicit Comprehension

The most basic type of language comprehension is explicit comprehension—the sentence is clear and unambiguous. When someone says "I need a haircut," the interpretation is unmistakable. The listener knows exactly what the speaker means and does not need to draw any inferences or elaborate further. Adults tend to use explicit sentences with children to avoid ambiguity. "Eat your vegetables," and "Please be quiet" are clear statements. Whether the child complies, of course, is another story.

Inferred Comprehension

A more sophisticated form of language comprehension requires the listener to make inferences about meanings that go beyond what the speaker explicitly said. A principal who says to a tardy teacher, "Our school really gets off to a great start in the morning when all the staff is here by 8:15," is really saying, "Be on time." The teacher has to infer the statement's real intent by reading between the lines of what the principal explicitly said.

Young children have difficulty with inferred comprehension. If the parent says, "Vegetables are good for you," the child may not pick up on the underlying intent of this statement—eat your vegetables. Consequently, the child may not finish the vegetables and the parent may mistake this behavior as disobedience when it was really a lack of inferred comprehension.

Teachers sometimes use language requiring inferred comprehension when explicit comprehension would be much easier. A teacher who says, for example, "Do you think I should speak if someone else is talking?" may provoke a variety of responses in the minds of the children. One could think absolutely not, while another might hope she would just speak louder than everyone else so the lesson could move along. A few might get the real intent—oh, she wants us to be quiet.

Context Clues. We discussed earlier how context can be an important clue for determining the meaning of vocabulary words in a sentence. Context can also help with inferred comprehension. A first grade teacher who is telling her spouse over dinner how crowded her class is and that there are too many students who need special help may just be seeking sympathy. But in having the same conversation with her principal, she is really saying she needs an instructional aide. She never says that explicitly; the principal must infer the teacher's intent from her statement and the context.

Children need to develop an awareness that language comprehension exists on several levels. It involves different styles of speech that reflect the formality of the conversation, the context in which it occurs, and the explicit as well as underlying intent of the speaker. When children gain a good understanding of these patterns in speech, they will be better able to comprehend what they read.

What's Coming?

The child's brain has now acquired the fundamentals of spoken language. Neural networks are developing rapidly in Broca's and Wernicke's areas, and every day brings new vocabulary and understanding to the expanding mental lexicon. How will these newly-acquired language skills and knowledge help the child accomplish the next major cognitive task: learning to read? All the steps the brain must go through to progress from spoken to written language are unveiled in the next chapter.

CHAPTER 2

Learning to Read

This chapter addresses several basic questions about how the human brain learns to read. They include:

- *What must a child be able to do in order to read effectively?*
- *What role does working memory play in learning to read?*
- *What happens in the brain when a child goes from a non-reader to a novice reader, and finally to a skilled reader?*

One of the first things to recognize is that intelligence generally does not play a critical role in learning to read. Three sources of evidence indicate this. First, studies of children who learn to read before entering school indicate that there is not a strong relationship between IQ and early reading. Second, studies have shown that IQ is only weakly related to reading achievement in grades 1 and 2. Finally, children who have difficulty learning to read often have above-average IQs (Rawson, 1995; Shaywitz, 2003). It appears then that, to a large degree, learning to read is independent of intelligence.

READING IS NOT A NATURAL ABILITY

Humans have been speaking for tens of thousands of years. During this time, genetic changes have favored the brain's ability to acquire and process spoken language, even setting aside specialized areas of the brain to accomplish these tasks. Consequently, the brain's proficiency at hearing and quickly remembering words is natural, though no l ess r emarkable. Children begin to learn words before their first birthday and during their second year are acquiring them at the rate of 8

> To a large degree, learning to read is independent of intelligence.

to 10 per day. By the time they enter school, they have a well-developed language system consisting of an active vocabulary of about 3,000 words and a total mental lexicon of over 5,000 words. At some point, the child's brain encounters the written word and wonders, "What are those symbols? What do they mean?"

Speaking is a normal, genetically-hardwired capability; reading is not. No areas of the brain are specialized for reading. In fact, reading is probably the most difficult task we ask the young brain to undertake. Reading is a relatively new phenomenon in the development of humans. As far as we know, the genes have not incorporated reading into their coded structure, probably because reading, unlike spoken language, has not emerged over time as a survival skill. If reading were a natural ability, everyone would be doing it. But in fact, there are nearly 40 million adults in the USA alone who are functionally illiterate.

> Speaking is a normal, innate ability; reading is not.

Renewed emphasis in recent years on improving the basic cognitive skills of students has increased pressure to start reading instruction sooner than ever before. In many schools, reading instruction starts in kindergarten. Some neuropsychologists are now debating whether kindergartners are developmentally ready for this challenging task. Are we creating problems for these children by trying to get them to read before their brains are ready? Because boys' brains are physiologically one or two years less mature than girls' brains at this age, are boys at greater risk of failure? To answer these questions, let's examine what researchers have discovered about how the brain learns to read, and the problems that can develop.

Some children—perhaps 50 percent—make the transition from spoken language to reading with relative ease, once exposed to formal instruction. It appears, however, that for the other 50 percent, reading is a much more formidable task, and for about 20 to 30 percent, it definitely becomes the most difficult cognitive task they will ever undertake in their lives.

Answer to Test Question # 2

Question: Learning to read, like learning spoken language, is a natural ability.

Answer: *False.* Unlike spoken language, the brain has no areas specialized for reading. The skills needed to link the sounds of language to the letters of the alphabet must be learned through direct instruction.

EARLY STAGES OF READING

Before children learn to read, they acquire vocabulary by listening to others and by practicing the pronunciation and usage of new words in conversation. Adult correction and other sources help to fine-tune this basic vocabulary. Because the ability to read is strongly dependent on the word forms learned during this period, a child's beginning reading will be more successful if most of the reading material contains words the child is already using. The phoneme-grapheme connection can be made more easily. Reading, of course, also adds new words to the child's mental lexicon. Consequently, there must be some neural connections between the systems that allow the brain to recognize spoken words and the system that recognizes written words.

Learning to read starts with the awareness that speech is composed of individual sounds (phonemes) and a recognition that written spellings represent those sounds (*the alphabetic principle*). Of course, to be successful in acquiring the alphabetic principle, the child has to be aware of how the phonemes of spoken language can be manipulated to form new words and rhymes. The neural systems that perceive the phonemes in our language are more efficient in some children than in others. Just because some children have difficulty understanding that spoken words are composed of discrete sounds doesn't mean that they have brain damage or dysfunction. The individual differences that underlie the efficiency with which one learns to read can be seen in the acquisition of other skills, such as learning to play a musical instrument, playing a sport, or building a model. To some extent, neural efficiency is related to genetic composition, but these genetic factors can be modified by the environment. Nonetheless, being aware of sound differences in spoken language is crucial to learning to read written language.

Phonological and Phonemic Awareness

Phonological awareness is the recognition that oral language can be divided into smaller components, such as sentences into words, words into syllables and, ultimately, into individual phonemes. This recognition includes identifying and manipulating onsets and rimes as well as having an awareness of alliteration, rhyming, syllabication, and intonation. Being phonologically aware means having an understanding of all these levels. In children, phonological awareness usually starts with initial sounds and rhyming, and a recognition that sentences can be segmented into words. Next comes segmenting words into syllables and blending syllables into words.

Phonemic awareness is a subdivision of phonological awareness and refers to the understanding that words are made up of individual sounds (phonemes) and that these sounds can be manipulated to create new words. It includes the ability to isolate a phoneme (first, middle, or last) from the rest of the word, to segment words into their component phonemes, and to delete a specific phoneme from a word. Children with phonemic awareness know that the word *cat* is made up of three phonemes, and that the words *dog* and *mad* both contain the phoneme */d/*. Recognition of rhyming and alliteration are usual indications that a child has phonological awareness, which develops when children are read to from books based on rhyme or alliteration. But this awareness does not easily develop into the more sophisticated phonemic awareness, which is so closely related to a child's success in learning to read (Chard and Dickson, 1999). Nonetheless, reading programs that emphasize phonological and phonemic awareness have proved to be successful in schools (Wise, Ring, and Olson, 1999).

Phonemic awareness is different from *phonics*. Phonemic awareness involves the auditory and *oral* manipulation of sounds. A child demonstrates phonemic awareness by knowing all the sounds that make up the word *cat*. Phonics is an instructional approach that

> Simply learning letter-sound relationships during phonics instruction does not necessarily lead to phonemic awareness.

builds on the alphabetic principle and associates letters and sounds with *written* symbols. To demonstrate phonics knowledge, a child tells the teacher which *letter* is needed to change *cat* to *can*. Although phonemic awareness and phonics are closely related, they are not the same. It is possible for a child to have phonemic awareness in speech without having much experience with written letters or names. Conversely, a child may provide examples of letter-sound relationships without ever developing phonemic awareness. In fact, simply learning these letter-sound relationships during phonics instruction does not necessarily lead to phonemic awareness (SEDL, 2001).

The terms phonological awareness, phonemic awareness, and phonics have different meanings, but they can be easily confused. Table 2.1 defines these terms. In this book, I will refer mainly to phonemic awareness because many of the research studies on learning to read focus specifically on phonemes.

Phonemic Awareness and Learning to Read

New readers must learn the alphabetic principle and recognize that words can be separated into individual phonemes, which can be reordered and blended into words. This enables learners to associate the letters with sounds in order to read and build words. Thus, phonemic awareness in kindergarten is a strong predictor of reading success that persists throughout school. Early instruction in reading, especially in letter-sound association, strengthens phonological awareness and helps in the development of the more sophisticated phonemic awareness (Snow, Burns, and Griffin, 1998).

Numerous research studies over the past two decades have established a strong positive link between phonemic awareness and success in early reading. About 70 to 80 percent of children are able to learn the alphabetic principle after one year of instruction. For the rest, additional study is needed (Shaywitz, 2003).

Table 2.1 Definitions of Terms Related to Speech and Reading		
Term	**Definition**	**Example**
Phonological awareness	The awareness of any size unit of sound, including the ability to separate words into syllables, to count syllables, to identify phonemes in words, and to generate and recognize rhyming words	The word *carpet* has two syllables, each one composed of three phonemes
Phonemic awareness	The awareness that spoken language is made up of individual units of sound	The word dog has three phonemes, /d/-/ŏ/-/g/
Phonics	An instructional approach for teaching reading and spelling that emphasizes sound-symbol relationships	The symbol *p* is used to represent the italicized sounds in the words *p*ot, jum*p*, and co*p*y

Source: Yopp and Yopp, 2000

Sounds to Letters (Phonemes to Graphemes)

To be able to read, the brain must memorize a set of arbitrary squiggles (the alphabet) and identify which symbols, called *graphemes,* correspond to the phonemes already stored in the mental lexicon. Many European languages use abstract letters (i.e., an alphabetic system) to represent their sounds so that the words can be spelled out in writing. The rules of spelling that govern a language are called its *orthography.* How closely a language's orthography actually represents the pronunciation of the phoneme can determine how quickly one learns to read that language correctly. Some languages, like Spanish, Italian, and Finnish, have a very close correspondence between letters and the sounds they represent. This is known as a *shallow* orthography. Once the rules of orthography in these languages are learned, a person can usually spell a new word correctly the first time because there are so few exceptions.

English, on the other hand, often has a poor correspondence between how a word is pronounced and how it is spelled. This is called a *deep* orthography. It exists because English does not have an alphabet that permits an ideal one-to-one correspondence between its phonemes and its graphemes. Consider that just when the brain thinks it knows what letter represents a phoneme sound, it discovers that the same symbol can have different sounds, such as the *a*'s in *cat* and in *father.* Consider, too, how the pronunciation of the following English words differs, even though they all have the same last four letters, and in the same sequence: *bough, cough, dough* and *rough.* This lack of sound-to-letter correspondence makes it difficult for the brain to recognize patterns and affects the child's ability to spell with accuracy and to read with meaning. Eventually, the brain must connect the 26 letters of the alphabet to the 44-plus sounds of spoken English (phonemes) that the child has been using successfully for years. Table 2.2 illustrates the complexity of English orthography, compared to some other related languages. There are more than 1,100 ways to spell the sounds of the 44 phonemes in English.

Table 2.2 Language Sounds and Their Spellings		
Language	Number of Sounds (Phonemes)	Number of Ways to Spell Sounds
Italian	33	25
Spanish	35+	38
French	32	250+
English	44	1,100+

Alphabetic Principle

The alphabetic principle describes the understanding that spoken words are made up of phonemes and that the phonemes are represented in written text as letters. This system of using letters to represent phonemes is very efficient in that a small number of letters can be used to write a very large number of words. Matching just a few letters on a page to their sounds in speech enables the reader to recognize many printed words: for example, connecting just four letters and their phonemes /a/, /l/, /p/, and /s/ to read *lap, pal, slap, laps,* and *pals.*

Despite the efficiency of an alphabetic system, learning the alphabetic principle is not easy because of two drawbacks. First, the letters of the alphabet are abstract and thus unfamiliar to the new reader, and the sounds they represent are not natural segments of speech.

Answer to Test Question # 3

Question: There are about 200 ways to spell the sounds of the 44 phonemes in English.

Answer: *False.* Actually, there are more than 1,100 ways to represent the sounds of the 44 English phonemes. This condition, known as deep orthography, is one major reason that English is a difficult language to learn, especially for those whose native language has a more reliable letter-to-sound correspondences, such as Spanish.

Second, because there are about 44 English phonemes but only 26 letters, each phoneme is not coded with a unique letter. There are over a dozen vowel sounds but only five letters, *a, e, i, o,* and *u,* to represent them. Further, the child needs to recognize that how a letter is pronounced depends on the letters that surround it. The letter *e,* for example is pronounced differently in *dead, deed,* and *dike.* And then there are the consonant digraphs, which are combinations of two consonants, such as *ch, sh,* and *ph,* that represent a single speech sound. There are also three-letter combinations, called trigraphs, such as *tch* and *thr.* With more practice at word recognition, the reader must work toward fast and accurate word recognition in order to increase reading fluency.

Unfortunately, the human brain is not born with the insight to make sound-to-letter connections, nor does it develop naturally without instruction. Children of literate homes may encounter this instruction before coming to school. Others, however, do not have this opportunity during their preschool years. For them, classroom instruction needs to focus on making the phoneme-phonics connections before reading can be successful. If children cannot hear the *-at* sound in *bat* and *hat* and perceive that the difference lies in the first sound, then they will have difficulty decoding and sounding out words quickly and correctly.

> The human brain is not born with the insight to make sound-to-letter connections, nor does it develop naturally without instruction.

Whether children learn the alphabetic principle by direct or implicit instruction, the problems of inconsistent orthography are resolved the same way other learning challenges are—through practice. With sufficient, effective practice, children develop a context-sensitive understanding of letter-to-sound correspondence. Eventually, they learn that *-ough* in the context of *c_ _ _ _* is pronounced differently from the context *thr_ _ _ _.*

Letters to Words

Decoding

Phonological awareness helps the beginning reader decipher printed words by linking them to the spoken words that the child already knows. This process is called *decoding.* It involves realizing that a printed word represents the spoken word through a written sequence of letters (graphemes) that stand for phonemes, and then blending the phonemes to pronounce the word. Research studies indicate that a child must be able to decode with accuracy and fluency in order to read proficiently (Moats, Furry, and Brownell, 1998).

Decoding starts with learning the letters of the alphabet and the basic sounds they represent. There has been some discussion among researchers over whether beginning readers should learn the letters of the alphabet by their *names* (that is, *ay, bee, cee, dee,* etc.) or whether they should learn the letters by how the generally *sound* (that is, *ah, beh, cuh, duh,* etc.). Some linguists believe that learning how the letter sounds will accelerate the child's ability to link sounds to letters. At the time of this writing, the research literature was mixed as to whether either method is more effective.

Early decoding most likely starts when children match symbols in their environment to concrete objects in contextual situations. For example, many children recognize the golden arches and the McDonald's sign as a place they like to eat, yet they might not be able to read the word *McDonald's* out of context. Children might also recognize the word *corn* on a cereal box, but might not recognize it in a story. This situation is called *environmental print reading.*

Exactly how the human brain developmentally makes the connections between sounds and words needed for successful decoding is still unclear. But research studies, including some that used brain scans, have helped neurolinguists gain a better understanding of how written word knowledge develops in the beginning reader. One model was developed by Ehri (1998), who proposed four phases of word recognition during early reading (Figure 2.1). The phases are described as follows (Morris, Bloodgood, Lomax, and Perney, 2003):

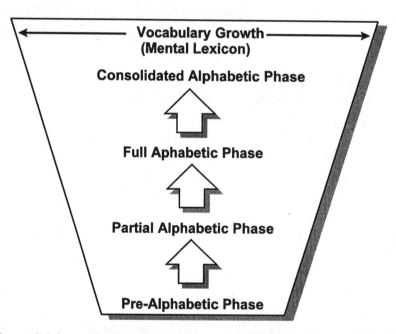

Figure 2.1 As word recognition develops over time from the pre-alphabetic phase to the consolidated alphabetic phase, the reader's vocabulary (the mental lexicon) grows dramatically (Ehri, 1998).

1. *Pre-alphabetic phase.* In this phase, children remember words by connecting visual cues in the word (such as the two *l*s in *bell* or the curve at the end of *dog*) with the word's meaning and pronunciation. There is no systematic letter-sound connection. Consequently, the child's ability to commit new words to memory or

retain old words is overwhelmed when visually similar words (such as *bell, ball, will,* or *dog, bug, dig*) are encountered in the text.

2. ***Partial alphabetic phase.*** In this phase, the child commits printed words to memory by connecting one or more printed letters with the corresponding sound(s) heard during pronunciation. For instance, a child might remember the word *talk* by joining the beginning and ending letters (*t* and *k*) with their corresponding spoken sounds *tuh* and *kuh.* New readers enter this phase when they know some letter-sound correspondences and can separate the beginning or ending sounds from the word. Words now become easier to remember because they can be processed through a more reliable letter-sound system rather than the unreliable visual cues used in the pre-alphabetic phase. This phase is sometimes called *sight-word reading* and the readers develop the ability to recognize certain familiar and high-frequency words. However, because these readers still have a limited memory, the ability to remember new words diminishes. They will confuse letters, misreading *take* or *tack* for *talk,* and usually cannot read text that has words outside their mental lexicon.

3. ***Full alphabetic phase.*** As reading progresses, phonemic awareness improves and the reader moves into this phase. Here, the child remembers how to read a specific word by making accurate connections between the letters seen in the word and the phonemes that are used in the word's pronunciation. For example, when reading the word *trap*, the child recognizes the initial consonant blend, */tr/,* then the medial vowel, */u/,* and then to the final consonant, */p/.* This complete phoneme-grapheme connection will facilitate committing this word to long-term memory, thus leading to more accurate reading.

4. ***Consolidated alphabetic phase.*** In this phase, the beginning reader begins to notice multi-letter sequences that are common to words stored in memory (such as the ending *-ake* in *cake, make,* and *take,* or the *-ent* in *bent, cent,* and *tent*). By forming a chunk for each common sequence, word reading becomes faster and more efficient. When encountering a new word containing the chunk (such as *dent*), the child just processes the beginning consonant and the chunk, instead of processing each letter separately. Chunking is particularly helpful when reading longer, multisyllable words like *practice, measurement,* and *traditional.*

As children master each phase, their mental lexicons grow dramatically. Ehri's model is consistent with others (Gough and Juel, 1991), all of which describe an increasing degree of phoneme awareness that occurs in stages. Beginning readers focus on the initial sound of a word *(bug = /b/ /-/ /-/).* Then they progress to processing the beginning and ending sounds *(bug = /b/ /-/ /g/),* and finally to each sound in the word *(bug = /b/ /u/ /g/).*

It should be noted that not all researchers believe that children acquire word recognition skills in a series of stages identified by different decoding strategies. Another theory suggests that children develop these skills gradually on the basis of many experiences with language and reading (Munakata, McClelland, Johnson, and Siegler, 1997). The idea is that children's decoding skills improve based on exposure to many examples and increased sensitivity to the internal structure of words, their components, and their corresponding pronunciations. In other words, progress in decoding is incremental and based on repeated word exposure rather than separated into stages that are based on the manipulation of letter cues. Regardless of whether decoding skills are acquired in stages or incrementally, no one doubts that a firm understanding of the alphabetic principle is essential for early success in learning to read.

Morphemes

What Are Morphemes and Morphology? As reading practice continues, the neural systems are no longer decoding words letter by letter, but are becoming better at recognizing *morphemes*. Morphemes are the smallest word elements that can change a word's meaning, such as the *-ing* that changes *signal* to *signaling*. They can stand on their own as a complete word (free morphemes) or exist as prefixes and suffixes (bound morphemes) that must be added to a root word. When readers understand morphemes, they can separate unfamiliar words into comprehensible parts. If the reader understands what *hate* means and also what *-ful* means, then the reader is likely to comprehend the meaning of *hateful*. This component of grammar that builds words out of pieces (morphemes) is called *morphology*.

There are two types of bound morphemes:

1. *Inflectional morphemes.* These are suffixes that provide information such as case (*Tommy's dog*), number (*dog/dogs*), tense (*he called*), and person (*she calls*).
2. *Derivational morphemes.* These are affixes (prefixes and suffixes) that create new words by changing the meaning of the root words. Some derivational morphemes change the root word's part of speech (*attend* is a verb, add *-ance* and *attendance* becomes a noun). Others, like *un-* and *re-*, change the root word's meaning but not the part of speech.

Morphology is an important component of our language, even to young brains. Research studies confirm that before they learn to read, children are more cognizant of morphology than phonology (Mann, 2000). This means they comprehend more easily that the inflectional morpheme *-s* in *dogs* represents the plural of *dog* than that the *-s* in *yes* represents a phoneme. They also understand more easily that the *-er* in *bigger* is a comparison to something that is already big than that the *-er* represents the second syllable in a word like *power*.

Morphological and Phonemic Awareness. Of course, when students first learn to read, phonemic awareness becomes all important as the young brain tries to match letters to sounds. But by grade 3, morphological awareness begins to surpass phonemic awareness in the development of decoding skills (Singson, Mahony, and Mann, 2000). Morphological awareness helps these students when they encounter multisyllabic words. A word like *indisputable* will be separated into its affixes and root word: *in-, dispute, -able.* Because such words do not appear frequently in their texts, the ability to understand these words will depend far more heavily on the reader's morphological awareness than on word recognition skills (Mahony, Singson, and Mann, 2000).

Other than helping to decode unfamiliar words, morphemes can also help the reader decide whether a word is an adjective (*singing*), noun (*singer*), or verb (*sing*), and thus assist in determining the word's meaning. The syntactic position of the word also helps determine its grammatical aspects, and this redundant information makes the sentence easier to understand and increases reading speed. At this point, word recognition is largely automatic and the reader can understand familiar words without consciously analyzing and decoding their phonemic characteristics. When a student can recognize enough words, the next step is to read sentences and paragraphs fluently.

Is Spelling Crucial to Reading?

Spelling becomes important almost as soon as the child has mastered phonemic awareness and begins to make the letter-sound correspondences. Now the new reader must match the variety of spellings to their sounds. Research studies have found that preschool children are sensitive to patterns in the way words are spelled and the pieces (morphemes) that can be attached to them (Treiman and Cassar, 1997). By grade 1, children note that *ck* never comes at the beginning of a word, and it is always preceded by a short vowel. Older children are not likely to spell *dirty* as *dirdy* because they recognize the morpheme *dirt* and a suffix.

As children progress in mapping letters and sounds, they discover an important reality about spelling: Usually, the mapping from spelling to pronunciation is more reliable than from pronunciation to spelling—the same sound can be spelled in different ways. This fact apparently causes some hesitation in word identification during reading. Recent research has shown that the more ways a sequence of phonemes can be spelled, the longer it takes to read a sentence containing that sequence. For example, *shelf* is read more quickly than *sneer* because the rime unit /ɛlf/ is always spelled *elf* whereas the rime unit /ir/ can be spelled as *ere, eer, ier,* or *ear* (Stone, Vanhoy, and Van Order, 1997; Peereman, Content, and Bonin, 1998). The researchers suspect that the hesitation is caused by a feedback mechanism in the reader's brain that verifies whether past experience supports the pronunciation of *eer* as /ir/. This notion demonstrates at least one way in which reading and spelling may be closely related.

> Success in reading does not automatically result in success in spelling.

Success in reading does not automatically result in success in spelling. Reading requires recognition whereas spelling requires production—a more complex skill that utilizes additional mental processes. Indeed, many skilled readers consider themselves to be terrible spellers. This is because so many English words do not adhere to strict phonetic rules. Almost every spelling-to-sound convention has exceptions. Nonetheless, good spelling is crucial for recognizing and decoding the meaning of words. To become an expert decoder, the reader will need to learn how to correctly identify and spell the exceptions. Studies show that the accuracy of a student's spelling in kindergarten and grade 1 is a predictor of later reading ability (Moats et al., 1998).

As students develop their spelling skills, they also increase their word recognition speed during reading. Word recognition becomes automatic, and skilled readers are now able to recognize new words based on their morphemes. For example, a student who recognizes the spelling of *react* in *reaction*, will realize that the words are related and make connections between their meanings. This is the primary way in which students expand their lexicon in grade 3 and beyond (Anglin, 1993). In sum, good spelling skills often lead to rapid word recognition and comprehension.

READING COMPREHENSION

Words to Sentences

Comprehension of reading material occurs when readers are able to place the meaning of individual words into the structure and context of the entire sentence. Furthermore, the reader's ability to remember the sentence's structure (syntax) relies on working memory. Let's examine first the role of syntax in sentence comprehension; working memory is discussed later in this chapter.

Syntax and Comprehension

When children read simple sentences, they grasp meaning mainly through simple associations that are already stored in the brain's word form area and the mental lexicon. The syntax is easy and there is little risk of ambiguity of meaning. In the sentence "The cat is white," only one interpretation is possible. But as sentences get more complex, syntax plays an important role in comprehension. Readers are more likely to encounter ambiguity in reading than in speech because written texts tend to use complex grammatical structures more often than casual conversation.

Before beginning to read, children already have a good sense of syntax as a result of speaking and listening. They learn that "I want cookie" sounds better (and may get more results) than "Cookie, I want" or "I cookie want." Their brains soon recognize a speech pattern: Who's acting? (subject), What's the action? (predicate), What's being acted upon? (object). Interestingly enough, this syntax pattern is common to many Indo-European languages. Sentence structure gets more complicated in reading, however. There are three types of syntactic structure for sentences, as follows (SLC, 2000):

- *Simple:* A simple sentence contains just one main clause, for example, "The boy rowed the boat."
- *Compound:* A compound sentence has two or more main clauses joined by connecting words, for example, "The boy rowed the boat while his mother watched."
- *Complex:* A complex sentence contains a main clause and one or more dependent or relative clauses. An example would be: "The boy who rowed the boat waved to his mother."

Many syntactic changes can occur within these three categories that change the meaning of these sentences. Some clauses can include negation ("The boy didn't row the boat.") or contain prepositional phrases ("to his mother"), or conjunctions ("The boy and his mother rowed the boat."). Using the passive voice will reverse the relative position of the subject and the object ("The boat was rowed by the boy."). Relative clauses can further complicate the matter, by being relative to the subject ("The boy who rows the boat is lost.") or relative to the object ("The boy rows the boat that is leaking.").

So how is a beginning reader going to deal with differences in meaning that result from variations in syntax? The following six syntactic variations can be particularly troublesome and require some basic strategies that, by the way, do not always work (SLC, 2000).

- Word order
- Minimum-distance principle
- Analysis of conjoined clauses
- Passive voice
- Negation
- Embedding

Word Order. As mentioned earlier, prereading children are accustomed to the subject-verb-object (SVO) sequence and rely heavily on it to decode early reading. This reliance is fine as long as the sentences are in the active voice, such as "He chased the dog." Difficulties arise, however, when sentences are in the passive voice, such as "He was chased by the dog." In the latter case, order of the words, *He, chased,* and *dog* was preserved, so the reader might misinterpret the sentence to mean "He chased the dog."

Minimum-Distance Principle. Beginning readers assume that words in a sentence refer to their closest related words, verbs referring to their closest preceding nouns, and pronouns to their closest noun of the same gender. The minimum-distance principle is easily applicable to the sentence "He rowed the boat all by himself," but not to "He rowed the boat that belonged to the fisherman all by himself." Readers are apt to rely more on the minimum-distance principle when the number of words they have to remember in the sentence exceeds the capacity of their working memory.

Analysis of Conjoined Clauses. While attempting to comprehend a sentence with two clauses, the young reader may assume that the two clauses are conjoined by a conjunction such as "and." Consequently, the reader may misinterpret the sentence "The man chased the dog that ate the steak" to mean "The man chased the dog, and the man ate the steak."

Passive Voice. For the young reader, the passive voice is particularly difficult to understand and learn. They violate the SVO sequence, and they can be particularly troublesome if they are reversible, such as "She was called by him," which could be mistakenly read as "She called him." Sometimes, common sense helps the reader to comprehend passive voice sentences correctly. For example, in the sentence "The window was broken by the baseball," it is clear that the window couldn't break the baseball, so only one interpretation makes sense.

Negation. Sentences written in the negative are usually more difficult for the young brain to comprehend. That is because the brain tends to interpret the sentence in the positive sense, and then moves to the second phase to process the negative sense. Consequently, the young reader will find the sentence, "Circle the picture that shows cows and sheep" easier to understand than "Circle the picture that has cows but not sheep." Substantial practice with negation can improve a reader's comprehension and fluency with these types of sentences.

Embedding. Embedded clauses can lead to ambiguity or misinterpretation. In grades 2 and 3, readers encounter the following three types of embedded clauses:

1. *The subject of the main clause is the same as the subject of the embedded clause.* Example: "The boy rowed the boat and waved to his mother." These are usually easy for young readers to understand.
2. *The object of the main clause is the subject of the embedded clause.* Example: "The man chased the dog that ate the steak." These are more difficult to comprehend accurately. The reader may incorrectly apply the conjoined-clause strategy here and read the sentence as "The man chased the dog, and the man ate the steak."
3. *The subject of the main clause is the object of the embedded clause.* Example: "The boat that the boy rowed belongs to the fisherman." Ambiguity arises because these types of sentences violate both the SVO sequence as well as the minimum-distance principle.

As students read more and as their working memory becomes more efficient, they gradually switch from using these rudimentary strategies to paying closer heed to the actual syntax of sentences.

Morphology and Comprehension

Morphology, you will recall, studies how words are put together from pieces (e.g., prefixes and suffixes), and how these pieces can change the meaning of words or create new ones. Morphological awareness contributes to reading comprehension in the following ways (Mahony et al., 2000):

- *Meaning.* The reader is able to distinguish the difference between nouns formed by adding *-tion* and nouns formed by adding *-ive.* Thus, *operation* and *operative* are formed from the same root word but have different meanings.
- *Syntactic properties.* The reader understands that a particular suffix indicates a part of speech. For example, *-y* indicates an adjective (*noisy*) and *-ly* indicates an adverb (*noisily*).
- *Phonological properties.* The reader understands that derivational suffixes can alter the pronunciation of the root word. For example, adding *-ic* to *hero* involves a shift in emphasis from the first syllable of *heroic* to the second, and adding *-al* to *hymn* involves pronouncing the previously silent consonant *-n* in *hymnal.*
- *Relational properties.* The reader understands the relationship between words formed by adding different prefixes and suffixes to the same root word, as in *import* and *export* or in *operation* and *operative.* When readers use relational properties effectively, their reading fluency, pronunciation, and comprehension improve. Furthermore, they get better at distinguishing between true morphological relationships, such as *sail-sailor,* and false ones, such as *may-mayor.*

Decoding Ability, Intelligence, and Comprehension

Research studies have shown that phonemic awareness is a stronger predicator of success with reading comprehension than intelligence during the stages of early reading (Torgesen, 1999). As children progress, however, the research evidence suggests that decoding speed as well as intelligence (as measured by standard IQ tests) are closely related to reading comprehension. One recent study involving 124 children found that decoding ability was the best single predictor of how well the child comprehended the reading. The child's IQ was also a significant predictor, although not as strong as decoding ability (Tiu, Thompson, and Lewis, 2003).

> Research studies show that during early reading phonemic awareness is a stronger predictor of success in reading comprehension than intelligence.

Reading Comprehension
and Language Comprehension

Research studies have demonstrated that reading comprehension is very closely related to spoken language comprehension. If that is the case, how do we explain those children who can read words but whose comprehension in reading is not as good as their spoken language comprehension? One possible explanation is that children learn spoken language in settings that are different from where they learn to read. Written language generally adheres to stricter grammatical structures and uses more formal vocabulary than spoken language. Consequently, how well a child comprehends a written text is determined by how well that child comprehends the same text when it is spoken.

> How well a child comprehends a written text is determined by how well that child comprehends the same text when it is spoken.

HOW MEMORY AFFECTS LEARNING TO READ

To understand how memory affects reading, we need a brief review of the brain's memory components. As researchers gain greater insight into the brain's memory processes, they have had to devise and revise terms that describe the various stages of memory. If you took a psychology course more than a decade ago, you learned that we had two memories, short-term (temporary) memory and long-term (permanent) memory. Neuroscientists now believe that we have two temporary memories that perform different tasks. It is a way of explaining how the brain deals briefly with some data, but can continue to process other data for extended periods of time. For now, short-term memory is used by cognitive neuroscientists to include the two stages of temporary memory: immediate memory and working memory (Squire and Kandel, 1999). Figure 2.2 illustrates the stages of temporary and permanent memory.

Immediate Memory

Immediate memory is one of the two temporary memories and is represented in Figure 2.2 by a clipboard, a place where we put information briefly until we make a decision on how to dispose of it. Immediate memory operates subconsciously or consciously and holds data for up to about 30 seconds. (Note: The numbers used in this chapter are averages over time. There are always exceptions to these values as a result of human variations or pathologies.) The individual's experiences determine its importance. If the information is of little or no

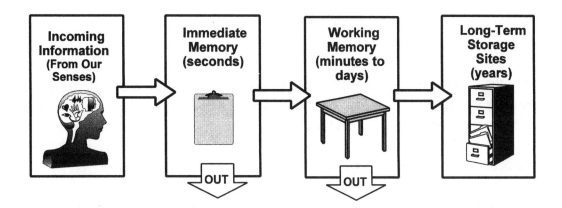

Figure 2.2 The diagram illustrates the theory of temporary and permanent memories. Information gathered from our senses lasts only a few seconds in immediate memory. Information in working memory usually endures for minutes or hours, but can be retained for days if necessary. The long-term storage sites (also called permanent memory) store information for years.

importance within this time frame, it drops out of the memory system. For example, when you look up the telephone number of the local pizza parlor, you usually can remember it just long enough to make the call. After that, the number is of no further importance and drops out of immediate memory. The next time you call, you will have to look up the number again.

Working Memory

Suppose, on the other hand, you can't decide whether to call the pizza parlor or the Chinese take-out place, and you discuss these options with someone else in the room. This situation requires more of your attention and is shifted into working memory for conscious processing. Working memory is the second temporary memory and the place where conscious, rather than subconscious, processing occurs. In Figure 2.2, working memory is shown as a work table, a place of limited capacity where we can build, take apart, or rework ideas for eventual storage somewhere else. When something is in working memory, it generally captures our focus and demands our attention. Scanning experiments show that most of working memory's activity occurs in the frontal lobes, although other parts of the brain are often called into action (Goldberg, 2001; Sousa, 2001a).

Capacity of Working Memory

Working memory can handle only a few items at one time. This functional capacity changes with age. Preschool infants can deal with about two items of information at once. Preadolescents can handle three to seven items, with an average of five. Through adolescence, further cognitive expansion occurs and the capacity increases to a range of five to nine, with an average of seven. For most people, that number remains constant throughout life.

This limited capacity explains why we have to memorize a song or a poem in stages. We start with the first group of lines by repeating them frequently (a process called *rehearsal*). Then we memorize the next lines and repeat them with the first group, and so on. It is possible to increase the number of items within the functional capacity of working memory through a process called *chunking*. In spoken language, chunking occurs when the young child's mind begins to combine phonemes into words, such as when *can* and *dee* become *candy*.

Time Limits of Working Memory

Working memory is temporary and can deal with items for only a limited time. For preadolescents, it is more likely to be 5 to 10 minutes, and for adolescents and adults, 10 to 20 minutes. These are average times, and it is important to understand what the numbers mean. An adolescent (or adult) normally can process an item in working memory intently for 10 to 20 minutes before fatigue or boredom with that item occurs and the individual's focus drifts. For focus to continue, there must be some change in the way the individual is dealing with the item. As an example, the person may switch from thinking about it to physically using it, or making different connections to other learnings. If something else is not done with the item, it is likely to drop from working memory.

This is not to say that some items cannot remain in working memory for hours, or perhaps days. Sometimes, we have an item that remains unresolved—a question whose answer we seek or a troublesome family or work decision that must be made. These items can remain in working memory, continually commanding some attention and, if of sufficient importance, interfere with our accurate processing of other information. Eventually, we solve the problem and it clears out of working memory.

Reading Comprehension and Working Memory

Spoken language uses memory systems for meaning. Memory helps students remember a set of oral directions: "Take out you math book and do the even-numbered problems on pages 18 and 19, and then check your answers on page 237." But reading is a far more complicated skill involving a number of brain systems. When reading a word, the decoding process breaks the word into its segments and, while being retained in working memory, the phonemes are blended to form words that the reader can recognize. The ability to retain verbal bits of information is referred to as *phonologic memory*.

When reading sentences, the visual and memory systems of the brain must decode and then retain the words at the beginning of a sentence for a period of time while the reader's eyes move to the end of the sentence. In a short sentence like "See the dog run," that is no problem because the memory time-span requirement is minimal. However, when reading complex sentences, such as "The boy ran down the street to tell his friend that the ice cream truck was just around the corner and would be here soon," requires much more memory time. Furthermore, the brain must pay attention to syntax and context in order for the sentence to be accurately understood. Because of working memory's limited capacity, beginning readers will have difficulty understanding long sentences or sentences with complex structure or syntax. They may be able to read the sentence aloud, but may not comprehend its meaning.

A child's ability to store words temporarily in working memory depends on several factors, such as age, experience, and language proficiency. But the code that readers of any age use to store written words and phrases is a phonological code. Consequently, phonological coding skills are crucial for using and developing the ability of working memory to store representations of written words. A reader with efficient phonological decoding skills will be able to quickly generate and retain phonetic representations of written words as well as preserve the words themselves and their sequence in the sentence. By developing these working memory skills, the reader with appropriate background knowledge can comprehend not only the sentence, but also the paragraph and the chapter (SLC, 2000).

> **Because of working memory's limited capacity, beginning readers will have difficulty understanding long sentences.**

During reading, working memory helps comprehension in the following two ways.

- *Understanding complex structure.* In complex sentences, such as "The woman who is getting into the blue car dropped her key," working memory holds the decoded results of the first part of a sentence while the visual cortex processes the words and phrases in the rest of the sentence. Working memory then puts all the pieces together to establish the sentence's meaning.
- *Preserving syntax (word order).* Take the sentence "The driver of the blue car, not the red car, honked his horn." Here, working memory preserves the word order so that the reader can process the sequence, recognize negation, and correctly identify who honked the horn.

As reading progresses, the meaning of each sentence in a paragraph must be held in memory so that they can be associated with each other to determine the intent of the paragraph and whether certain details need to be remembered. Working memory must then link paragraphs to each other so that, by the end of the chapter, the reader has an understanding of the main ideas encountered. With extensive practice the working memory becomes more efficient at recognizing words and at chunking words into common phrases. As a result, the child reads faster and comprehends more.

Forming Gists

Because working memory has a limited capacity, it cannot hold all the words of a long sentence. To deal with this limitation, working memory merges words within a clause to form a *gist* (the memory device known as *chunking*) that is then temporarily stored in place of the words. As reading continues, the brain adds new gists of clauses until the sentence is completed. Then a gist of the sentence is generated. Gists from other sentences in the paragraph are chunked to form a higher level gist of the paragraph. Then, gists of paragraphs are chunked to form an even higher level gist of the chapter, and eventually for the entire text. Table 2.3 shows how gists at one level combine to form gists of the next level.

Table 2.3 Levels of Reading Comprehension Gists in Working Memory		
4th Level: Chapter #1 gist ✚ Chapter #2 gist ✚ Chapter #3 gist ➡ **Text gist**		
3rd Level: Paragraph #1 gist ✚ Paragraph #2 gist ✚ Paragraph #3 gist ➡ **Chapter #1 gist**		
2nd Level: Sentence #1 gist ✚ Sentence #2 gist ✚ Sentence #3 gist ➡ **Paragraph #1 gist**		
1st Level: Clause #1 gist ✚ Clause #2 gist ✚ Clause #3 gist ➡ **Sentence #1 gist**		

Source: SLC, 2000

Early reading makes heavy demands on both the processing and storage functions of a young working memory. Chunking the representations of word forms into gists is an efficient way of managing the competition for space and time in working memory. Gists take up less space and are retained while individual word forms are deleted. Sentence gists are then deleted when paragraph gists are formed, and so on. Clause gists endure for about 30 seconds; chapter gists can last for 15 minutes or more (SLC, 2000).

Other factors affect the ability of working memory to retain or lose information during reading (Figure 2.3). New reading that the child finds interesting is likely to make it past immediate memory to working memory for conscious processing. And if the new reading activates material recently learned, long-term storage retrieves that information and moves it into working memory where it enhances the acquisition of the new learning. This process is called *transfer* and represents one of the most powerful principles of learning (Sousa, 2001a).

Reading information can also leave working memory. This can occur if

- Too many minutes have elapsed since the information was last activated. For instance, just after reading the first sentence of a lengthy paragraph, the reader gets involved in a brief conversation with another child. When the reader returns to the text, the previously-read material has faded and the child must start again from the beginning.

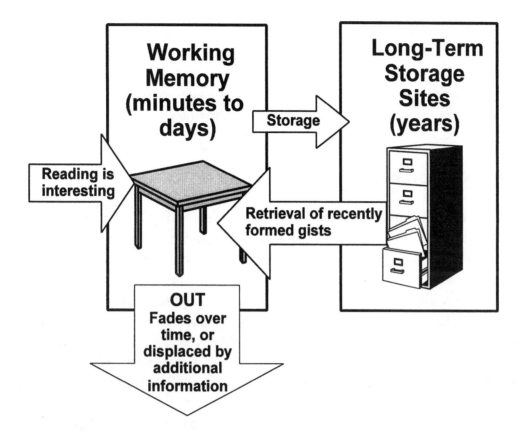

Figure 2.3 Reading and memory interact in several ways. Reading that is interesting to the reader will pass through immediate memory into working memory for conscious processing. New reading may activate long-term storage to retrieve related gists already learned. Reading information can fall out of working memory by fading or by being displaced by additional information.

- The information is displaced when additional information is placed in working memory and its capacity is exceeded. This can happen if the child is reading faster than he can comprehend, thus giving the brain insufficient time to form the necessary gists and then clear out the individual words. In this case, the words are removed from memory before the gist is generated, and comprehension suffers.

As more demands are placed on working memory during reading, other difficulties may arise. A young child who is just learning to read using a book with advanced vocabulary words will have trouble with comprehension because so much memory capacity is being used trying to decode unfamiliar words. Research studies on the pace at which people read have offered further insights into how memory affects comprehension. For example, the studies found that readers spent more time reading the topic sentence of a paragraph. This may indicate that working memory is exerting more effort to generate and ensure the retaining of this gist because it is most useful in understanding the rest of the passage, and for creating the gist of the entire paragraph. The research studies also demonstrated, to no one's surprise, that readers remembered best those ideas and concepts that were referenced repeatedly, as well as those that were linked through cause and effect (SLC, 2000). On the other hand, readers spent the least amount of time reading the details of a paragraph and, thus, had difficulty recalling them. They were able to recall, however, details related to a humorous or vivid event, probably because such events evoke emotion, a powerful memory enhancer.

Memory and Comprehension: Schema Theory

A reader's ability to comprehend gists is largely dependent on that individual's past experiences and the mental models that have evolved as a result of those experiences. We all use mental models to help us interpret the world and to predict situations occurring in our environment. These models, first suggested by Jean Piaget in 1926, are called *schemata* (singular, *schema*). They develop over time and represent frameworks or scripts that use general concepts stored in long-term memory to help us make meaning out of situations. For example, if some friends are telling you about the quality of food at a new restaurant, there is no need for them to also tell you that they sat at a table, got menus, and left a tip. These incidentals are filled in because they are part of your general model, or schema, about your past experiences at restaurants, and are implicitly understood.

Schemata are important in helping to comprehend text. Readers use their schemata to interpret cause and effect, to compare and contrast, and to make inferences about the author's meaning. Information that does not fit into these schemata may not be understood or may be understood incorrectly. This is one reason why readers may have problems comprehending text on a subject in which they have no experiences even though they understand the meaning of every word in the text (Driscoll, 1994). Schemata are greatly influenced by an individual's culture. Thus, young readers who were not brought up in the United States may have a difficult time reading and answering questions about George Washington.

Modifying Schemata

Schemata are created through repeated experiences with events, people, and objects that we encounter in our world. When we encounter a new experience, our schemata can be modified in any of the following three ways (Figure 2.4):

- *Accretion:* The learner incorporates the new information into an existing schema without altering that schema. For example, suppose I visited a public library and all that I experienced there fit into my long-held schema of a library as a place with just print material and a card catalog. As a result, I did not alter my library schema in any appreciable way.

Figure 2.4 This illustration shows how a stored schema helps us to interpret new information. As the new information is processes, the schema can be returned to long-term memory unchanged or altered to accommodate the new experience. In some cases, the new information cannot be accommodated by the current schema, so a new one is created.

- *Tuning:* The learner realizes that the existing schema is inadequate to accommodate the new information, and alters the existing schema to be more consistent with the experience. For example, when I visited a modern public library and realized that the card catalog was replaced by a computer database, I had to modify my library schema to accommodate this experience.

- *Restructuring:* The learner realizes that the new information is so inconsistent with the existing schema that a new schema has to be created. For example, now my ability to access the print information at the local public library directly from my computer at home any time of the day or night has forced me to create a new schema.

Using Schema Theory in Teaching and Learning

Schema theory reaffirms the importance of the role of prior knowledge in learning. Teachers of reading should consider using strategies that activate the reader's prior knowledge, thus enabling them to better understand the text. Effective strategies include the following (Armbruster, 1996):

✓ Read the heading and title. Have the readers examine visuals in the text, and make predictions based on the title and visuals.

✓ Provide content that has unifying themes, because information that lacks a theme can be difficult to understand, especially for readers with limited experiences.

✓ Use analogies and comparisons to elicit the readers' existing schema and to help them make connections between their schema and the new learning. Ask readers specific questions that can help in this process: "How does what you have read compare to what you already know about this subject?" "Does what you have read change any of your ideas?"

✓ Pay attention to the students' answers and comments. They may give clues about how the students are organizing information and what schemata they are using.

✓ Keep in mind how cultural differences may affect the reader's ability to interpret text, and avoid text that is so culture-biased as to interfere with a reader's ability to correctly comprehension the passage.

WHAT DO BRAIN SCANS REVEAL ABOUT READING?

Reading Pathways

Using functional imaging scans, neuroscientists have discovered the neural mechanisms involved in reading. As would be expected, the scans have shown that all readers use neural circuitry dedicated to visual processing, because the curves and lines of the alphabet need to be visually analyzed to distinguish one letter from another. In addition to the visual processing area, Shaywitz (2003) and other researchers (Indefrey et al., 1997; McCandliss, Cohen, and Dehaene, 2003) noted that three other areas of the brain were involved in reading. However, which of these three areas the brain used was dependent on how skilled the person was at reading. Apparently, beginning readers use different neural pathways than skilled readers, most likely because their needs are different. Here is what the researchers found.

> Beginning readers use different neural pathways than skilled readers.

Pathway for Novice Readers

The brain of a beginning reader needs to analyze each new word it encounters. It must pull it apart and associate the letters with their sounds. A region of the brain that overlaps portions of the parietal and temporal lobes—called the parieto-temporal area—is shown in Figure 2.5 and is the area where this important word analysis occurs. In this area, located

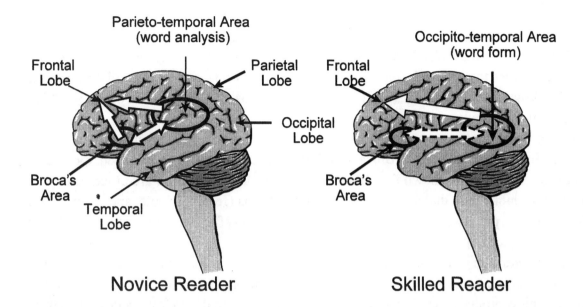

Figure 2.5 These diagrams show the brain systems used for reading. The novice reader uses the parieto-temporal area to slowly analyze new words with considerable help from Broca's area. However, the skilled reader uses the occipito-temporal area to quickly identify previously learned word forms, with just a little help from Broca's area, as indicated by the dotted arrow. Both types of readers activate the frontal lobe to generate meaning (McCandliss et al., 2003; Shaywitz, 2003).

above and slightly behind the ear, the brain begins to recognize certain relationships between the sounds of spoken language and the letters of the alphabet that represent them. Broca's area, specialized region for language located behind the left temple, is also significantly involved in this word analysis.

When, for example, the child's brain first sees the word *dog* in print, the word analysis area (parieto-temporal area) records the three alphabetic symbols and matches the *duh-awh-guh* sounds to their appropriate letters, *duh=d, awh=o,* and *guh=g.* We know this developing sound-to-letter relationship as the alphabetic principle. Eventually, a mental image of a furry animal is conceptualized in the mind's eye, adding meaning to the symbolic representation, *d-o-g.*

Pathway for Skilled Readers

With repeated encounters of the same word, the child's brain makes a neural model—called a word form—that encompasses the spelling, pronunciation, and meaning of that word. Current interpretation of the functional imaging scans supports the notion that word forms are stored in a region that overlaps the occipital and temporal lobes—called the occipito-temporal area—located toward the lower rear part of the brain. Here, all the important information about a word is stored, including its spelling, pronunciation, and meaning. Thus, when the word form is produced, the child can read this word far more quickly. Just seeing it activates all the components at once without any conscious thought on the part of the reader. As more word forms collect in this cerebral region, reading becomes more fluent and reading skill levels rise dramatically. Broca's area now plays only a minor role in assisting this region. The more skilled the reader, the more quickly this area responds to seeing a word—in less than 150 thousandths of a second (150 milliseconds), much faster than the blink of an eye (Price, Moore, and Frackowiak, 1996).

It is important to note that the occipito-temporal region is not an area specialized for reading in the same way that Broca's and Wernicke's areas are specialized for spoken language. Studies have shown that other types of sensory information are processed by the occipito-temporal area that are not related to word forms (Joseph, Noble, and Eden, 2001). However, with practice, this area can become exceptionally efficient at generating visual word forms during reading.

To summarize: Beginning readers use both Broca's area and the word analysis region to slowly analyze each word. Skilled readers, on the other hand, rely mainly on the word form area to rapidly produce meaning from words, with only marginal help from Broca's area when needed. As we shall see later on, children and adults with reading difficulties, including dyslexia, show distinctly different patterns of brain activation when reading from those described here.

MODELS OF READING PATHWAYS

Now that functional imaging scans have given us a clearer picture of the neural areas involved in reading, we can develop models that represent how the novice and skilled brains read.

The Novice Reader

Figure 2.6 shows the pathway and the components for the novice reader, one who usually sounds out new words while reading. The visual cortex records the word *dog* and sends the visual information to the word analysis region (parieto-temporal area). Working with Broca's area, these two networks analyze the word for its component phonemes and pronunciation. The pathway is indicated in the diagram by the white arrows labeled "N" (Shaywitz, 1996).

A visual word form is then produced and the mental lexicon is activated to identify the visual form. If the visual form for dog is retrieved, a conceptual representation is generated of a furry, barking animal. This is a relatively slow process because each step—spelling, pronunciation, and meaning—is treated separately. In the event that the lexicon cannot identify the visual form, a feedback loop may reactivate the visual cortex as well as the decoding and

Pathway for the Novice Reader

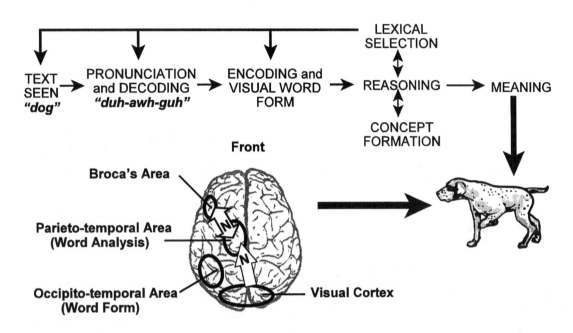

Figure 2.6 The diagram represents the neural pathways and linguistic components of the novice reader. The printed word stimulates the visual cortex, which passes the visual input information to the word analysis region (parieto-temporal area). Working with Broca's area, these two networks slowly analyze the word for its constituent phonemes and pronunciation (pathway indicated by the white arrows marked "N"). A visual word form is produced and the mental lexicon is activated to identify the word form and generate the concept of a furry animal that barks. If the lexicon cannot retrieve the word form, the visual cortex and coding areas may be reactivated to provide more input, thus slowing down the process.

encoding areas to provide more information, adding further delay. Although this feedback process takes more time, it can still be completed correctly.

The Skilled Reader

Following repeated encounters with the same word, the child's brain forms a composite neural model of the word that includes its spelling, pronunciation, and meaning. This word form model gets stored in the occipito-temporal area. As the number of words in the word form area grows, the child becomes a more skillful reader.

Figure 2.7 shows the neural pathway and components for the skilled reader. Note that the visual information about *dog* is sent to the word form region (occipito-temporal area) where all the relevant linguistic information is stored (indicated in the diagram by the white arrow labeled "S"). The mental image can be generated quickly, and the reader moves on to the next word. Imaging scans show that the word form area is in full activation when highly-

Pathway for the Skilled Reader

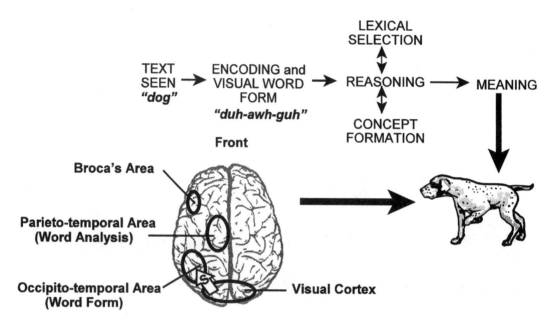

Figure 2.7 This diagram shows the pathway for the skilled reader. Visual information about the word *dog* is passed along to the word form region (occipito-temporal area) where all the linguistic and visual information about a dog is generated, indicated by the white arrow labeled "S." The lexical representation is quickly activated and a mental concept is formed.

skilled readers are moving through text. This indicates that reading skill relies heavily on the word form area (McCandliss, et al., 2003; Shaywitz, 2003). Keep in mind that although the processes outlined in Figures 2.6 and 2.7 appear linear and singular, they are really bidirectional and parallel, with many phonemes being processed at the same time.

Eye Movements During Reading

When we read, our eyes make rapid movements across the page, stopping for certain periods of time, called *fixations*. It is during these fixations of about 200 to 250 milliseconds that the eyes actually acquire information from the text. Then the eyes take about 20 to 40 milliseconds to move to the next fixation point, a distance of about nine letter spaces. During this time, vision is suppressed and no new information enters the processing system. Skilled readers also move their eyes backwards about 10 to 15 percent of the time in order to reread material. These *regressions* are needed when the reader has difficulty comprehending the text (Rayner, Foorman, Perfetti, Pesetsky, and Seidenberg, 2001).

Research studies on eye movements during reading lend further support to the notion that novice and skilled readers are processing written information differently. Novice readers fixate on every word in a text and they often fixate on the same word several times. Their fixation points are only about three letter spaces apart and their fixation periods run longer, from 300 to 400 milliseconds. Furthermore, up to 50 percent of their eye movements are regressions. These eye movements most likely indicate the difficulty the novice reader is having encoding the text. The longer fixation time may also result from the slower process of word analysis that occurs in the brain's parieto-temporal area. Table 2.4 shows a comparison of the eye movements of novice and skilled readers.

Table 2.4 Comparison of Eye Movements of Novice and Skilled Readers			
Reading Skill Level	Fixation Time (in milliseconds)	Fixation Span (in letter spaces)	Percentage in Regression
Novice	300 to 400	3	Up to 50
Skilled	200 to 250	9	10 to 15

Source: Rayner et al., 2001

Combining Written and Spoken Words

You will recall in the previous chapter we discussed a schematic representation of how the brain processes and recognizes spoken language (Figure 1.11). We mentioned then that written language must share some of the steps with the spoken language model. Figure 2.8 is a schematic representation of how the spoken and written language processing systems might interact. Words can enter the system through either pathway. However, words entering through the spoken word pathway are more likely to be learned easier because that process is facilitated by genetic influences and by Broca's and Wernicke's areas that specialize in spoken language processing.

The processing of written words, however, is not facilitated at the lower levels by any brain areas specialized for reading. Remember that to the occipito-temporal area, reading is just another collection of sensory stimuli that must be decoded and encoded in order to derive meaning. Several fMRI studies have shown that both Broca's and Wernicke's areas (sites of phonologic processing) were activated when participants were asked to generate written words (Joseph et al., 2001). Apparently, as you can see from the model, the formation of visual word forms (orthographic coding) relies

> How well and how quickly a child learns to read even common words depends a great deal on how well that child has acquired and practiced spoken language.

strongly on the ability to generate auditory word forms (phonologic coding). How well and how quickly a child learns to read even common words depends a great deal on how well that child has acquired and practiced spoken language.

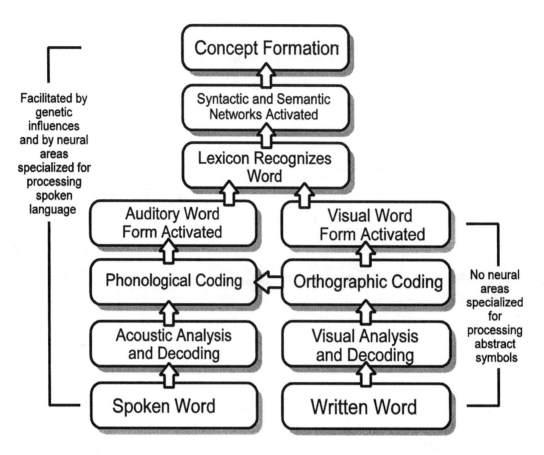

Figure 2.8 This is a schematic representation of the components involved in spoken and written language processing. Words can enter the system through either pathway. Words entering through the spoken word pathway are learned quicker because that process is facilitated by genetic influences and by brain areas specialized for spoken language. Note the horizontal arrow at the third step, which indicates that the ability to encode visual word forms (orthographic coding) relies strongly on the brain's ability to generate auditory word forms (phonological coding) (Gazzaniga et al., 2002).

THE IMPORTANCE OF PRACTICE

For most children, reading improves with practice. Experience in reading improves several components of the decoding and comprehension processes (Rayner et al., 2001). For example, practice

- Allows the mental lexicon and word form areas of the brain to acquire increasingly accurate representations of a word's spelling, thereby strengthening the connection between how the word sounds (the phonological form) and its spelling (the orthographic representation). This is called the *phonological-orthographic connection*. The stronger this connection, the faster one reads.

- Results in an increasing facility with words because it increases the quality of the words' representation in the lexicon, thereby enhancing comprehension.
- Turns low-frequency words into high-frequency words, improving the fluency of reading. Fluency involves developing rapid and automatic word-identification processes as well as bridging the gap between word recognition and comprehension.
- Increases familiarity with the patterns of letters that form printed words, thereby improving spelling. This is referred to as the *lexical-orthographic connection*. It is not the same as the phonological-orthographic connection. Both contribute in their own way to support the brain's ability to read words.
- Improves comprehension because the reader is exposed to both familiar and new words used in many different contexts. This helps the reader recognize that two words can have the same spelling, but have different meanings, grammatical functions, and pronunciation, such as: "I *lead* a team that tests our drinking water for *lead* and other metals."

Less able readers are likely to get less practice than more able readers. Consequently, the gap between more and less able readers increases over time. It was not surprising, then, that Cunningham and Stanovich (1997) found that reading ability in grade 1 was a strong predictor of reading ability in grade 11. This evidence contradicts a common belief that initial differences in reading ability wash out over time.

> Reading ability in grade 1 is a strong predictor of reading ability in grade 11.

Being a Skilled Reader

Skilled readers do not read each word individually, nor do their eyes move from word to word until they reach the end. Rather, they scan the text searching for patterns that will make the task of reading easier. To illustrate this, look at the following block of text and note any irregularities:

```
Q Q Q Q Q Q Q Q
Q Q Q Q Q Q Q Q
Q Q Q Q Q P Q Q
Q Q Q Q Q Q Q Q
Q O Q Q Q Q Q Q
Q Q Q Q Q Q Q Q
```

What did you notice? Most people will spot the letter "P" almost immediately, but miss the letter "O" in the fifth line. This illustrates the selectivity of vision. We notice something that violates the pattern but skim over something that very closely resembles it. These expectations of conformity guide our reading and allow us to increase our reading speed. This activity also shows the faster we read, the more detail we miss.

Another interesting characteristic of skilled reading is that the phonologic module becomes so adept at recognizing common words that it can do so even if the word is significantly misspelled. Can you understand the following text?

> Aoccdrnig to rseerach at an Elingsh uinervtisy, it deosn't mttaer in waht order the ltteers in a wrod are, the olny iprmoetnt tihnh is taht the frist and lsat ltteer is in the rghit pclae. The rset can be a total mses and you can sitll raed it outhit a porbelm. Tihs is bcuseae we do not raed ervey letetr by itslef, but the wrod as a wlohe.

Most skilled readers can read this paragraph despite the misspellings. Apparently, the beginning and ending letters as well as the context supply enough clues for the phonologic module to recognize the words and determine meaning.

What's Coming?

That the brain learns to read at all attests to its remarkable ability to sift through seemingly confusing input and establish patterns and systems. For a few children with exceptional language skills, this process comes naturally; most, however, have to be taught. In the next chapter, we discuss some considerations that parents and teachers should keep in mind when teaching children to read.

CHAPTER 3
Teaching Reading

This chapter addresses several basic questions about teaching reading. They include:

- *What are the basic characteristics of the various approaches to reading instruction?*
- *What strategies are effective for teaching phonemic awareness, phonics, spelling, fluency, vocabulary, and comprehension?*
- *What strategies are effective for teaching reading to students who have limited English proficiency?*

BRIEF HISTORY OF TEACHING READING

Reading instruction in the United States over the past 130 years has involved two general methods: an analytical method called the *phonics* approach and a global method called the *whole-word* (now, *whole-language*) approach (Figure 3.1). Phonics instruction was the earliest method for teaching reading. Children were taught the letter names and simple syllables from which they then constructed words. Emphasis was on phonics drill. In this analytical approach, bits of words were used to build syllables, then words and meaningful phrases.

At the beginning of the twentieth century, the emphasis shifted to a more global approach and choral reading emerged. Students would spell the syllable aloud together and then pronounce it. A few decades later, the pendulum swung back and phonics drill returned. But dissatisfaction with this method arose again in the 1940s, and the emphasis shifted back to a global approach known as whole-word instruction. The whole-word method placed little emphasis on phonics drill and more on recognizing entire words as the meaningful units of reading. The teacher showed the students a flash card with a word on it. After the teacher

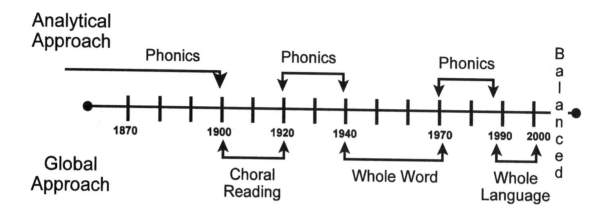

Figure 3.1 The timeline from 1870 to the present shows how the predominant method of reading instruction has alternated between analytical and global approaches. Today, the emphasis has shifted toward a balanced approach that seeks to combine phonics instruction with enriched reading text.

pronounced the word, the children would say it aloud. The small set of beginning vocabulary words was gradually expanded.

One major reason for advocating the whole-word approach was that the irregularities in the pronunciation of common words, such as *pint* (violates the pattern of *hint, mint, tint,* etc.) and *have* (violates the pattern of *gave, pave, save,* etc.) meant that the letter-to-phoneme correspondence was not very reliable. Therefore, emphasis should be on learning to memorize the pronunciation of whole words, not parts of words. Another argument for whole-word instruction was that it promoted comprehension early in the learning of reading: words have meaning, speech sounds do not (Rayner et al., 2001).

In the early 1970s, concerns over the poor results on standardized reading tests prompted a shift in emphasis back to phonics drill. At the same time, a psycholinguistic approach to reading was emerging, based on the work of Smith and Goodman (1971). Psycholinguistic advocates suggested that reading was like a guessing game in which readers determined meaning through a variety of redundant cuing systems present in rich literature. This approach, which became known as the whole-language method, also suggested that phonics not be taught separately because they were boring and failed to show the child that learning to read could be enjoyable. The proponents of phonics, however, were not convinced that the whole-language method (sometimes called the literature-based method) was effective. Thus, the so-called "reading wars" began in earnest and continued through the 1990s.

> For over a century, reading instruction in the United States has shifted between the phonics and whole-language approaches.

Basic Rationale for Phonics Instruction

Phonics instruction is based on the following concepts:

- Learning to read is not a natural ability for the human brain.
- Spoken language and written language are very different, and thus require the mastery of different skills.
- The alphabetic principle must be taught because it is not learned merely by exposure to print.
- The most important skill at the beginning stages of reading is the ability to read single words accurately, completely, and fluently.
- Context is not the primary factor in beginning word recognition.

Basic Rationale for Whole-Language Instruction

Whole-language instruction is based on the following concepts:

- Reading knowledge can be developed in the same natural way as spoken language.
- Children can often determine the meaning of an unfamiliar word by searching for semantic, syntactic, and phonetic cues in the text.
- Experiencing words in context leads to greater improvement in word reading than experiencing words out of context.
- Phonics knowledge is important but should not be explicitly taught.
- Reading should be a pleasurable experience for the child.

Figure 3.2 shows a comparison between the phonics and whole-language approaches to teaching reading. Obviously, the methods used to teach reading will dramatically affect the young brain's ability to decode abstract symbols into sounds and words that will result in obtaining meaning from print. Despite the passion of the supporters for both the phonics and whole-language approaches, experience has taught us that no one mix of instructional strategies and curriculum materials will work for every child. As a result of the reports of the National Research Council (Snow et al., 1998) and the National Reading Panel (NRP, 2000), many educators now suggest that the teaching of reading should use a balanced approach that includes a phonics component as well as enriched text. Figure 3.3 shows one way to look at the balanced approach to teaching reading.

> Experience has taught us that no one mix of instructional strategies and curriculum materials on teaching reading will work for every child.

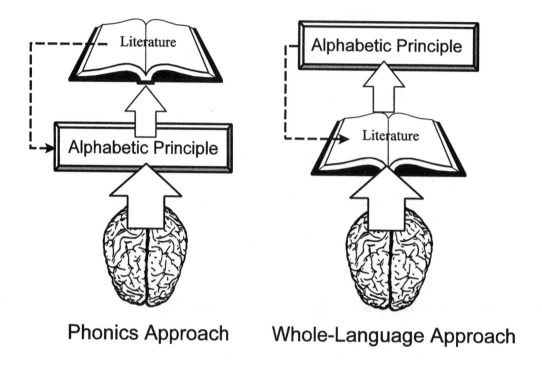

Figure 3.2 A comparison of the phonics and whole-language approaches to teaching reading. The phonics approach focuses on developing the alphabetic principle through decoding text before moving on to enriched literature. As reading progresses, letter-to-sound correspondences are strengthened and new ones learned (dotted arrow). The whole-language method focuses on reading literature early so that letter-to-sound correspondences develop naturally. As the alphabetic principle strengthens, more unfamiliar words can be read (dotted arrow).

Figure 3.3 In the balanced approach to teaching reading, students learn the alphabetic principle and use enriched literature together.

Basic Rationale for the Balanced Approach

The balanced approach is based on the following considerations:

- No one reading program is the best program for all children.
- Children need to develop phonemic awareness in order to learn to read successfully.
- Children need to master the alphabetic principle.
- Phonics are important but should not be taught as a separate unit through drill and rote memorization.
- Phonics should be taught to develop spelling strategies and word analysis skills.
- An important component is learning to read for meaning.
- Enriched literature helps students develop a positive dispositions toward reading and develops their ability to think imaginatively and critically.

There is still some persistent debate about what constitutes a balanced reading program. The question now is whether reading programs built around a balanced approach are based sufficiently on scientific research to meet the requirements of the No Child Left Behind Act. Regardless of their biases and perspectives, educators, parents, and policymakers must now recognize that reading is a *learned* skill, and the curriculum programs selected to teach reading must reflect what science continues to learn about how we acquire skills.

BRAIN RESEARCH AND LEARNING A SKILL

Research in cognitive neuroscience indicates that learning any skill, including reading, requires some basic elements if such learning is to be successful. These elements include the following (SLC, 2000):

- *Practice.* For the brain to build and strengthen the neural pathways required to learn a new skill, the learner must be repeatedly exposed to, and process, the material being learned. But the practice cannot be haphazard. Practice leads to permanency, so it is important that the activities associated with practice be carefully planned to ensure that the learning being stored is correct. As for reading, practice brings about true accomplishment. Studies show that the more a person reads, the better that person will be at reading at any age and at any level of proficiency.
- *Intensity.* Learning a new skill requires focus and concentration. Intense focus on a new skill allows the learner's brain to build more neural support for that skill in a short period of time. If you are planning on running a marathon, occasional

jogging will not have sufficient intensity to prepare and train your body. To become a skilled reader, the learner must first focus intently on the basic skills needed to learn the correct letter-to-sound relationships.

- *Cross-training.* Learning any skill is easier if it can be supported by other skills the student already knows or is learning at the same time. Cross-training involves bringing together a wide range of skills that reinforce overall comprehension of the material. Accomplished reading requires that the learner be simultaneously proficient in many different skills, such as spoken language fluency and comprehension.

- *Adaptivity.* When teaching a new skill, the teacher needs to assess the student's current skill level and adapt the new instruction accordingly. If the instructional skill level is too low, the learner may get bored and lose interest. If the skill level is too high, the learner may get frustrated and lose motivation. Reading instruction should include constant monitoring of the learner's progress so that the teacher can adapt the instructional strategies as needed.

- *Motivation and attention.* Motivation is the key to successfully learning a skill because it keeps students interested in paying attention and in practicing the skill. Reading instruction needs to include motivational strategies and texts that keep students interested and thus sustain attention.

None of the elements mentioned above will come as a surprise to any person who has taught. Nonetheless, they are worth reviewing. With so many reading programs available, these elements become important measures that teachers can use to assess the effectiveness of materials designed to support the teaching of reading.

MODERN METHODS OF TEACHING READING

With the growing support in the late 1990s for the balanced approach to teaching reading, the reading wars abated. But now a new war seems to have taken its place. The reports of the National Research Council (Snow et al., 1998) and the National Reading Panel (NRP, 2000) concluded that, based on scientific evidence, reading programs that included a strong phonics component were more likely to be successful with more beginning readers than programs lacking this component. At the same time, the research using fMRI technology described in Chapter 2 offered new insights into how the brains of novice, skilled, and struggling readers differed. Furthermore, intensive interventions with struggling readers (described later in Chapter 5) changed their fMRI images to resemble those of typical readers.

It did not take long for some researchers to question the findings of the National Reading Panel (Camilli and Wolfe, 2004; Krashen, 2001, 2002; Yatvin, 2003). Their criticisms included (1) concerns over whether the Panel's methodology was truly scientific, (2) suggestions that the results were crafted to fulfill a political agenda, and (3) cautions that the Panel's conclusions would promote one philosophical view of reading (i.e., phonics) over others. Even the results of the fMRI studies were challenged (Coles, 2004) as being of questionable value and deliberately misinterpreted to support the prescriptive approaches mandated by the No Child Left Behind legislation. Not surprisingly, other researchers responded in defense of the Panel's two years of work (Ehri, Shanahan, and Nunes, 2002; Shaywitz, 2003). Consequently, a new debate is in progress, this one over what constitutes good research in reading. School districts, meanwhile, are caught in the middle. The No Child Left Behind legislation requires districts to use scientifically-based reading programs just as researchers and politicians debate the meaning and intent of scientific evidence.

Where Do We Go From Here?

So, where do we go from here? Educators should become familiar with all positions so that they can understand the major issues involved in the debate. Ultimately, however, they need to make important recommendations regarding the type of reading program that is most likely to help young children learn to read successfully. Accordingly, let's consider what the major research studies have revealed about how the brain learns to read. The evidence presented here comes from the following sources:

- *The National Research Council (NRC) (Snow et al., 1998).* This 1998 report from the research arm of the National Academy of Sciences focused on how to reduce children's reading difficulties. It looked at how parental influences, family literacy, and preschool environments affect reading development. Although it did not make specific suggestions for reading curriculum, the report did make recommendations about teacher preparation, both in preservice and inservice training programs. However, the NRC report did not specifically address how critical reading skills are most effectively taught.

- *The National Reading Panel (NRP, 2000).* The report the NRP issued in 2000 was the result of two years of effort that included reviewing thousands of research studies on reading, interviewing parents and teachers, and recommending the most effective and scientifically proven methods for teaching reading. The NRP report took into account the report of the National Research Council and focused on the specific topics of alphabetics (phonemic awareness and phonics), fluency, vocabulary and text comprehension, teacher preparation, and the use of computer technology in reading instruction. Many of the recommendations of the NRP were translated into teaching strategies in a publication developed by the Center for the Improvement of Early Reading Achievement and funded by the National Institute for Literacy (NIFL, 2001).

- *Laboratory Studies.* Experimental studies conducted in laboratories are also providing new information about the reading process. Using brain imaging and mapping technologies, scientists are learning more about the brain regions associated with the different stages of learning to read. These studies include looking at the brains of people with reading problems.

- *Best Practices Research.* Best practices research on reading conducted in schools involved case studies that assessed whether certain instructional practices were more effective than others. These studies examined the practices of exemplary teachers to sort out what they were doing differently from others that resulted in greater student achievement. Several of these reports have been published recently, and they offer valuable insights into the effectiveness of various strategies for teaching reading. Although some of the studies involved a small sample of students, their results cannot be dismissed.

- *Evidence-based Practices.* Other research studies have looked at the effectiveness of practices in longitudinal and multi-level designs rather than just at exemplary teachers. Results from these types of studies are particularly valuable because they generally involve a large sample of students whose achievement is monitored for a year or more.

In this chapter, we will discuss the findings of these research studies and reports as they apply to the teaching of reading to children without any reading difficulties. Diagnosing children with reading problems, and how to address those problems, will be discussed in subsequent chapters. Figure 3.3 reminds us that reading involves the two major processes of decoding and comprehension. Successful decoding includes phonemic awareness, phonics, and fluency. Comprehension requires a developed vocabulary, interaction with the text, and a teacher whose training provides strategies for advancing the learner's ability to understand what is read.

RESEARCH FINDINGS ON READING INSTRUCTION — DECODING

Phonemic Awareness Instruction

Phonemic awareness, you will recall, is the ability to manipulate individual sounds in *spoken* language. Children have phonemic awareness when they can (1) recognize words beginning with the same sound, (2) isolate and say the first and last sounds in a word, (3) combine and blend sounds in a word, and (4) break a word into its separate sounds. Phonemic awareness and letter knowledge are the two best predictors of how well children will learn to read during their first two years of instruction. Even for middle and high school students, phonemic

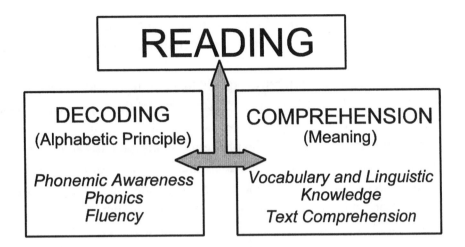

Figure 3.3 Successful reading is the result of the interaction between the decoding and comprehension processes. Decoding includes phonemic awareness, phonics, and fluency. Comprehension requires adequate vocabulary and linguistic knowledge, and interaction with text to capture meaning.

awareness is a good predictor of their ability to read accurately and quickly (Shaywitz, 2003). Phonemic awareness can be taught and learned.

The findings in the research examined by the NRC were (Snow et al., 1998):

- Learning to read depends critically on mapping the letters and the spellings of words onto the sounds of speech and speech units they represent.
- Explicit instruction in the phonological structure of speech and of phonemes and their spellings helps children acquire the alphabetic principle and use it appropriately when they encounter unfamiliar words in text.

> Even for middle and high school students, phonemic awareness is a good predictor of their ability to read accurately and quickly.

The findings in the research examined by the NRP showed that phonemic awareness instruction (NIFL, 2001):

- Helps children learn to read. Phonemic awareness is the first step in mastering the alphabetic principle, the ability to map letters onto the spoken sounds of language. As their mapping skills get better, they can read faster and with greater comprehension.

- Helps children learn to spell. Children who have phonemic awareness understand that letters and sound are related in a particular way, and that these relationships are important in spelling.

- Is most effective when children are taught to manipulate phonemes while handling cutouts of the letters of the alphabet that represent those phonemes. This allows children to see how phonemic awareness relates to their reading and writing. Learning how to blend letters with phonemes helps them to *read* words, and learning to segment letters with sounds helps them to *spell* words.

- Is most effective when it focuses on only one or two types of phoneme manipulation, rather than several types. Teaching too many types at once confuses children and may not allow enough time to teach each type well. Another possibility is that it may inadvertently result in teaching more difficult types before the children have learned the simpler ones.

> **After children are introduced to new letter-sound relationships, practice ensures that the learning is committed to long-term memory.**

- Is effective under a variety of teaching conditions with a variety of learners across a range of grade and age levels. Furthermore, the improvements in reading lasted well beyond the end of the phonemic awareness training, indicating mastery in most children.

Recent brain imaging studies have shown

- How effective practice can build new neural circuits. After children are introduced to new letter-sound relationships, additional practice is necessary to ensure that the learning is committed to long-term memory.

How Do I Teach Phonemic Awareness?

✓ Assess each child's phonemic awareness capabilities before beginning instruction. This will help identify which students should start with simple manipulation and which can move on to more advanced manipulation activities.

✓ A complete phonemic awareness program provides activities that include matching, isolating, substituting, blending, segmenting, and deleting sounds in words (Yopp and Yopp, 2000).

✓ Teach one or two types of phoneme manipulation to produce a greater benefit rather than teaching several types at once.

✓ Teach students to manipulate phonemes along with letters to enhance their mental lexicon. Have them say the whole word aloud and then the individual phonemes. Then write each letter on the board as they sound out its phoneme. This helps the students acquire the alphabetic principle.

✓ Remember that phonemic awareness instruction can benefit **all** children, including preschoolers, kindergartners, first graders, and even less able readers.

✓ Avoid spending too much time on phonemic awareness activities. The whole program should average out to about 10 minutes per day. Obviously, some students will need more time than others, perhaps up to 30 minutes per day (Brady and Moats, 1998).

✓ Small groups are usually more productive for phonemic awareness instruction. Children can benefit from hearing their classmates and receiving feedback from the teacher.

✓ Preschool (and parental) instruction should focus on
  • developing an awareness of rhyme
  • separating words into syllables and syllables into phonemes

✓ Kindergarten instruction should focus on
  • practicing the sound structure of words
  • the recognition and production of letters
  • knowledge of print concepts.

✓ Grade 1 instruction should provide
  • explicit instruction and practice with sound structures that lead to phonemic awareness
  • familiarity with sound-spelling correspondences and common spelling conventions and their use in identifying written words
  • sight recognition of frequent words
  • independent reading, including reading aloud

✓ Remember that phonemic awareness instruction is only one important part of a reading program. How well students learn to read and comprehend will depend not just on phonemic awareness but also on the effectiveness of the other components in the literacy curriculum.

> Phonemic awareness is only one important part of a literacy curriculum.

✓ Keep in mind the importance of practice. When children learn new letter-sound correspondences, they should practice them in isolation and then in reading aloud simple sentences and books. With every bit of practice and corrective feedback, the word form that will be stored in the brain's memory is likely to be accurate in pronunciation, spelling, and meaning. Through additional practice in spelling-sound patterns, a precise replica of the word form will be established in the neural circuits, and recognition of that word again in the future becomes easier.

Phonics Instruction

Phonics instruction teaches the relationship between phonemes of spoken language and the graphemes of *written* language, and how to use these relationships to read and write words. It includes helping children use the alphabetic principle to recognize familiar words automatically and accurately, and to decode unfamiliar words. Critics of phonics say that English spellings are too irregular for phonics instruction to be of any value. Nonetheless, phonics instruction teaches children a system for remembering how to read words. For example, when children learn that *ghost* is spelled this way and not *goast,* their memory helps them to remember the spelling and to recognize the word instantly. Although many words are spelled irregularly, most of them contain some regular letter-sound relationships that help children learn to read them. Moreover, students at risk for reading failure, such as those in special education and Title I programs, benefited the most from phonics-based programs (Foorman, Francis, Fletcher, Schatschneider, and Mehta, 1998). The NRP report summarizes the research on phonics instruction as follows (NIFL, 2001).

Phonics instruction that is systematic and explicit

- Makes a bigger contribution to a child's growth in reading than little or no phonics instruction.
- Significantly improves kindergarten and grade 1 children's word recognition and spelling when compared to children who do not receive systematic instruction. It should be noted that the effects of phonics instruction on students in grades 2 through 6 are limited to improving their oral text and word reading skills. Explicit phonics instruction beyond grade 6 is not generally productive for most students.
- Significantly improves children's reading comprehension. This is because their increased ability for automatic word recognition allows them more time to focus on and process the meaning of text. Contrary to what some believe, research studies indicate that phonics instruction contributes to comprehension skills rather than inhibiting them.
- Is effective for children from various economic and social levels.

- Particularly helps children who are having difficulty learning to read and who are at risk for developing future reading problems.
- Is most effective when introduced in kindergarten or grade 1.

How Do I Teach Phonics?

✓ Systematic instruction is characterized by the direct teaching of the letter-sound relationships of both consonants and vowels in a clearly defined sequence. Such programs give children substantial practice in applying these relationships as they read and write, as well as opportunities to spell words and write their own stories. Several approaches to teaching phonics exist, depending on the unit of analysis or how letter-sound combinations are presented to the student. They include
  - *Analogy-based phonics* - using parts of word families to identify unknown words that have similar parts
  - *Analytic phonics* - analyzing letter-sound relationships in previously learned words
  - *Embedded phonics* - learning letter-sound relationships during the reading of connected text
  - *Onset-rime phonics* - identifying the sound of the letter or letters before the first vowel (onset) in a one-syllable word and the sound of the remaining part of the word (the rime)
  - *Phonics through spelling* - learning to segment words into phonemes and to make words by writing letters for phonemes
  - *Synthetic phonics* - learning how to convert letters or letter combinations into sounds, and then how to blend the sounds together to form recognizable words.

✓ Effective programs for phonics instruction
  - Include knowledge of the alphabet, phonemic awareness, vocabulary development, the reading of text, and systematic instruction in phonics.
  - Help teachers systematically and explicitly instruct students in how to relate sounds and letters, how to break words into sounds, and how to blend sounds to form words.
  - Help children understand why they are learning relationships between sounds and letters.
  - Help children apply their knowledge of phonics as they read text.
  - Help children apply what they learn about sounds and letters to their own writing.
  - Can be adapted to the needs of individual students.

✓ Systematic programs in phonics introduce the child to different letter-sound pairings, starting with the simplest and most frequent combinations and then progressing to more complex and unusual ones. One approach (Carnine, Silbert, and Kame'enui, 1997) suggests

- *Start with one-to-one letter-sound relationships.* Introduce consonants that are predictable in their relationships between the letter and their sounds. A possible sequence could begin with : *m, t, s, f, d,* and *r,* and ending with *k, v, w, j, p, y.*

- *Continue with vowel sounds.* Vowels are needed to help make up words, but they can be more difficult for young children to pronounce than consonants. Identify long vowels that say their name, as the /a/ in *made,* the /e/ in *be,* the /i/ in *mine,* the /o/ in *row,* and the /u/ in *used.* Short vowels do not say their name, such as in *dad, tell, kid, top,* and *run.*

- *Phonic units.* These usually contain six to eight consonants and two vowels. As the children master more phonic units, they should be able to pronounce a larger number of words.

- *Complex letter-sound combinations.* Introduce common digraphs, such as *sh-* in *should, ch-* in *chip, th-* in *thing,* and the *wh-* in *what.* Later, the children will recognize larger phonetic combinations, such as *-tch* (*witch*), *-dge* (*fudge*), and *-ough* (*cough, rough*).

✓ Practice materials should include stories that contain words using the specific letter-sound correspondences the children are learning (often called decodable texts). They should also have practice writing letter combinations and using them to write their own stories.

✓ Phonics instruction can be taught effectively to individual students, small groups, or the whole class, depending on the needs of the students and the number of adults working with them.

✓ Phonics lessons should last typically from 15 to 20 minutes a day, but should also be reinforced during the remainder of the day with other activities in the child's reading program, including opportunities to read and write.

✓ Phonics instruction should be taught for about two years for most students, usually kindergarten and grade 1. If begun in grade 1, it should be completed by grade 2.

✓ Phonics instruction is but one of the necessary components of a comprehensive reading program, including phonemic awareness, fluency, and text reading and comprehension skills.

✓ Role reversal can be an effective strategy for helping children acquire the alphabetic principle. Ask the students to make up vocabulary words for you to write down. They should be nonsense words that the children create. Ask them to clearly enunciate each sound so that you can write the word down accurately (SEDL, 2001).

✓ Pay close attention to how children write. To assess their understanding of the alphabetic principle, it is not necessary for them to write accurately. It is important, however, that they write one symbol per sound; that is, a word with three phonemes should be represented in writing by three symbols.

Spelling and Invented Spelling

Spelling is closely linked to reading because it involves breaking apart a spoken word into its sounds and encoding them into the letters representing each sound. While learning to read words, children also learn how to spell those words. As children try to represent words with the alphabet, they often encode words by their initial consonants, followed by their ending sounds. Middle sounds, usually vowels, are omitted at first. Thus, *horse* might be written as *hrs,* and *monster* as *mstr.* The pronunciation of this *invented spelling* is very close to that of the intended word. Invented spelling allows children to practice applying the alphabetic principle and gain in phonemic awareness. It serves as a transitional step and assists in the development of reading and writing.

> Invented spelling allows children to practice applying the alphabetic principle and gain in phonemic awareness.

Studies on early literacy development have shown that invented spelling is a reliable measure of early reading achievement. One study found that preschool and kindergarten children who were inventive spellers performed significantly better on word reading and on storybook readings. In a literacy study of four grade 1 classrooms, two teachers encouraged invented spelling while the other two teachers encouraged traditional spelling. The inventive spellers scored significantly better than the traditional spellers on several measures of word reading that were administered during the second semester in grade 1 (Ahmed and Lombardino, 2000). Uhry (1999) found that invented spelling was the best predictor of how well kindergartners could match, through finger-point reading, spoken words to printed words in reading a sentence—a skill known as *concept of a word in text.*

When their invented spelling is accepted, children feel empowered to write more and with purpose, communicating their messages from the very beginning of school. Writing slows down the process of dealing with text, allowing children more time to recognize and learn about sound-letter relationships. For some children, writing may be an easier way to literacy than reading. In reading, the process involves changing letter sequences to sounds, whereas in writing the process is reversed—going from sounds to letters. Accordingly, writing may be a simpler task because it involves going from sounds in the child's head that are already known and automatic, to letters, rather than from the unknown letters in reading to what is known (Chomsky, 1979).

Some researchers in the past have raised concerns about whether the persistent use of invented spelling leads to confusion and the formation of bad spelling habits. But research studies indicate that, with appropriate teacher intervention, the invented spellings gradually come closer to conventional forms. Consequently, spelling errors should not be seen as an impediment to writing but as an indication of the child's thought processes while making sense of letter-sound relationships. From that perspective, the errors could yield important information about a child's internal reading patterns (Sipe, 2001). On the other hand, remember that practice eventually makes permanent. The consistent repetition of incorrect spellings will, in time, lead to their storage in long-term memory. Therefore, teachers should use strategies that will help children transform invented spelling into conventional spelling.

How Do I Teach Spelling?

✓ Effective spelling instruction focuses on helping children go from sound to letter, which strongly reinforces their reading—going from letter to sound. Spelling instruction is more than memorizing word lists. It should follow a logical sequence that starts with phonemic awareness, demonstrates which letters represent which sounds, and introduces the notion that the same sound can have different spellings (Shaywitz, 2003).

✓ *Moving away from invented spelling.* Techniques, such as using sound boxes (also known as Elkonion boxes) drawn on paper, can help the child enunciate the word slowly and recognize other sounds that need to be represented by letters. For example, if the child spells *dog* as *dg,* you draw a box for the first sound /d/ = *duh* and the child enters the letter *d* and puts a marker or coin on it. By stretching out the pronunciation of the word, the child hears the /ô/ = *auh* sound. Now draw another box, enter the letter *o* and ask the child to push a marker into it. This continues until the last phoneme, /g/ = *guh* is represented by the letter *g.* The process can be repeated until the child is confident in hearing the middle vowel sound (Figure 3.4).

✓ Another technique for correcting spelling is the Have-a-Go chart (Bolton and Snowball, 1993). Students use this chart (Figure 3.5) when they need your assistance with words they have misspelled. The student writes the misspelled word in the first column. Use the sound box (Figure 3.4) to stretch the word and

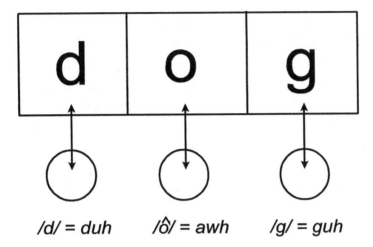

/d/ = duh   /ô/ = awh   /g/ = guh

Figure 3.4 This sound (Elkonion) box technique requires the student to move a marker (or coin) into the box several times while pronouncing the letter's sound. It helps the child detect the middle vowel sounds and thus represent them in spelling (Sipe, 2001).

ask the student to listen for phonemes. After sounding out the word several times, the student writes the word again in the Have-a-Go column. If incorrect, you can write the word correctly. The student then writes the correct word in the third column. Now encourage the student to recall the correct spelling mentally and to write it again in the fourth column to enhance retention of the correct spelling in long-term memory.

Have-a-Go Chart

Misspelled Word	Have-a-Go	Correct Spelling	Copied Spelling
Bots	Boats		Boats
Clen	Cleen	Clean	Clean

Figure 3.5 Students write the misspelled word in the first column. The teacher might use the sound box (Figure 3.4) to stretch the word and ask the student to listen for phonemes. The student writes the word again in the Have-a-Go column. If incorrect, the teacher either writes the word or refers the student to a dictionary. The student then writes the correct word in the third column and copies it again in the fourth column to enhance retention in long-term memory (Bolton and Snowball, 1993).

✓ As spelling progresses, introduce children to spelling strategies they can use to help spell new words. Later, tell them about words, like *colonel* and *could,* that do not match the spelling rules they were taught.

✓ A study conducted by Ahmed and Lombardino (2000) analyzed the spelling of 100 kindergarten children for letter omission, letter substitution, as well as letter voicing and devoicing. Based on their spelling scores, the children were identified as low, middle, or high in spelling acquisition. The researchers suggested that teachers consider the following strategies, based on the students' spelling acquisition levels:

Low-level spellers:

✓ Teach that a monosyllabic word must be spelled with a vowel (Example: *cat*, not *ct*).
✓ Show children how to distinguish between the name of a vowel letter and its sound in closed monosyllabic words (Example: the letter *a* has a different sound from its name in the word *cat.*
✓ Help children master spelling consonants that have only one letter form and a corresponding letter name (Examples: *b, d, m, p, t*).
✓ Have children practice closed monosyllables consisting of the five vowel sounds (*a, e, i, o, u*) and the consonants that have one corresponding letter (Examples: *bat, met, sit, not,* and *put*).

Mid-level spellers:

✓ Teach the vowel lengthening rule by adding the silent letter *e* after a consonant (Examples: in *lake* and in *time*).
✓ Help children learn to spell consonants that do not have a corresponding letter name (Examples: *ch-* as in *child,* and *sh-* as in *shop*).
✓ Teach how to spell consonant blends (Examples: *dr-* as in *drink, tr-* as in *trap*, *-mp* as in *damp, -ng* as in *wing,* and *-nk* as in *think*).

High-level spellers:

✓ Have children practice the spelling of frequently occurring vowel digraphs (Examples: *-ai* as in *sail, -ee* as in *bee, -oa* as in *coat*).
✓ Then practice the floss rule—double a word's final *-f, -l,* or *-s* if it follows a short vowel (Examples: *buff, fill,* and *toss*).
✓ Help children understand the meaning of the suffixes *-ed* and *-ing,* and practice their spellings.

In the past, writing was often delayed until children could spell every word correctly. Such an approach inhibited the flow of thoughts necessary for children to attain literacy. Accepting invented spelling allowed children to engage in meaningful writing more than they ever expected. Furthermore, the processes used by teachers to correct spelling develops phonemic awareness and reading. The key to corrective spelling lies with the interventions that teachers *purposefully* use to guide children's writing from invented to conventional spellings. If left alone to grapple with the bizarre nature of English orthography, children will grow frustrated with spelling. But with appropriate teacher interventions, children can overcome the orthography maze and eventually learn the rules, patterns, and exceptions that control spelling in English.

How Teaching Writing Can Affect Spelling and Reading

Few research studies have examined the links between beginning writing and its influence on spelling accuracy and reading. Nonetheless, there is growing evidence that these skills are interrelated. Handwriting is not just a motor skills process or exercise in penmanship. It draws on letter knowledge because to write a letter, the child must attach a verbal label (the letter's name) to the letter symbol, have a precise image of the letter in memory, and be able to retrieve that letter from memory when needed. Some researchers suggest that this direct link between letter knowledge and writing letter forms may indicate that poor handwriting is the result of weak letter knowledge rather than the result of motor difficulties (Berninger et al.,1997).

> Studies have found that explicit instruction in spelling for kindergarten children improved both their spelling and reading abilities.

Studies by O'Connor and Jenkins (1995) and Vandervelden and Siegel (1997) found that explicit instruction in spelling for kindergarten children not only improved the children's spelling ability but also improved their reading ability. The explicit instruction in these studies included using magnetic letters to spell words, speech-print matching of words, Elkonion boxes (Figure 3.4) for spelling, and onset deletion and substitution activities.

What should be the nature of writing instruction in kindergarten classes? Despite the limited research, some suggestions do emerge from these studies (Berninger et al., 1997; Graham, Harris, and Fink, 2000; Vandervelden and Siegel, 1997).

✓ Writing instruction is equally effective whether it is distributed throughout the kindergarten day or taught as a single daily activity.

✓ The instruction should include components related to handwriting, letter writing accuracy and fluency, spelling, and, if appropriate, simple compositions.

✓ Kindergarten children, even those with reading and writing difficulties, can be taught how to form and write letters. This can be accomplished by modeling newly introduced letters, practicing letter names while writing letters, tracing letters with numbered arrow cues, practicing letters from memory, and asking children to circle letters that represent their best work.

✓ Kindergarten children can learn to spell consonant-vowel-consonant (CVC) words as they learn beginning reading skills related to letter-sound correspondences, blending, and segmenting.

✓ At the beginning of the year, writing lessons in kindergarten that feature specific instruction in letter formation and spelling could be extended to include short compositions later in the year; for example, write a sentence describing a picture, or write a short story explaining what is happening in the wordless picture book.

Fluency Instruction

Fluency is the ability to read a text orally with speed, accuracy, and proper expression. Case studies report that fluency is one component that is often neglected in the classroom. Children who lack fluency read slowly and laboriously, often making it difficult for them to remember what has been read (recall the limited capacity of working memory) and to relate the ideas expressed in the text to their own experiences. Frequent practice in reading is one of the main contributors to developing fluency.

Fluency bridges the gap between word recognition and comprehension. Because fluent readers do not need to spend much time decoding words, they can focus their attention on the meaning of the text. With practice, word recognition and comprehension occur almost simultaneously. Of course, a student will usually not read all text with the same ease. Fluency depends on the reader's familiarity with the words, and with the amount of practice reading the text. The fluency of even skilled readers will slow down when encountering unfamiliar vocabulary or topics. To read with expression, readers must be able to divide sentences into meaningful chunks that include phrases and clauses. As comprehension speed increases, readers develop a sense of knowing when to pause appropriately at the ends of sentences, and when to change tone and emphasis.

> Frequent practice in reading is one of the main contributors to developing fluency.

Fluency and Automaticity. Although the terms are often used interchangeably, it should be noted that fluency is not the same as automaticity. Automaticity is the fast and effortless word recognition that comes after a great deal of reading practice. It does not refer to reading with expression. Thus, automaticity is necessary, but not sufficient, for fluency. Two approaches, each of which has several variations, have been used to teach fluency.

- *Guided repeated oral reading.* This approach encourages students to read passages aloud several times and receive systematic and explicit guidance and feedback from the teacher.
- *Independent silent reading.* This approach encourages students to read silently on their own, inside and outside the classroom, with minimal guidance and feedback.

Researchers have investigated these two main approaches and have found the following (NIFL, 2001):

- *Repeated oral reading.* Monitored repeated oral reading improves reading fluency and overall reading achievement. Students who read passages aloud and receive guidance from their teachers become better readers because this process improves word recognition, speed, accuracy, and fluency. It also improves reading comprehension, but to a lesser extent. This approach even helps struggling readers at the higher elementary grade levels.
  - Round-robin reading—where students take turns reading parts of a text aloud, but not repeatedly—in itself does not increase fluency. This may be because students usually read a small amount of text and only once. Furthermore, the children are likely to pay attention only when it is their turn to read.
  - Children become good readers when they gain an increased sensitivity for how the printed word relates to how it is pronounced. This ability requires the child to pay attention to letter strings and the phoneme sequences in those strings. Children who have attained this ability can read pronounceable nonwords, and the pronunciation errors that they make in reading are plausible. When this occurs, the child's brain is apparently doing some form of phonological recoding, that is, recoding the spellings so they can be pronounced. Opportunities for this recoding occur when children read aloud to a parent or teacher. Feedback from these attempts build up the child's recognition of the written (orthographic) form of unfamiliar words. Several research studies conclude that reading aloud promotes the acquisition of printed word representations in the child's mental lexicon (Share and Stanovich, 1995).
  - Many studies indicate that good readers read the most and poor readers read the least. The suggestion here is that the more children read, the better their fluency, vocabulary, and comprehension. However, these findings do not indicate cause and effect. It is possible that the more children read, the better their fluency. But it may just be that better readers simply choose to read more.
  - The popular belief that fluency was a direct result of proficiency in word recognition is not supported by recent research. Although word recognition is a necessary skill, fluency is now seen as a separate component that can be developed through instruction. Informal Reading Inventories (IRIs), running

records, and miscue analysis are appropriate measures for identifying problems that students are having with word recognition, but are not suitable measures of fluency. Simpler measures, such as calculating words read correctly per minute, are more appropriate for monitoring fluency.

- *Independent silent reading.* No research evidence is currently available to confirm that instructional time spent on silent, independent reading with minimal guidance and feedback improves fluency and overall reading achievement in young readers. Given that instructional time is limited, there may be better ways to spend reading time in the classroom than silent reading. Nonetheless, you should encourage students to read more outside of school rather than devote instruction time to independent reading. Students could also read on their own in class during independent work time when, for example, they have finished one activity and are waiting for another one to begin. Independent reading does build a reader's vocabulary. Some researchers estimate that young readers who engage in independent reading for just 10 minutes a day read over 600,000 more words each year than students who do no independent reading. Increasing the reading time to 20 minutes a day raises the words read to over two million a year (Cunningham and Stanovich, 1998; Hart and Risley, 2003).

How Do I Teach Fluency?

✓ Have students read aloud and provide effective guidance and feedback to improve their fluency. Students need instruction in fluency when
  - Their word recognition errors exceed 10 percent when reading a text they have not practiced.
  - They cannot read orally with expression.
  - Their comprehension is poor after reading a text orally.

✓ *Literature Circles.* Combine reading instruction with opportunities for them to read books at their independent level of reading ability. One technique is to use literature circles where small groups of students discuss a piece of literature in depth. The group is formed by the choice of the book rather than by ability. Literature circles allow students to discuss, on their own, events, characters, and their own personal experiences related to the story. This process helps students engage in reflection and critical thinking as well as construct meaning in their interactions with other students. For more information on literature circles, see the **Resources** section.

✓ Read aloud daily to your students. By your being a good model of fluent reading, students learn how a reader's voice can help text make sense. Then have the students reread the text, perhaps up to four times to improve fluency. Students can practice reading aloud in several ways. The methods are listed in Figure 3.6 in the order of increasing student independence and of decreasing teacher involvement (Carbo, 2003).

- *Shared reading.* This is an interactive reading activity in which students join in the reading of a large book as guided by the teacher. After placing the book on an easel so it can be easily seen, the teacher uses a pointer to guide the reading, pointing to the words as they are read. The teacher may wish to read the text first, asking students to predict a word or phrase or summarize what is happening. Later, the teacher and students take turns reading, and choral reading may also occur. The goal is to work toward phrase fluency rather than reading the text word by word.

- *Student-adult reading or neurological impress.* In this one-on-one method, the adult provides a model of fluent reading by reading the text first. The student then reads the text and the adult provides encouragement and assistance as needed. The student rereads the passage three or four times until fluency is attained. In a variation of this method, called neurological impress, the teacher reads a passage softly into the student's dominant ear as they both use their fingers to follow along in the text.

- *Tape-assisted reading.* An audiotape of a fluent reader is used for this strategy. The reader should read at a speed of about 80 to 100 words per minute to ensure that the students can follow the words and gain meaning. At first, the students read the passage to themselves. Then they listen to the tape and follow along, pointing to the words in their books as the reader says them. Next, the students read aloud along with the tape several times until they can read the text independently.

More Student Independence
Less Teacher Involvement

Readers' Theatre

Partner Reading

Choral Reading

Tape-Assisted Reading

Student-Adult Reading

Shared Reading

Less Student Independence
More Teacher Involvement

Figure 3.6 The diagram illustrates the range of teacher and student involvement for various models of teaching reading (Adapted from Carbo, 2003).

- *Choral (unison) reading.* Students read along as a group with an adult reader, either from a big book or from their own copy. Choose a text that is short and aimed at the independent reading ability of most students. Begin reading and invite students to join in as they recognize the words you are reading. After three or four readings, the children should be able to read the text independently.

- *Partner or paired reading.* This technique pairs a more fluent reader with a less fluent reader. The more fluent student reads first, providing a model of fluency. Then the less fluent student reads aloud while the stronger partner provides assistance with word recognition and feedback. Another format is to pair readers of similar fluency to reread parts of a story to each other.

- *Readers' theatre.* In this activity, students rehearse (but not memorize) and then perform a play in front of their classmates. They read from scripts that have been taken from books rich in dialogue. A narrator may be used to give any necessary background information, and the students read lines as characters in the play. This novel approach provides an enjoyable opportunity for rereading text, practicing fluency, and promoting cooperation among the students in the class. In one study, students participating in this activity for a period of ten weeks made an entire year's gain in improving their reading rates (Martinez, Roser, and Strecker, 1999). Readers' theatre is appropriate for students in second grade through high school.

✓ Consider having other adults, such as parents and other family members, read to the class and to their children at home. The more models of fluent reading the children hear, the better. Such an approach increases the children's vocabulary, their familiarity with written language, and their knowledge of the world.

✓ In primary grades, read aloud from a big book while pointing to each word as you read it. The children will notice when you are raising or lowering your voice, and you may need to explain to them why you are reading a sentence in a certain tone.

✓ Fluency develops when students can read a text repeatedly with a high degree of success; that is, they can decode and understand about 95 percent of the words. If the text is more difficult, students will spend so much effort and time on decoding that they will not develop fluency. Restrict text to 50 to 200 words, depending on the age of the reader, and include a variety of nonfiction, poetry, and stories to maintain interest.

✓ Because they contain rhyme, rhythm, and meaning, poems are an easy and enjoyable way for children to practice reading.

✓ One measure of fluency is the average number of words the student can read correctly in a minute. Graphing words correct per minute (WCPM) throughout the year can show a student's reading growth. These values can be compared to published norms to determine whether students are making suitable progress in their reading fluency. Table 3.1 explains how to calculate words correct per minute. After making the calculation, compare the result to average oral reading frequency norms. Some local school districts have set their own norms to help teachers assess their students' progress in fluency. Table 3.2 lists oral reading frequency norms compiled from Hasbrouck and Tindal (1992), Mather and Goldstein (2001), NAEP (2003), and NIFL (2001). Figure 3.7 suggests a sample graph for grade 2 that you could use to show a student's progress in WCPM throughout the school year.

Decoding and the Balanced Approach

In response to the renewed interest in phonemic awareness, some schools adopted a modified form of whole-language that includes teaching modules for explicit phonics instruction in addition to the literature-based instruction. A few studies have shown that reading achievement for students in these "balanced" programs improved more than those in the pure whole-language programs, provided certain conditions were met (Fitzgerald and Noblit, 2000; Pressley, 1998). The programs that showed improvement were those where the instruction in phonological awareness followed a scope and sequence with texts based on developing letter-sound correspondences. Further, the phonological and literature-based components represented an integrated balance of skills and meaningful applications of the research on reading and reading instruction.

It seems, then, that a balanced approach involving adequate, purposeful instruction in phonological awareness (including phonemic awareness) and supplemented later by literature is a workable framework for teaching young children to read. Children bring a knowledge of spoken language when they encounter the printed page. They need to learn the written symbols that represent speech, and to use them accurately and fluently. Reading instruction should begin with phonics, using decodable text, and then move to contextual and enriched reading as the student gains competency and confidence. Thus, some of the principles of whole language can be incorporated later as part of reading development.

> Reading instruction should begin with phonics, using decodable text, and then move to enriched texts as the student gains competency and confidence.

Table 3.1 Calculating Words Correct Per Minute (WCPM) and Reading Accuracy	
Steps	**Example**

Select three brief passages from a grade-level basal text. Have the student read each passage aloud for exactly one minute. Count the total number of words the student read for each passage.	Words read per minute:
	    Passage 1: 88
	    Passage 2: 83
	    Passage 3: 85

Compute the average number of words read per minute.	Average is: 88 + 83 + 85 = 256 / 3 = 85.3

Count the number of errors the student made on each passage.	Errors made per minute:
	    Passage 1: 10
	    Passage 2: 7
	    Passage 3: 8

Compute the average number of errors per minute.	Average is: 10 + 7 + 8 = 25 / 3 = 8.3
Subtract the average number of errors read per minute from the average number of words read per minute. The result is the average number of words correct per minute (WCPM).	Average words less average errors: 85.3 – 8.3 = **77.0 WCPM**
The WCPM can also be used to calculate a student's average percentage of accuracy when reading. Simply divide the WCPM figure by the average number of words read per minute and multiply by 100.	Percent accuracy: 77.0 / 85.3 x 100 = **90.3%**

Table 3.2 Average Reading Rates for Students in Grades 1 to 12	
Grade Level	Words Correct per Minute by End of Year (50th Percentile and Above)
1	50 – 75
2	90 – 120
3	110 – 135
4	115 – 145
5	125 – 165
6	177
7	191
8	205
9	219
10	233
11	247
12	261

Sources: Hasbrouck and Tindal (1992), Mather and Goldstein (2001), NAEP (2003), and NIFL (2001).

Words Correct Per Minute for Student X

Grade 2

Figure 3.7 This is a sample graph of a student's words correct per minute scores throughout the school year. It is an easy way to show progress in developing reading fluency. In this example, the student's progress was monitored monthly, but less frequent assessments are also appropriate.

Answer to Test Question # 4

Question: Research studies have concluded that neither the phonological approach nor the whole-language approach is more effective in teaching most children how to read.

Answer: *False.* Numerous research studies have found that mastering the alphabetic principle does not come naturally to most children, and that instructional techniques that explicitly teach this principle through phonological awareness are more effective with most children than those that do not.

RESEARCH FINDINGS ON READING INSTRUCTION — COMPREHENSION

The ultimate goal of reading is for children to become sufficiently fluent to understand what they read. This understanding includes literal comprehension as well as more sophisticated reflective understandings, such as "Why am I reading this?" and "What is the author's point?" Reading comprehension depends heavily on spoken language comprehension. As children master the skill of word identification, their reading comprehension improves dramatically. Reading comprehension is a complex cognitive process that relies on several components to be successful. To develop reading comprehension skills, children need to

- Develop their vocabulary and linguistic knowledge
- Thoughtfully interact with the text to derive meaning

Let's take a look at each of these areas and review the relevant research.

Vocabulary and Linguistic Knowledge Instruction

Vocabulary refers to the words we know that allow us to communicate effectively. Words that we use in our speech or that we recognize when listening comprise our oral vocabulary. Words we recognize or use in print comprise our reading vocabulary. Oral vocabulary becomes the basis for comprehension in reading. A child with a good grasp of the alphabetic principle can encounter an unfamiliar printed word and decode the word into

---

What Are Decodable Texts?

Some confusion exists about what constitutes a decodable text. Two reasons may explain the confusion. First, the word "decodable" is used differently by researchers and by educators and policymakers. In research studies, "decodability" is a measure of the regularity of word pronunciation as decoded by the reader's phonological module. It does not refer specifically to phonics instruction. To educators and policymakers, however, decodable text contains a certain number of words that could be expected to be pronounced (i.e., decoded) as a result of phonics lessons already taught.

Second, the documents issued by educators and policymakers offer many different definitions of a decodable text. In general, the documents state that a decodable text should be composed of words that use the letter-to-sound correspondences that have already been taught, but there is no agreement on what the percentage of such words should be. There is no research available at this time to support any specific recommendation of a particular proportion of decodable words in beginning reading texts (Allington and Woodside-Jiron, 1998).

---

speech. If the word is in the mental lexicon, the child will be able to understand it. However, if the word is not in the lexicon, the child will have to determine its meaning by other means. Consequently, the larger the child's oral vocabulary, the more easily the child will comprehend text. As children learn, pronounce, and use more words in their speech and reading, their linguistic knowledge develops. They get more confident in their understanding of letter-sound combinations, more adept at recognizing semantic differences, and more aware of the various classes of words (e.g., adjectives, nouns, and verbs) used in a sentence.

The scientific research on vocabulary instruction reveals that some vocabulary must be taught directly but that most vocabulary is learned indirectly. The research also has shown the following:

- Children learn the meanings of most words indirectly, through everyday experiences with oral and written language. These experiences include conversations with other people, listening to adults read to them, and reading on their own. They learn vocabulary words directly when they are explicitly taught individual words and word-learning strategies.

- Some vocabulary should be taught directly. Direct instruction is particularly effective for teaching difficult words representing complex concepts that are not part of the children's everyday experiences.

- Repeated exposure to vocabulary in many contexts aids word learning and linguistic knowledge. The more children see, hear, and read specific words, the better they learn them and their various meanings.
- Vocabulary acquisition can be affected by several factors. In a broad review of the research literature on vocabulary, Swanborn and de Glopper (1999) found that factors such as ability, age, and text density had an impact on the chances that students will learn new words in context. Table 3.3 shows the factors and their influence on vocabulary acquisition. Low-ability students have only an 8 percent chance of learning new words in context, but that number climbs to 19 percent for high-ability students. Not surprisingly, older students in grade 11 have a 33 percent chance of learning new words while fourth-graders have only an 8 percent chance. Text density measures the number of new words per given number of words. The lower the text density (1 new word in 150), the greater the chances of learning a new word (30 percent). The chances drop to only 7 percent when the text density reaches to 1 new word in 10.

Table 3.3 Factors Influencing Chances of Learning New Words in Context	
Factor	**Chances of Learning New Word**
Ability: Low Medium High	8 percent 12 percent 19 percent
Age: Grade 4 Grade 11	8 percent 33 percent
Text Density: 1 new word in 10 words 1 new word in 74 words 1 new word in 150 words	7 percent 14 percent 30 percent

Source: Swanborn and de Glopper, 1999

- Linguistic knowledge includes one's ability to (1) hear, distinguish, and categorize the sounds of speech (phonology), (2) understand the rules that constrain how words are put together in phrases and sentences (syntax), and (3) understand the meaning of individual words and sentences and the relationships between them (semantics).

How Do I Teach Vocabulary?

Selecting Vocabulary. Selecting which vocabulary words to teach separately is an important instructional decision. To help in this selection process, consider the following:

✓ Be sure to teach those terms that are central to the unit of study. These should be terms that are so important that students who do not understand them will have difficulty comprehending the text. Avoid selecting words that will have little value to students after they complete the unit test.

✓ Remember the capacity limits of working memory and keep the number of new words per lesson to no more than five for elementary students and up to seven for secondary school students. This will give you more time to teach each word in depth, resulting in greater student comprehension.

✓ Choose other new words with care. Although a chapter may have 10 to15 new words, only 3 or 4 may address critical components of the chapter. Avoid selecting words in the text just because they are italicized or in boldface print, or words that the student will never encounter again.

✓ Include words that will be used continually throughout the text or unit of study. Having a deep understanding of these words will allow students to build on them as they develop new information over the long term.

Other Guidelines. Here are some other guidelines for teaching vocabulary.

✓ You can promote indirect learning of vocabulary by
   • Reading aloud to your students, regardless of the grade level or subject that you teach. Students of all ages will learn vocabulary better if you read text containing difficult words. Discuss the text before, during, and after you read to help students attach meaning to unfamiliar words by connecting them to past knowledge and experiences. Then ask the students to use the newly-learned words in their own sentences.
   • Encouraging students to read extensively on their own.

✓ You will not have time to teach directly all the words that students might not know in a text. In fact, it is better not to try to teach all the unknown words so that students can develop their own word-learning strategies. Word-learning strategies include using

- *Dictionaries and other reference aids.* Students need to learn how to use dictionaries, thesauruses, and glossaries to deepen and broaden their knowledge of words. You can show them how to find an unknown word in the classroom dictionary and note that there may be several different definitions for the word. Read the definitions one at a time and have the class discuss which one is more likely to fit the context of the story. For example, in the sentence "The workers went into the mine," the children may confuse *mine* with the possessive word form. After you finish reading the various definitions from the dictionary, the students can eliminate the inappropriate definitions and settle on "a hole made in the earth to find coal or minerals."

- *Information about word parts to figure out the meanings of words in text.* Word parts include affixes (prefixes and suffixes), base words, and word roots. Students learn that certain affixes change the meaning of words in a specific way. For example, the prefix *dis-* usually means the negative or reverse of the root word's meaning (*disrespect* means showing no respect). Base words are words from which many other words can be formed. The base word *complete* can form the words *completely, incomplete, incompleteness, completion, completing.* Word roots are the words from other languages (mainly Latin and Greek) that are the origin of many English words.

- *Context clues to determine the meaning of words.* Context clues are hints about the meaning of an unknown word that are provided by the words, phrases, and sentences that surround the word. The clues may be descriptions, examples, definitions, or restatements. However, not all context clues are helpful, because they give little information about a word's meaning. Descriptive words that are used in a literary or obscure way are particularly difficult to comprehend through context clues. For example, in the sentence "She gave a strained response," *strained* could have a number of meanings in this context, such as *squeaky, hoarse, noisy, difficult, tense,* and so on.

- *Associating an image with a word.* Imagery is a powerful memory device. Whenever students can associate an image (or other symbolic representation) with a new word, they are more likely to remember the word and its meaning.

✓ With early readers you will probably be able to teach about 10 new words per week. Focus your teaching time on the following types of words:
  - *Important words.* Directly teach those new words that are important for comprehending a concept or the text. Give the students some word-learning strategies to figure out the meanings of other words in the text.
  - *Useful words.* Teach directly words that students are likely to encounter and use repeatedly. For example, it is more useful for students to learn the word *biology* than *bionic,* and the word *journey* is more useful than *excursion.*

- *Difficult words.* Provide instruction for words that are particularly difficult for the students. Especially challenging are words that are spelled or pronounced the same but have different meanings, depending on the context. Here are but a few examples of words that are spelled the same but have different meanings in a sentence:

  > The bandage was *wound* around the *wound.*
  > When shot at, the *dove dove* into the bushes.
  > She did not *object* to the *object.*
  > They were too *close* to the door to *close* it.

  Problems also arise with words that are spelled and pronounced the same, but have different meanings, such as *store* (place to buy things) and *store* (to put away), *land* (piece of ground) and *land* (bring down an airplane), and *arms* (limbs) and *arms* (weaponry).

> With early readers you will probably be able to teach about 10 new words per week.

✓ When selecting reading texts, it is important to know the level of word knowledge that students will have for those texts. Students know the vocabulary words in their mental lexicon in varying degrees that researchers divide into the following three levels:

- *Unknown.* A word that is completely unfamiliar and its meaning is unknown.
- *Acquainted.* A word that is somewhat familiar and the student has some idea of its basic meaning.
- *Established.* A word that is very familiar and the student can immediately recognize its meaning and use the word correctly.

Assess the child's level of familiarity with the words in a specific text according to these three categories. If the assessment indicates few or no unknown words, consider selecting a more difficult text to challenge the child and to build vocabulary.

How Do I Teach Linguistic Knowledge?

✓ Linguistic knowledge (SEDL, 2001).

- *Phonology.* To assess phonological skill, play the "same or different" game by generating pairs of words that are either identical or differ in some subtle way. Say them aloud and ask if they are the same or different. Most children should not miss hearing the different ones. Sometimes children can hear the differences between similar sounding words, as *glow* and *grow,* but have difficulty articulating that difference in their own speech. Difficulty with articulation does not mean difficulty with perception. When a child mispronounces a word, say the mispronounced word back to the child as a question. The child with normal phonologic skills will repeat the statement, trying to make you understand the meanings.

- *Syntax.* The rules of English prohibit the haphazard arrangement of words in a sentence. Poor syntax can make meaning ambiguous (see Chapter 2). One way to assess syntactic skill is to give the children sentences with a key word missing. Ask them to supply the word that would correctly fill the blank. Remember that a child's answer may not make sense, yet still be syntactically correct. Develop syntactic skills by helping children build more complex sentences. For example, after showing a short video, ask students to describe something they saw or heard ("I saw a tree" or "I heard a bird."). Then ask them to build their sentences ("I saw a tree and heard the bird singing.").

- *Semantics.* Semantics describes meaning. One way to assess semantics is to create sentences and stories that have logical inconsistencies and see if the children can detect them ("Mary went to the store because she enjoys staying home."). Instructional activities that develop semantics include asking children to substitute words (synonyms) that would have the same meaning in context, and suggesting that they use context to guess the meaning of unknown words.

Text Comprehension

Just because readers are able to sound out words does not guarantee that they will comprehend what they read. Many reading teachers have witnessed group reading sessions where students could sound out a story with great effort but really had little understanding of what had been read. Children who are first learning to sound out words are using substantial mental effort, so fewer cerebral resources remain for the cognitive operations needed to comprehend the words being read aloud. It is critical for children to develop fluency in word recognition. When they are fluent, word recognition requires far less mental effort, freeing up the child's cognitive capacity for understanding what is read. Thus, explicit instruction in word recognition to the point of fluency is a vital component for text comprehension.

Tan and Nicholson (1997) conducted a study that showed the importance of word-recognition instruction to the point of fluency. Struggling primary-level readers who were taught new words with instruction that emphasized word recognition to the point of fluency (i.e., they practiced reading the individual words until they could recognize them automatically) answered more comprehension questions correctly than did students who experienced instruction emphasizing individual word meanings (i.e., instruction involving mostly student-teacher discussions about word meanings).

Text comprehension occurs when readers derive meaning as a result of intentionally interacting with the text. Such comprehension is enhanced when readers actively relate the ideas represented in print to their own knowledge and experiences and can construct mental representations in their memory. Hence, good readers are both purposeful and active. Purposeful means they may read to find out how to use a computer, read a magazine for entertainment, read a classic novel for enjoyment, read a guidebook to gather information about a tourist spot, or read a text book needed for a course. Good readers are active in that they get the most out of their reading by using their experiences and knowledge about the world, their understanding of vocabulary and language structure, and their knowledge of reading strategies. When problems with reading occur, they know how to solve them.

The scientific research on text comprehension reveals the following:

✓ Comprehension is a complex interactive process that begins with identifying words by using knowledge outside the text, accessing word meaning in context, recognizing grammatical structures, drawing inferences, and self-monitoring to ensure that the text is making sense. When confronted with several meanings for a word in a sentence, the brain needs to select the one that makes sense in context. How this happens is the subject of much research. One possible mechanism, called the *structure-building framework* (Gernsbacher, 1990), suggests that readers construct meaning by activating mental representations of concepts that are relevant to the text and blocking those that are irrelevant. Figure 3.8 illustrates the cognitive mechanism, using the example of a reader encountering the sentence "The man planted a tree on the bank." *Bank* has two common meanings, but only one fits the context of this sentence. The mental lexicon may activate both at first, but skilled readers quickly suppress the irrelevant meaning. Less skilled readers, however, spend more time considering alternative meanings and may not make the correct selection in the end. Many English words have dozens of meanings, depending on their context. Thus, developing the ability to quickly block irrelevant meanings becomes a necessity for reading fluency and comprehension. (This process is similar to the syntactic blocking described in Chapter 2, whereby syntactic rules are blocked for the formation of irregular verbs.)

✓ Text comprehension is improved by direct, explicit instruction that helps readers use specific strategies to make sense of the passage. These strategies represent the purposeful steps that enable readers to reason strategically whenever they encounter barriers to understanding what they are reading. Comprehension strategies include self monitoring, graphic and semantic organizers, answering questions, generating questions, recognizing story structure, and summarizing.

✓ Teaching comprehension strategies in the context of specific academic areas can be effective at all grade levels. Cooperative learning is a particularly useful technique for helping students to understand content-area texts (see Chapter 6).

"The man planted a tree on the bank."

```
                        ┌─────────────────────────────┐
                        │          Experience:         │
                        │                              │
                        │   Activates      Blocks      │
                        │   relevant       irrelevant  │
                        │   concept        concept     │
                        └──────┬──────────────┬────────┘
                               │              │
                               ▼              ▼
   ┌──────────┐
   │ "bank"   │──►  "bank" = Side of a river ──►(Correct)
   │          │
   │ Mental   │──► "bank" = Financial institution  (Incorrect)
   │ Lexicon  │
   └──────────┘
```

Figure 3.8 The diagram illustrates how the brain deals with multiple meanings of a word. Spoken language experience activates the relevant meaning while blocking the irrelevant meaning.

How Do I Teach for Text Comprehension?

Text comprehension occurs when the brain's frontal lobe is able to derive meaning by processing the visual and auditory input that resulted from reading with the reader's prior knowledge. Teachers should emphasize text comprehension as early as the primary grades, rather than waiting until children have mastered reading basics. The basics of decoding can be learned in a few years, but reading to learn subject matter does not occur automatically and requires constructing meaning at all grade levels.

Start Teaching Comprehension Strategies Early. At what grade level can teachers begin to include instruction in comprehension strategies? Tradition curricula have favored honing word-recognition skills in the primary grades while developing comprehension skills in the later grades. Recent research (NRP, 2000; Snow et al., 1998) studies suggest, however, that instruction aimed at improving comprehension (i.e., instruction beyond word-recognition) does make a significant impact on literacy during the primary years. Student reading achievement in the primary grades improved when decoding and word recognition were taught systematically with comprehension strategies. This approach was particularly effective in raising reading achievement for children in high-poverty schools (Taylor, Pearson, Clark, and Walpole, 2000).

The instructional approaches that have received the strongest support from scientific research are the following (NIFL, 2001):

✓ *Comprehension monitoring.* This is a self-monitoring strategy to help students recognize when they understand what they are reading and when they do not. They also learn appropriate strategies for resolving problems in comprehension. Metacognition (thinking about our own thinking) is an effective means of monitoring comprehension. Before reading, simply ask them to clarify their purpose for reading this text and preview the text with them. As part of the preview, ask the students what they already know about the content of the selection. During reading, they should monitor their understanding and adjust their reading speed to match the difficulty of the text. Students can use several different forms of monitoring, such as

- Identifying where the difficulty occurs ("I don't understand the third paragraph on page 10.").
- Identifying what the difficulty is ("I don't know what the author means when he says...").
- Restating the difficult passage in their own words ("Oh, so the author means...").
- Looking back through the text ("The author talked about . . . in the previous chapter. Maybe I should reread that chapter to find out what he is talking about now.").
- Looking ahead in the text for information that might help resolve the difficulty ("Oh, the next section seems to have some information that may help me here.").

After reading, they should summarize in their own words what they understood from the passage. Their summaries can be addressed to the teacher or shared with other students in cooperative learning groups.

✓ *Using graphic and semantic organizers.* Graphic organizers are effective visual tools for illustrating the interrelationships among concepts in a text. Known by many different names (e.g., frames, clusters, webs, text maps, visual organizers), they provide cues about connections between and among ideas that can help students better understand difficult concepts. Semantic organizers look a little like a spider web. They have lines connecting a main idea to a variety of related ideas and events. Both of these types of organizers help students read to learn subject matter in all content areas because they capitalize on the brain's innate aptitude for remembering patterns. Figure 3.9 illustrates examples of a spider map and a semantic map that can be used to enhance reading comprehension. Chapter 6 contains more on different types of graphic organizers.

> Graphic organizers are effective visual tools for illustrating how concepts in a text are related.

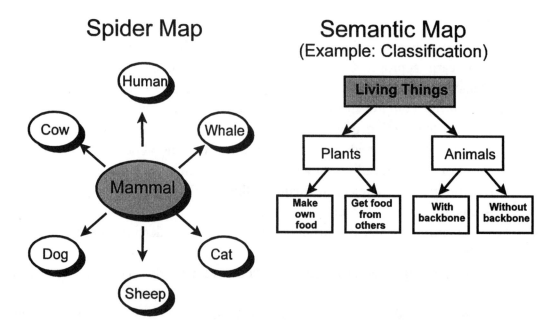

Figure 3.9 Visual organizers come in many forms. Here are examples of a spider map of types of mammals (left) and a semantic map for a simple classification of living things.

✓ *Answering questions.* Research studies show that teachers' questions strongly support and advance how much students learn from reading. The questions are effective because they
  • Give students a purpose for reading
  • Focus the students' attention on what they are to learn
  • Help students to interact with what they read
  • Encourage students to monitor their comprehension
  • Help students relate what they are learning to what they already know. The instruction helps readers learn to answer questions that require an understanding that is
       Text explicit – stated explicitly in a single sentence
       Text implicit – implied by information presented in two or more sentences
       Scriptal – not found at all in the text, but part of the reader's prior knowledge or experience.

✓ *Generating questions.* Teaching students to ask their own questions helps them become aware of whether they understand what they are reading. By generating their own questions, students focus on the purpose of the reading, improve their active mental processing, and learn to integrate information from different segments of the text.

✓ *Recognizing story structure.* Story structure describes how the events and content of a story are organized into a plot. Teaching about story structure helps student learn to identify categories of content, such as initiating events, goals, setting, internal reactions, and outcomes. How this content is organized into a plot can often be revealed through story maps. Story maps are a type of graphic organizer that illustrates the sequence of events in a simple story. They can be powerful aids for understanding and remembering stories (see Figure 5.2).

✓ *Summarizing.* When summarizing, students synthesize and integrate the most important information and concepts in the text. To do this successfully, students must identify the main ideas, connect them to each other, eliminate unnecessary information, and remember what they read.

✓ *Mental imagery.* Readers (especially young readers) who form mental pictures, or images, during reading understand and remember what they read better than readers who do not visualize. Urge readers to form visual images of what they are reading, such as picturing a character, event, or setting described in the text. This will not be easy because children today are exposed to technology that provides many images for them. Consequently, they have little practice at imaging and need to be given clear directions on how to do it.

✓ *Paraphrasing.* This strategy aids in comprehension by having students first hear the text read aloud, then reading it quietly themselves and taking notes, rewriting it in their own words, and discussing their paraphrased text with their classmates. Paraphrasing is effective because it involves reading, writing, speaking, and listening, all of which lead to a deeper understanding and greater memory of the text (Fisk and Hurst, 2003).

Another particularly effective strategy for developing comprehension focuses on reading and other activities related to a central theme. Because the varied classroom activities center around this theme, students can more easily comprehend their related readings (NIFL, 2001).

✓ *Concept-oriented reading instruction (CORI).* The teaching framework for CORI includes four phases: (1) observe and personalize, (2) search and retrieve, (3) comprehend and integrate, and (4) communicate to others. Here is an example of how CORI was implemented in one school. First, the teachers identified a conceptual theme for instructional units to be taught for 16-18 weeks in the fall and spring. The themes selected by third-grade teachers were the adaptations and habitats of birds and insects for the fall. In the spring, the third-grade units were weather, seasons, and climate. Fifth-grade units in the fall were life cycles of plants and animals, and the spring units emphasized earth science, including the solar system and geological cycles.

At the beginning of each unit, students performed observation and hands-on activities both outside and inside the classroom. Third and fifth graders participated in such activities as collecting and observing crickets, constructing spider webs, dissecting owl pellets, and building weather stations. Within each activity, students personalized their learning by composing their own questions as the basis for observing, reading, and writing. Student questions included a structural focus, such as, "How many types of feathers does a bird have?" Then conceptual questions, such as, "Why does that bird have such a long beak?" evolved as students attempted to explain the phenomena they had observed. These questions generated opportunities for self-directed learning. Students chose their own subtopics, found particular books, selected peers for interest-based activities, and constructed their goals for communicating to others.

The second phase of the CORI framework consisted of searching and retrieving information related to the students' questions. Students were taught how to use the library, find books, locate information within expository texts, and use a diversity of community resources. In addition, direct strategy instruction was provided to help students integrate information across sources including texts, illustrations, references, and human experts. Along with informational texts, woven through the instruction were stories, folklore, novels, and poetry. Most of the teachers began the units with a narrative related to the theme that students read at the same time they were conducting science observations. Following observation and the formation of conceptual questions, teachers moved to the informational texts. As students concluded their indepth study of multiple informational texts, teachers introduced novels, novelettes, and poetry related to the conceptual theme of the unit.

The last phase of the CORI framework is communicating to others. Having gained expertise in a particular topic, students were motivated to speak, write, discuss, and display their understanding to other students and adults. In both third- and fifth-grade classrooms, students made posters, wrote classroom books, and composed extended displays of their knowledge. One class made a videotape of its weather unit, providing a lesson on weather prediction and an explanation for the rest of the school.

✓ *Transactional strategies.* Transactional strategies combine some of the preceding strategies with whole-language instruction to improve reading comprehension. They begin with the teacher explaining to students how they can

- Make predictions about upcoming contents

- Relate the text to prior knowledge
- Ask questions about the information
- Seek clarification when the meaning is not clear
- Visualize the meaning
- Summarize along the way.

Students learn to use these strategies, especially in small reading groups that focus on high-quality literature. As students have trouble decoding a word, the teacher helps them use fix-up strategies they have learned, such as sounding out the word, rereading it, looking it up, and even skipping the word. Skipping the word is acceptable because main ideas are often expressed in several different ways in the text. This approach empowers students to read more challenging material by suggesting that they should not avoid reading texts that contain some unfamiliar words. For transactional strategies to be successful, teachers need to thoroughly understand the components of skilled reading and how to teach the related strategies (Pressley and Afflerbach, 1995).

✓ *The SAIL program.* Transactional strategies can even be used in the primary grades. One comprehensive program for reading comprehension instruction is known as SAIL (Students Achieving Independent Learning). In this program, the teachers

- Use explicit instruction, modeling, and discussion as a means of teaching comprehension strategies, focusing particularly on visualizing, questioning, predicting, clarifying, and making associations between the text and the students' experiences
- Emphasize not only the nature of the strategy but also when and how to apply it in actual reading
- Model the use of the strategies by thinking aloud in the presences of students about their own use of comprehension strategies
- Encourage students to discuss their comprehension of texts as well as the strategies they are using to achieve that comprehension
- Teach students to attend to their own reading processes, to the context in which they are reading, and to the text.

SAIL suggests a menu of strategies that can be used to enhance comprehension. Teachers and students select from this menu the strategies that are best suited to promoting understanding of the text being read. The menu includes (Pearson and Duke, 2002)

- Thinking aloud (talking about character development, identifying with a character, imaging how a character might feel)
- Constructing images (using visualization to create themes)
- Summarizing (especially reading for multiple meanings)

- Predicting (activating prior knowledge)
- Questioning (looking for different points of view)
- Clarifying (including relating text to personal experience)
- Story grammar analysis (relating one text to another)
- Text structure analysis (looking for specific text features, such as point of view, tone, or mood)

A study of SAIL with low-achieving students in second-grade classrooms (Brown, Pressley, Van Meter, and Schuder, 1996) found that the SAIL students performed considerably better on standardized measures of reading comprehension and word attack than the students of teachers who were not using the SAIL methods. Furthermore, the SAIL students made richer interpretations of text and acted like more strategic readers. (For more information on SAIL, see the **Resources** section.) SAIL is only one member of a family of approaches that use transactional strategy instruction. There is no indication that primary-grade students are unable to handle this approach to text comprehension instruction.

Developing Critical Reading Strategies in Older Students

Students read thousands of pages of text as they progress through secondary school. They often need to make judgments about what they are reading. These judgments are based largely on the prior knowledge, beliefs, and values that students bring to the reading process.

> Critical readers assess the reliability and validity of the text, and ask questions about themselves, the writer, and the writing.

The brain's frontal lobe is thought to be the place where critical thinking occurs. Here, past experiences are mingled with the reading to construct meaning and to acquire new knowledge. Critical readers assess the reliability and validity of the text, and ask questions about themselves, the writer, and the writing. They read beyond the obvious meanings to the assumptions, strategies, and arguments behind them. How does the writer reason with readers and manipulate them? Reading critically helps learners separate nonfiction from fiction, creativity from fantasy, fact from opinion, and is thus a valuable lifelong skill. Regrettably, not enough time is devoted to teaching students how to become critical readers.

If teachers want students to develop critical reading strategies, they should create a classroom climate that fosters inquiry by encouraging students to question, to make predictions, and to support their value judgments. Students employ higher-order thinking skills to evaluate evidence, draw conclusions, make inferences, and defend their line of thinking. This process is made somewhat easier if, when reading text critically, the students (Paterno, 2001)

- Underline key words, phrases, and sentences
- Write comments or questions in the margin
- Number related points in sequence
- Bracket important sections of the text
- Connect ideas with lines or arrows
- Make note of anything important, questionable, or interesting

Critical reading strategies include the following:

Previewing. This strategy allows students to get an overview of the content and organization of the reading by skimming the headnotes, captions, summaries, and other introductory material.

Contextualizing. As students read, what they comprehend is colored by their own experiences and by living in a particular time and place. But some of the texts they read were written in a radically different place and time. To read critically, they need to put the text in its biographical, cultural, and historical contexts to recognize the differences between their own contemporary values and those represented in the text.

Questioning to Understand and Remember. Students write down questions that come to mind as they read the material for the first time. The questions should focus on main ideas, not details, and should be expressed in their own words. This activity also helps in retention of new learning.

Challenges to the Students' Beliefs and Values. Students put a mark next to sections that challenge their attitudes, beliefs, and values. They make notes in the margin about how they feel or about what particularly challenged them. Then they review their notes and look for any patterns.

Evaluating an Argument. Writers make assertions that they want the reader to accept as true. Critical readers do not accept anything at face value but evaluate the claim and support for each argument. Students assess the reasoning process as well as its truthfulness. The support should be appropriate to the claim, and the statements should be consistent with each other.

Outlining and Summarizing. Students use an outline to reveal the basic structure of the text, its main ideas, subtopics, and supporting details. This requires a close analysis of each paragraph and a listing of the main ideas. In summarizing, however, the students write a synopsis in their own words of what they have read. Thus, students experience creative synthesis by putting ideas together in a condensed and new form.

Comparing and Contrasting Related Readings. Different authors discuss the same issues in different ways. Comparing and contrasting the arguments of various authors on a particular issue helps to better understand the approach each author used.

Questions That Promote Critical Reading

Critical reading can be prompted by specific questions that relate to the reader, the author, and the writing. Students can use the following questions to sharpen their critical reading skills (Paterno, 2001):

About the reader
- What do I know about this topic?
- What are my beliefs and values about this topic?
- Why am I reading this material?

About the writer
- What is the writer's background?
- How might that background affect the writer's approach to the topic as well as the selection and interpretation of the evidence presented?
- What are the writer's value assumptions about this topic?

Writer's arguments, evidence, and conclusions
- What is the basis for the writer's argument?
- What evidence does the writer present to support the argument?
- What is the writer's conclusion?

Writer's use of evidence to support the conclusion
- Are there any logical fallacies?
- What evidence does the writer use to support the conclusion(s)?
- Are the writer's sources credible?
- If the writer uses research studies:
  - Is the research timely?
  - Is the sample group representative of the target population?
  - Who conducted the research and what was its purpose?
  - Has the research been replicated?
  - Do the graphic illustrations represent the data in a truthful manner?
  - What is the source of the data in the illustration?
  - Do the physical dimensions of the graphic illustration accurately portray numerical relationships?

- Are the statistical findings and the writer's conclusion focused on the same topic?

Reader's reaction to the reading
- Do I accept the writer's evidence as reliable and as a valid support of the conclusion?
- How does the conclusion relate to what I already know about this topic?
- How has the writer's argument changed my views on this topic?

Teaching students to read, write, and think critically takes time and may represent a shift from what happens in many secondary school language arts classes. Teachers feel pressed for time and face the ever-increasing demands of high-stakes testing. Nonetheless, critical reading strategies can make reading much more productive and satisfying and thus help the students handle difficult material well and with confidence.

Students Who Are English Language Learners (ELL)

Children for whom English is a new language have been entering schools across the country in ever-increasing numbers, posing unique challenges to teachers of reading. These challenges have been intensified by recent state and federal policy initiatives mandating that all students demonstrate adequate yearly progress. Thus, schools with large English language learner populations are under pressure to help these students succeed. One of the more vexing problems is whether it is better to promote literacy in these children's native or second language. The research evidence, though small, suggests that initial reading instruction in a child's home language (e.g., Spanish) contributes positively to that child's ability to attain literacy in both languages, and also to the prevention of reading difficulties. It is generally counterproductive to hasten young non-English-speaking children into reading in English without adequate

> It is generally counterproductive to hasten young non-English-speaking children into reading in English without adequate preparation in speaking English.

preparation. Reading in any language requires a solid mental lexicon of spoken vocabulary. Thus, learning to *speak* English becomes the child's first priority, because it provides the foundation for hearing and reflecting on the structure of spoken words and then to learning the alphabetic principle as it applies to the sounds of English. Likewise, learning to read for meaning depends on comprehending the language of the text being read.

The report of the National Research Council (Snow et al., 1998) suggested that if children come to school with no proficiency in English but speaking a language for which there are instructional guides, materials, and locally proficient teachers, then these children should be taught how to read in their native language while acquiring oral, and eventually, reading, proficiency in the English language. Those non-English speaking children with a native language for which there are no materials, should focus on developing their oral proficiency in English. Formal reading instruction should be postponed until the child can speak English with an adequate level of proficiency.

One format for providing this type of instruction is paired bilingual instruction whereby ELL students are taught to read in their native language and in English at different times of the day. This can be expanded to two-way bilingual instruction in which ELL and native English speakers both learn to read in both languages (Calderón and Minaya-Rowe, 2003). In an analysis of 17 research studies, Slavin and Cheung (2003) found that most studies showed significant positive effects of the bilingual approach, especially the two-way format, on the students' reading performance. Most of these studies evaluated the Success for All program, which is a comprehensive reading program emphasizing systematic phonics, cooperative learning, tutoring for struggling students, and family support programs. Evaluations of both the English and Spanish versions of the Success for All program have consistently found them to improve English and Spanish reading performance in beginning readers. Two other programs that have been successful with helping ELL students learn to read in their native language and then in English are the Spanish version of Reading Recovery (Escamilla, 1994) and the small-group version of Direct Instruction (Gunn, Biglan, Smolkowski, and Ary, 2000).

Cooperative Learning Strategies With ELL Students

As children with limited English proficiency begin to acquire English, cooperative learning seems particularly appropriate and effective for bilingual education. First of all, cooperative learning should improve the reading performance of students in their native language. In an analysis of nearly 100 studies, Slavin (1995) showed that student achievement in a variety of settings using cooperative learning methods increased significantly those of the control groups.

Answer to Test Question # 5

Question: Non-English-speaking children can be taught to read English even if their spoken English vocabulary is weak.

Answer: *False.* During reading, the brain relies heavily on a person's spoken vocabulary to decode words. With only a small number of English words in the mental lexicon, learning to read in English becomes very frustrating. Bilingual programs that build a child's native reading skills while also enhancing English language skills have shown success in helping the child learn to read English.

Research on second-language learning has found that students need to engage in a great deal of oral interaction, jointly solving problems and determining meaning, if they are to achieve a high level of proficiency in the new language. Because cooperative learning provides many opportunities for students to work together to share understandings, it is likely to be an especially beneficial strategy for students making the transition to reading in English.

One form of cooperative learning has been particularly successful with bilingual students. Known as Bilingual Cooperative Integrated Reading and Composition (BCIRC), this method assigns students to four-member heterogeneous learning teams. After their lesson, the students work in teams on cooperative learning activities including identification of main story elements, vocabulary, summarization, reading comprehension strategies, partner reading, and creative writing using a process writing approach. In a major study (Calderón, Hertz-Lazarowitz, and Slavin, 1998) of 222 students with limited English proficiency in grades 2 and 3, teachers used the BCIRC model, working first with students in their native language and then helping them to make the transition to English. As part of BCIRC, the teachers used a total of 15 different strategies before, during, and after reading. Most of the activities were completed in a five-day cycle. They were the following:

1. *Building background and vocabulary.* Teachers select vocabulary that might be particularly difficult, strange, or important. They write the words on chart paper and develop semantic maps with the students. The maps are displayed on a wall and are used later during reading, discussion, and writing activities.

2. *Making predictions.* Teachers model how to make and confirm predictions. Students then work in their teams with the title and illustrations of a story and predict the elements of that story.

3. *Reading a selection.* Students track as the teacher reads aloud the first part of a story. During the second part, the students are encouraged to read in a whisper with the teacher.

4. *Partner reading and silent reading.* For partner reading, the students sit in pairs and take turns reading alternate paragraphs aloud. They assist each other in pronouncing and decoding the meaning of words. Then each student reads the assigned text silently.

5. *Treasure hunting: Story comprehension.* After partner reading, pairs discuss the answers to questions about key elements of a narrative, such as characters, setting, problems, and problem solutions. Working together, students help each other to understand the questions, to look up the answers, to look for clues to support their answers, to make inferences, and to reach consensus.

6. *Mapping the story.* After the treasure hunts are done, each team reviews a variety of graphic organizers and chooses one to map the story. This visual aid helps to organize the story elements. After discussing story elements, such as character names, the setting, the main idea, major events of the story, and problems the

characters encountered, the team members represent these creatively in the story map. They can use the maps later to provide visual clues for retelling the story and for story-related writing later in the cycle.

7. *Retelling the story.* Students use the maps to retell the stories to the partners within their teams and evaluate their partners' verbal summaries. Afterward, the students discuss with their partners what they liked about the story.

8. *Story-related writing.* In this part of the lesson cycle, students engage in a variety of writing activities that are related to the selection they have been reading all week. For the students who are acquiring English, the teacher models the writing process extensively each time. Then, with a partner or in teams of four, students write in various genres. During this time, the students help each other to develop story lines and characters, to sequence events, and to give each other feedback. They are also learning to engage in a process of drafting, revising, rewriting, editing, and publishing.

9. *Saying words aloud and spelling.* Words from the story become the word bank to be used throughout the week. Students say the words aloud to ultimately master their meaning, pronunciation, and spelling. This activity includes 10 to 12 words from the story that students must be able to read fluently, spell, and use correctly in meaningful sentences.

10. *Checking the partner.* When students complete the activities listed above, their partners initial a student assessment form indicating that they have completed and achieved the task. The teacher gives the student teams the daily expectations about the number of activities to be completed. However, the teams can proceed at their own rate and complete the activities earlier if they wish, creating additional time for writing and for independent reading of other books on the same theme. Because the scores of individual students also become the team's score, the partners have a vested interest in making sure all students correctly finish their work.

11. *Making meaningful sentences.* The students carefully select five or more words from the story. They discuss their meanings and use these words to write meaningful sentences that denote the definitions and give a clear picture of the word's meaning.

12. *Taking tests.* After three class periods, the teacher gives the students a comprehension test on the story. It includes asking them to write meaningful sentences for each vocabulary word and to read the word list aloud to the teacher. Students are not permitted to help one another on these tests because the test scores and evaluations of the story-related writing are the major components of students' weekly team scores. These weekly tests provide teachers a progressive view of the students' listening, speaking, reading, and writing performance.

13. *Direct instruction in reading comprehension.* Throughout the lesson cycle, the teacher provides direct instruction in reading comprehension skills such as identifying main ideas, drawing conclusions, and comparing and contrasting. The students practice these skills in their teams and take quizzes on them individually (without the help of their teammates) to contribute to their team scores.

14. *Writing workshops.* These workshops consist of a series of mini-lessons on the writing process. First, the teacher gives step-by-step explanations and ideas for completing a writing assignment. Then the students work closely with their peers and with the teacher through the phases of pre-writing, writing, revising and editing.

15. *Independent reading.* The teacher asks students to read a book of their choice for at least 20 minutes each evening. Parents are encouraged to discuss the reading with their children and to initial forms indicating that the children have read for the minimum time. The students earn points for their team if they submit a completed form each week. Additional points can be earned by completing a book report every two weeks.

The students who were part of the BCIRC program in the second and third grades performed significantly better on tests of Spanish and English reading than comparison students. Second graders taught primarily in Spanish scored significantly higher on a Spanish writing scale and somewhat higher on the reading scale than comparison students. Third-grade students who had been in the program for two years were more likely than the comparison group to meet the criteria necessary for exiting the bilingual program in language and reading.

My purpose in this chapter was to present the latest research on the effectiveness of models that educators use for teaching reading. In the past few decades, methods for teaching reading have become highly politicized. The proponents of literature-based and skills-based programs have attacked each other's research and practices, leaving the classroom teacher confused about which program to use. Given the wide variation in the cognitive abilities of children and their environments as well as the complexities involved in learning to read, it is clear that no one approach will be successful for all children. Some preschool children will have had such rich exposure to spoken language and print that they are already mastering the alphabetic principle and are prepared for enriched reading experiences as early as kindergarten. Others can be so language deprived that instruction will need to focus mainly on developing phonemic awareness. And, of course, there are all the possible variations in between.

Faced with this heterogeneous mix, teachers of reading still need sound guidance, not rhetoric, regarding research-based methods for teaching beginning reading. Despite the controversy, the latest review of scientific research on reading leads us to the following three conclusions. For *most* children,

- Mastering the alphabetic principle is essential to learning how to read successfully.
- Instructional techniques that explicitly teach this principle are more effective than those that do not.
- The reading teacher remains the most critical component of any reading program.

These conclusions are even more important when applied to children who are at risk for having difficulty learning to read. This is not to deny that literature-based activities that supplement phonics instruction can help to ensure the application of the alphabetic principle to enriched readings. Such activities can make reading meaningful and enjoyable.

When children receive instruction in phonemic awareness and the alphabetic principle and learn to apply that knowledge to decoding words, they are likely to succeed at learning to read. But once they fall behind, they almost never catch up. As noted earlier, a child's reading level in first grade is an astonishingly reliable predictor of reading achievement in high school (Cunningham and Stanovich, 1997). Consequently, the sooner that parents and teachers can recognize children with reading problems, the better.

What's Coming?

We now know that many reading difficulties can be overcome with early diagnosis and systematic intervention. Just how to go about determining whether a child has a reading problem is the topic of the next chapter.

CHAPTER 4

Recognizing
Reading Problems

This chapter addresses several basic questions about how to recognize reading problems. They include:

- *What are the most common causes of reading problems?*
- *What have brain imaging scans revealed about struggling and dyslexic readers?*
- *What are some methods for detecting reading problems?*

THE READING GAP

Recent NAEP Assessments

About one student in three has reading problems. The 2003 report from the National Assessment of Educational Progress on reading described the reading achievement of students in the fourth, eighth, and twelfth grades (NAEP, 2003). It included comparisons between NAEP reading performance of students in 2002 and 2003 to the performance of their counterparts in previous assessments. Reading performance is reported in two ways: (1) average scale scores, and (2) achievement levels. The average scale score reflects the overall reading performance of a particular group, using a scale of 0 to 500 to provide information about student performance for all three grades. Achievement levels describe what students should know and be able to do at each of three levels, *Basic*, *Proficient*, and *Advanced*.

The Basic achievement level represents partial mastery of prerequisite knowledge and skills that are fundamental for efficient work at each grade. The Proficient achievement level indicates that students have demonstrated competency over challenging subject matter, including subject-matter knowledge, the application of such knowledge to real-world situations, and analytical skills appropriate to the subject matter. The Advanced achievement level represents superior performance in all these areas (NAEP, 2003).

National Scale Scores

Figure 4.1 shows the average reading scale scores for the three grades tested during 1992 through 2002 as well as the 2003 results for grades 4 and 8. In 1998, NAEP began testing the use of accommodations in reading, such as assessing these students in small groups or allowing them extra time as a way to increase participation. However, the NAEP does not allow having the reading assessment read aloud or translated because that would alter the skills being assessed.

In 2002, about 19 percent of grade 4 students selected for the NAEP were identified as special needs students. This is almost double the size of the special needs population tested in 1992. About 68 percent of these students participated in the 2002 testing, and 31 percent of them required accommodations.

Regrettably, little progress has been made in improving the average reading scale scores over the decade. The fourth-grade average score increased from 2000 to 2003, but it is not significantly higher than in 1992. NAEP explained these results by noting that more Hispanic and special needs students are now being assessed. When the scores of these students are removed from the totals, the average score is somewhat higher for the remaining fourth-grade population. The 2003 eighth-grade average score is the same as in 1998, but is an improvement over the 1992 score.

The twelfth-grade average score in 2002, however, is significantly lower than the 1998 score and represents a continuing decline since 1992. NAEP noted that fewer students in twelfth grade are participating in these assessments, and it has established a commission to examine the issues involving twelfth grade participation in future assessments (NAEP, 2003).

Achievement Levels for Fourth Grade

NAEP (2003) gives the following specific definitions of the Basic, Proficient, and Advanced achievement levels in reading for grade 4:

- *Basic:* Fourth-grade students at the Basic level should demonstrate an understanding of the overall meaning of what they read. When reading text appropriate for fourth-graders, they should be able to make obvious connections between the text and their own experiences and extend the ideas in the text by making simple inferences.

Average Reading Scale Scores
Grades 4, 8, and 12: 1992 to 2003

Figure 4.1 The chart shows the average NAEP reading scale scores for grades 4 and 8 for 1992 to 2003, and the grade 12 scores for 1992 to 2002. The tests were not administered in 1996. Grades 8 and 12 were not assessed in 2000. Scores from 1998 through 2003 reflect when testing accommodations were permitted (NAEP, 2003).

- *Proficient:* Fourth-grade students at the Proficient level should be able to demonstrate an overall understanding of the text, providing inferential as well as literal information. When reading text appropriate to fourth grade, they should be able to extend the ideas in the text by making inferences, drawing conclusions, and making connections to their own experiences. The connection between the text and what the student infers should be clear.
- *Advanced:* Fourth-grade students at the Advanced level should be able to generalize about topics in the reading selection and demonstrate an awareness of how authors compose and use literary devices. When reading text appropriate to fourth grade, they

should be able to judge text critically and, in general, to give thorough answers that indicate careful thought.

The fourth-grade results by reading achievement level are displayed in Table 4.1. They show that over one-third of these students are performing below Basic achievement levels, although that is an improvement over the percentages in 1998 and 2000 when accommodations are included. Thus, there are more fourth-grade students at or above Proficient in 2003 than in 1992. The report also noted that there were no differences between males and females in these results (NAEP, 2003).

Indications are that little progress is being made toward significantly increasing the number of elementary students who become Proficient readers, despite the large amounts of resources and time devoted to teaching reading. If school districts are to meet the expectations and deadlines regarding reading that are set forth in the No Child Left Behind Act, educators must reexamine how and when they are identifying students with reading problems, and what steps they are taking to help these at-risk students.

Table 4.1 Percentage of Fourth Grade Students by Reading Achievement Level NAEP 1992 to 2003 (*Accommodations Permitted)				
Year	Below Basic	At Basic	At Proficient	At Advanced
1992	36	34	22	6
1994	40	31	22	7
1998*	40	30	22	7
2000*	41	30	23	7
2002*	36	32	24	7
2003*	37	32	23	8

Source: NAEP, 2003

Achievement for Black and Hispanic Students

Of continuing concern is the consistently low achievement levels for Black (Figure 4.2) and Hispanic (Figure 4.3) students over the last decade when compared to White students. There were no significant changes in fourth-grade and eighth-grade average scores for Black and Hispanic students from 2002 to 2003, although the 2003 scores were slightly higher for both grade levels than in 1992. In 2003, Hispanic students scored higher on average than Black students. This persistent poor performance of minority students in reading can be explained only in part by specific cognizant impairments, such as dyslexia. After all, the White student

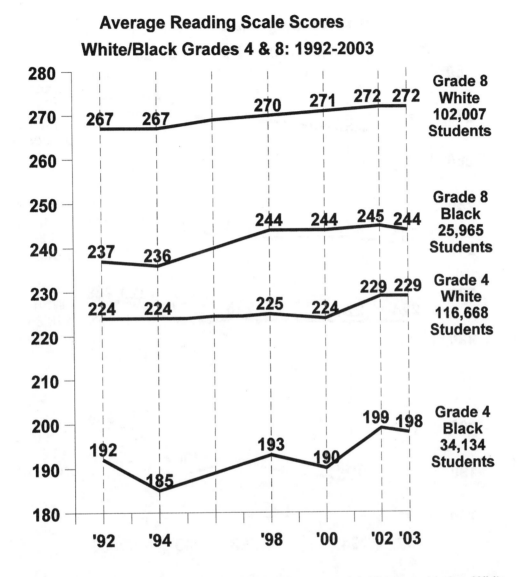

Average Reading Scale Scores
White/Black Grades 4 & 8: 1992-2003

Figure 4.2 Since 1992, grade 4 and 8 Black students consistently scored below White students. Grade 4 Black students have made some gains in the last three years but the scores of grade 8 Black students have changed little in recent years (NAEP, 2003).

population also includes children with reading problems, yet their average scores remain higher. Furthermore, there is little scientific evidence that Black and Hispanic children are at a substantially greater risk for developmental dyslexia than these testing results would suggest. The size of the reading gap and the number of students involved suggests that this problem has roots in at least three separate but related areas: inadequate reading instruction, social and cultural conditions, and physical causes.

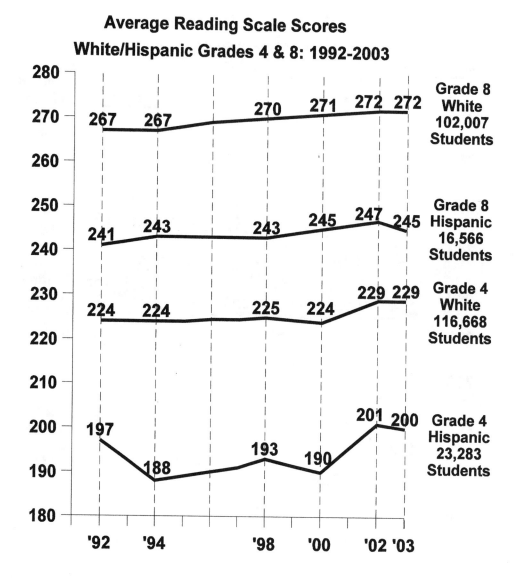

Figure 4.3 Since 1992, grade 4 and 8 Hispanic students consistently scored below White students. The scores of grade 4 Hispanic students have shown some improvement in the last four years but those of grade 8 Hispanic students have changed little (NAEP, 2003).

INADEQUATE READING INSTRUCTION

Some children have reading problems because they did not get adequate instruction in the skills needed for decoding, such as concepts about the nature of print, recognizing letters, and the alphabetic principle. They may not have had ample opportunities for systematic and focused practice in decoding real words. As a result, they failed to develop a rich mental lexicon, which is essential for promoting fluency and comprehension. To successfully understand a language, children need to develop a rich vocabulary and an appreciation for semantics, and combine that understanding with what they know about the real world. They also need to have a good understanding of the mechanics of language (syntax) and they need to be attuned to the phonology of the language so that they do not confuse similar sounding words, such as *chair* and *cheer*.

None of these areas can be described as social, cultural, or physical problems that lead to reading difficulties. These deficits are not intrinsic to the child, but to the classroom and to the school system that has not provided the appropriate instructional environment. Schools situated in high-poverty areas are often competing for limited materials and resources. Conscientious but inadequately trained teachers may be using outdated programs and methodologies. This unfortunate combination can be the cause of some children's reading difficulties. Children in this situation are not dyslexic. Their problem is that they were simply never taught the skills needed to learn how to read. To be successful in teaching all children, teachers need to become extremely knowledgeable about effective strategies as well as diagnostic in their approach to reading instruction.

SOCIAL AND CULTURAL CAUSES OF READING PROBLEMS

A large number of Black and Hispanic children performing below White children in reading display no signs of specific learning impairments. Clearly other factors are at work. Multiple studies have identified social conditions that have an impact on the achievement of children in inner-city schools. Limited teacher training, large class sizes, the absence of literature in the home, and poor parental support for schools have all been cited as causes for lack of student progress. Although these conditions cannot be ignored, schools need to focus more on the direct connections between what we are learning about how the brain learns to read and the *linguistic* barriers interfering with that learning.

Some researchers believe that these children are performing poorly on reading tests because their home language differs substantially from the language used in reading instruction (Labov, 2003). Bailey (1993) suggested a decade ago that Black children were being immersed in a language dialect that has become known as African-American Vernacular English (AAVE). Residential desegregation has increased the impact of AAVE. Meanwhile, as Spanish-speaking populations increase, children are faced with learning to read English in school while speaking Spanish at home.

> Teachers of reading should be trained to recognize when a child's reading problems are the result of linguistic clashes and not a pathology.

Consequently, some of the causes of poor performance by Black and Hispanic children can be attributed to impediments resulting from linguistic differences. That is, their native dialect or language is different in significant ways from what is being taught in school. They come to school with a mental lexicon whose word representations often do not match what they are trying to decode on the printed page. Learning to read involves determining which words *are* present in their mental lexicon, what they represent, and whether they can be comprehended in context. This is not a physiological deficit; it is a social and cultural problem. For these children, we should not be looking at what is wrong with them but how we can alter instruction to make them more successful in learning to read. Such alterations can be made when teachers of reading are properly trained to recognize when a child's reading problems are the result of linguistic clashes and not a pathology. Furthermore, that training should also help teachers understand how they can use some of the linguistic attributes of AAVE and Spanish to help children pronounce, decode, and understand standard English.

PHYSICAL CAUSES OF READING PROBLEMS

As noted earlier, nature long ago crafted sophisticated neural networks in the brain to process spoken language. But decoding written text is a wholly artificial creation that calls upon neural regions designed for other tasks. Because there is no single neural region for reading, numerous brain areas must be recruited to perform the task of decoding artificial symbols into sound. Reading is so complex that any small problem along the way can slow or interrupt the process. It is small wonder that children have more problems with reading than with any other skill we ask them to learn. Difficulties result essentially from either environmental or physical factors, or some combination of both. Environmental factors include limited exposure to language in the preschool years, resulting in little phoneme sensitivity, letter knowledge, print awareness, vocabulary, and reading comprehension. Physical factors include speech, hearing, and visual impairments and substandard intellectual capabilities. Any combination of environmental and physical factors makes the diagnosis and treatment more difficult.

> Successful decoding and comprehending of written text involves the coordination and integration of three separate neural systems.

Recent research into the causes and nature of reading problems has revealed more about the neural processes involved in reading. Recall that successful reading involves two basic processes—decoding and comprehension—that are generated by three neural systems. Figure 4.4 illustrates how these three systems interact. Decoding written text into sounds that represent words results when the visual and auditory processing systems see and sound out the words in the reader's head. The frontal lobe interprets the meaning conveyed by those word representations.

Problems with any one or more of these systems can cause reading difficulties. In some children, the problems occur during early brain development and affect their ability to process

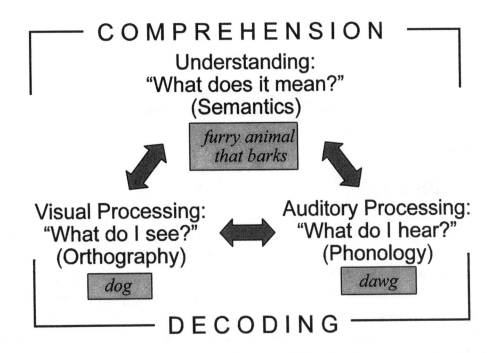

Figure 4.4 Successful reading requires the coordination of three systems: visual and auditory processing to decode the words, and frontal lobe processing to determine meaning.

the sounds of language and, eventually, to decode written text. This developmental deficit appears to be the most common cause of reading difficulties, and usually results in a life-long struggle with reading. Less common are problems with reading caused by impairments in hearing and vision that can occur at any time in a person's life.

Most research studies on reading have focused primarily on developmental reading problems that scientists refer to as *developmental dyslexia*. In developmental dyslexia, the child experiences unexpected difficulty in learning to read despite adequate intelligence, environment, and normal senses. It is a spectrum disorder, varying from mild to severe. Neuroimaging studies have established that there are significant differences in the way normal and dyslexic brains respond to specific spoken and written language tasks. Furthermore, there is evidence that these differences may weaken with appropriate instructional interventions.

Scientists have long been searching for the causes of reading problems. This has not been an easy task because of the large number of sensory, motor, and cognitive systems that are involved in reading. Struggling readers may have impairments in any one or more of these systems, but not all struggling readers have dyslexia. Specifically, dyslexia seems to be caused by deficits in the neural regions responsible for language and phonological processing or by problems in nonlinguistic areas of the brain.

Linguistic Causes

Several potential linguistic causes of developmental dyslexia that have emerged from recent research studies, including phonological deficits, differences in auditory and visual processing speeds, the varying sizes of brain structures, memory deficits, genetics, brain lesions, and word-blindness. It is possible that several of these causes are related to each other and can coexist in the same individual.

Phonological Deficits

The ability to sound out words in one's head plays an important role in reading familiar words and sounding out new ones. Phonological information is used by the working memory to integrate and comprehend words in phrases and sentences. Extensive evidence has existed for decades that phonological operations are impaired in many dyslexics (Harm and Seidenberg, 1999). But the causes of the impairment were not clear. Because many dyslexics have normal or above normal intelligence, researchers suspected that the phonological processing deficits appeared only when the brain was trying to decode writing. Exactly why that happens is not fully known. However, studies of the differences in auditory and visual processing speeds as well as fMRI scans of the brain during reading are shedding new light on the possible causes of the phonological impairments.

Differences in Auditory and Visual Processing Speeds

One of the more intriguing explanations of some reading difficulties, including dyslexia, has come from research studies using magnetoencephalography (MEG), a technique for measuring the electric signals emitted during brain activation as a result of mental processing. These studies noted abnormal auditory activation but normal visual activation during reading (Helenius, Salmelin, Richardson, Leinonen, and Lyytinen, 2002; Renvall and Hari, 2002; Tallal et al.,1996; Temple et al., 2003). Sometimes referred to as *temporal processing impairment,* the differences in the processing speeds could explain some of the symptoms common to dyslexia.

The explanation goes like this: When reading silently, our eyes scan the words on the page (visual processing) and we sound out those words in our head. This sounding out represents the auditory processing necessary for us to decode and interpret what we are reading. To read successfully, the visual and auditory processing systems have to work together, that is, be in synchrony.

When a child begins to learn to read, it is essential that the letter (grapheme) the child sees corresponds to what the child hears (phoneme) internally. In Figure 4.5, the child with normal auditory processing (left) is looking at the letter *d* and the auditory processing system is simultaneously sounding out /*d*/ or *duh.* As the eye moves to *o,* the phoneme /*ô*/ or *awh*

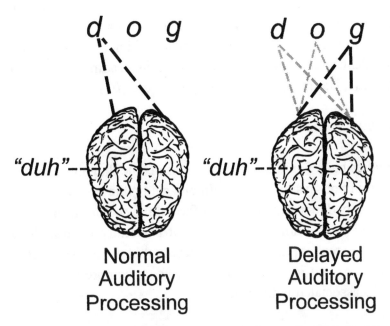

Figure 4.5 In normal auditory processing (left), the phoneme that the child hears correctly matches the letter that the eyes see—in this case, the sound "duh" corresponds to the letter "d." If the auditory processing system is delayed, however, the child's eyes are already on the letter "g" while the "duh" phoneme is still sounding in the child's head. The brain errs in matching "duh" with "g."

will sound out and then *g* produces the phoneme /*g*/ or *guh*. Later, when this child is asked to write *dog,* the /*d*/ phoneme will recall the letter *d,* and so on.

However, if the auditory processing system is impaired and lags behind the visual processing system, then the child's eye is already scanning to the letter *g* while the phoneme /*d*/ or *duh* is still being processed in the auditory system. As a result, the child's brain incorrectly associates the letter *g* with the phoneme sound of /*d*/ or *duh*. Now, when we ask the child to write the word *dog,* the child hears the first phoneme /*d*/ or *duh* but incorrectly recalls the letter *g,* perhaps eventually writing the word *god.*

If this notion is correct, then finding a way to bring the auditory and visual processing systems in closer synchrony should help to remedy the problem. That is exactly what several researchers tried. They developed a computer program, known as Fast ForWord, designed to help poor readers slow down visual processing to allow the auditory processing sufficient time to recognize the sound of the initial phoneme. Using this program with children who had reading problems produced surprisingly successful results. The program and process are discussed in greater detail in Chapter 5.

Some scientists are even suggesting that this time delay problem could lead to a simple test for early diagnosis of dyslexia. Researchers at Wake Forest University asked dyslexic and non-dyslexic people to tell which of two lights appeared first. Both groups performed much better when they heard sounds through headphones. For non-dyslexic participants, the sound needed to occur within 150 milliseconds of the light for them to perform better. Longer intervals did not improve their performance. However, dyslexic participants performed better with longer delays up to 350 milliseconds. Because the test did not involve reading, this time difference could help identify young children with potential reading problems before they reach school age (Burdette, Hairston, Flowers, and Wallace, 2003).

Structural Differences in the Brain

Some MRI studies have found that the brains of people diagnosed with dyslexia are structurally different from non-dyslexic brains. In one study, the researchers noted that the dyslexic brains of 16 men had less gray matter (surface of the cerebrum) in the left temporal lobe, the frontal lobe, and cerebellum than the brains of 14 non-dyslexic subjects (Brown et al., 2001). Having less gray matter (and thus fewer neurons) in the left temporal lobe (where Wernicke's area is located) and in the frontal lobe (where comprehension occurs) could contribute to the deficits associated with dyslexia.

Phonologic Memory Deficits

Skilled reading requires an ability to retain verbal bits of information (phonemes) in working memory. Recent studies have shown distinct deficits in this phonologic memory among poor readers. The deficits more commonly involve serial tasks, such as holding a string of phonemes to make a word and a sequence of words to generate a sentence (Howes, Bigler, Burlingame, and Lawson, 2003).

Genetics and Gender

Studies of genetic composition have shown strong associations between dyslexia and genetic mutations in twins and families (Pennington, 1990), and recent investigations may have actually identified some of the specific genes involved (Kaminen et al., 2003). Thus, dyslexia is a life-long condition and not just a "phase." The genetic mutations could impede the development of systems that the typical brain utilizes to decode written text, forcing the brain to construct alternate and less efficient pathways.

> Boys tend to be over-identified with reading problems; girls, on the other hand, tend to be under-identified.

Nationwide, there are three to four times more boys identified with reading problems than girls. Although this was once thought to be the result of genetic deficits, the true reason may be because boys are over-identified (often due to their rambunctious behavior) and girls are under-identified (sit quietly in class and obey the rules). Recent studies indicate that many girls are affected as well but are not getting help (Shaywitz, 2003).

Lesions in the Word Form Area

Researchers using PET scans have noticed that some developmentally dyslexic people have lesions in the left occipito-temporal area of the brain. You may recall from Chapter 2 that this area is identified as the word form area most used by skilled readers to decode written text. Another discovery in these studies was that the amount of blood flowing to this brain region predicted the severity of the dyslexia (Rumsey et al., 1999). Regardless of the cause, a lesion and reduced blood flow would likely hamper the ability of this patch of neurons to decode written text.

Word-Blindness

Word-blindness is the inability to read words even though the person's eyes are optically normal. Two forms exist: *Congenital word-blindness* involves a glitch in the wiring of neurons during embryonic development and is usually confined to those neural systems associated with reading. This disorder may go unnoticed for years, affecting reading and occasionally spoken language. *Acquired word-blindness* results from some traumatic insult to the brain, such as a stroke or a tumor, occurring during a person's lifetime and interfering with already established systems. The damaged area is usually on the left side of the brain, causing weakness in the right side of the body and difficulty pronouncing words or naming objects (Shaywitz, 2003).

Nonlinguistic Causes

Some people, who are otherwise unimpaired, have extreme difficulties in reading because of deficits in auditory and visual perception not related to linguistic systems. This revelation was somewhat of a surprise because conventional wisdom held that impairments in reading (and also in oral language) were restricted to problems with linguistic processing. The following are some possible nonlinguistic causes found in the research literature.

Perception of Sequential Sounds

The inability to detect and discriminate sounds presented in rapid succession seems to be a common impairment in individuals with reading and language disorders. These individuals also have difficulty in indicating the order of two sounds presented in rapid succession. This particular deficit is related to auditory processing of sound waves in general and is not related directly to distinguishing phonemes as part of phonological processing. Hearing words accurately when reading or from a stream of rapid conversation is critical to comprehension (Wright, Bowen, and Zecker, 2000).

Sound-Frequency Discrimination

Some individuals with reading disorders are impaired in their ability to hear differences in sound frequency. This auditory defect can affect the ability to discriminate tone and pitch in speech. At first glance, this may seem like only an oral language-related impairment. However, it also affects reading proficiency because reading involves sounding out words in the auditory processing system (Wright et al., 2000).

Detection of Target Sounds in Noise

The inability to detect tones within noise is another recently discovered nonlinguistic impairment. When added to the findings in the two deficits mentioned above, this evidence suggests that auditory functions may play a much greater role in reading disorders than previously thought (Wright et al., 2000).

Visual Magnocellular-Deficit Hypothesis

The interpretation of some research studies has lead to a hypothesis about the functions of the visual processing system. This proposes that certain forms of reading disorders are caused by a deficit in the visual processing system, which leads to poor detection of coherent visual motion and poor discrimination of the speed of visual motion. This part of the visual system involves large neurons and so is referred to as the magnocellular system. Impairment in this system may cause letters on a page to bundle and overlap, or appear to move—common complaints from some struggling readers and dyslexics (Demb, Boynton, and Heeger, 1998). Other scientists, however, question this interpretation of the research mainly because it is not known how the visual impairments relate to the phonological impairments (Amitay, Ben-Yehudah, Banai, and Ahissar, 2002). Current evidence suggests that visual impairments by themselves are a very small part of dyslexia (Rayner et al., 2001).

Motor Coordination and the Cerebellum

Several imaging studies show that many dyslexic readers have processing deficits in the cerebellum of the brain (Nicolson, Fawcett, and Dean, 2001). Another study determined that nearly 75 percent of the dyslexic subjects had smaller lobes on the right side of the cerebellum compared to non-dyslexic participants (Eckert et al., 2003). The cerebellum is located at the rear of the brain just below the occipital lobe (Figure 4.6). It is mainly responsible for coordinating learned motor skills. Deficiencies in this part of the brain could result, according to researchers, in problems with reading, writing, and spelling. Problems in reading may result if cerebellar deficits delay the time when an infant sits up and walks, and begins babbling and talking. Less motor skill coordination can mean less articulation and fluency in speech. This, in turn, leads to less sensitivity to onset, rime, and the phonemic structure of language.

Handwriting, of course, is a motor skill that requires the precise coordination and timing of different muscle groups. Lack of coordination of these muscles due to a cerebellar deficit would create difficulties in writing, a characteristic that many dyslexics display. Problems with spelling would arise from poor phonological awareness, trouble with word recognition, and difficulties in automating spelling rule skills.

Figure 4.6 The cerebellum is located at the rear of the brain and is responsible for coordinating learned motor skills.

The possibility of deficits in visual and auditory perception and memory as well as in motor coordination on various reading tasks accounts for the wide range of individual differences observed among those with reading disorders. Analyzing these differences leads to a better understanding of the multidimensional nature of reading disorders and possible treatment.

Attention-Deficit Hyperactivity Disorder

Attention-deficit hyperactivity disorder (ADHD) is a developmental disorder characterized by difficulty in focusing and sustaining attention. Children with ADHD are often assumed to also have developmental reading problems. But that is not usually the case. ADHD and developmental dyslexia are separate disorders, and less than 25 percent of ADHD children also have dyslexia.

Answer to Test Question # 6

Question: Most children with attention-deficit hyperactivity disorder (ADHD) are also dyslexic.

Answer: *False.* ADHD and developmental dyslexia are separate disorders. Only about 25 percent of ADHD children also have dyslexia.

Is Dyslexia Present in Readers of Other Languages?

Dyslexia appears in all languages, including those that are read from right to left, as Hebrew and Arabic. People with dyslexia who speak highly phonetic languages, such as Spanish and Finnish, are identified with the disorder later than those who speak deep morphological languages such as English, where the linguistic demands of the language are more challenging. English speakers experience the complex phonetic structure early on in their schooling. Readers can also experience difficulties in logographic languages, such as Chinese, due to visual confusion or problems with memory recall.

BRAIN IMAGING STUDIES

You will recall from the Introduction that brain imaging technologies are of two kinds: those that look at the structure of the brain (e.g., MRI and CAT scans) and those that look at how the brain functions (e.g., PET and fMRI scans). In recent years, these scans have revealed differences in both the structure and function of dyslexic brains compared to non-dyslexic brains. Eventually, these types of investigations may lead to more accurate diagnosis and treatment.

Studies of Brain Structure

MRI studies that have compared the brain structure of dyslexic individuals to normal readers have found some interesting differences. These differences were more evident in dyslexics who had early spoken language problems than in dyslexics whose speech progressed normally. The regions of the brain that showed structural variations were consistent across multiple MRI studies and were closely associated with those neural areas involved in spoken language processing (Beaton, 1997; Leonard, 2001). The implication here is that an individual with atypical brain structures that hamper speech is likely to have difficulties in learning to read as well.

Studies of Brain Function

Newer research in brain function is shedding more light on dyslexia. Because dyslexics often confused *b* and *d*, psychologists thought for many years that dyslexia was merely a vision problem. Researchers now believe that the letters can also be confused because they sound alike. This is the brain's inability to process what it hears, not what it sees. Other imaging studies show an imperfectly functioning system for dividing words into their phonological units—a critical step for accurate reading. Letter reversals can be the result of phonological missteps in the decoding of print to sound and back to print. It is likely that the learner has problems in assigning what he says or hears in his head (the phoneme) to the letters he sees on paper (the grapheme). Thus, remedial strategies should focus on reestablishing correct phonemic connections with intense practice.

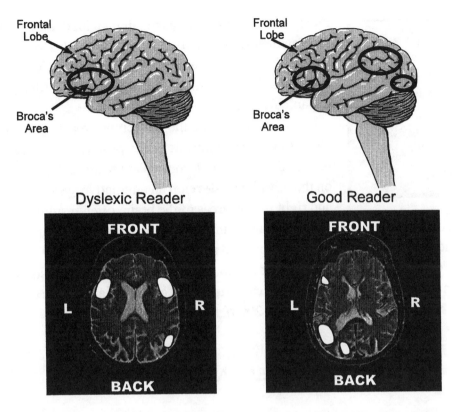

Figure 4.7 The brain regions that are activated during reading are shown as black ovals in the upper diagrams and as white areas in the lower representative fMRI scans. Dyslexic readers (left) use different brain regions during reading than do good readers (right). Note that dyslexic readers show little activation in the back of the brain but strong activation in the front regions, especially in Broca's area. Good readers, on the other hand, show strong activation in the back of the brain with lesser activation in the front (Richards, 2001; Shaywitz, 2003; Simos et al., 2000).

Numerous functional imaging studies clearly indicate that poor readers use different brain pathways than good readers. As discussed in Chapter 2, good readers of all ages rely more on the occipito-temporal areas in the back of the brain to decode word forms, and require only a little input from Broca's area (Figure 4.7). By using just these three left-side areas, their ability to recognize word forms, with practice, is automatic and their reading becomes fluent.

The studies further show that dyslexic readers at an early age do not use the word processing regions in the left rear part of the brain. Rather, they rely more on Broca's area for decoding text. This reliance increases with age so that, as adolescents, they are overactivating Broca's area and recruiting other frontal regions as they try to read. Apparently, the increased use of frontal brain areas is an attempt to compensate for the disruptions in the rear of the brain. In the cross-sectional picture in Figure 4.7, note how during reading a dyslexic reader's brain activates an area in the right frontal lobe—used primarily for visual memory—in addition to Broca's area. But rote-based learning of words can get a reader only so far before the memory systems begin to fail. This overreliance on memory results in slow and laborious reading because the disruption in the rear brain areas prohibit automatic word recognition.

> The different brain scan patterns between good and dyslexic readers are so consistent that they may one day allow for early diagnosis, perhaps even before a child begins to read.

Functional imaging studies of adults with dyslexia, including high-achieving university students, reveal this same pattern of strong frontal area use during reading (Richards, 2001; Shaywitz, 2003; Simos, Breier, Fletcher, Mergman, and Papanicolaou, 2000).

The results of the numerous imaging studies seem clear: Good readers use left-side posterior areas of the brain for rapid, automatic decoding and reading. Dyslexic readers, on the other hand, develop an alternative system that uses left and right frontal areas of the brain, often resulting in accurate but slow reading. Moreover, dyslexic brains during reading are working harder—that is, employing more neurons—than the brains of good readers (Brun et al., 2003). These different patterns between good and dyslexic readers are so consistent that neuroscientists believe that functional imaging may one day allow for early detection of dyslexia, perhaps even before a child begins to learn to read (Nandy et al., 2003).

DETECTING READING PROBLEMS

In recent years, researchers have made significant progress using fMRI scans to understand how novice, skilled, and dyslexic brains read. Yet, despite these advancements, fMRI scans are not a practical tool at present for diagnosing dyslexia in a single individual. That is because the results of fMRI studies are usually reported for groups rather than for individuals. Researchers have found some variations in the activated areas of the brain among individuals within both the dyslexic and control groups. More research is needed to clarify these differences before fMRI or any other imaging techniques can be used for diagnostic purposes (Richards, 2001). Until that time, however, researchers can use the information gained from imaging studies to develop other kinds of diagnostic tests that more closely align with our new understanding of dyslexia.

For the moment, critical observation of a child's progress in learning to speak, and eventually in learning to read, remains our most effective tool for spotting potential problems. Most difficulties associated with reading do not go away with time. Therefore, the earlier that parents and teachers can detect reading problems in children, the better. The problems often begin to reveal themselves first in spoken language and later while learning to read.

Spoken Language Difficulties

I discussed in previous chapters that learning to read is closely connected to fluency in spoken language. Both speaking and reading rely on the proper functioning of the phonologic module, that brain region where sounds are combined to form words and words are broken down into their basic sounds. Consequently, difficulties that children have with spoken language are often clues to potential reading problems. Parents and teachers should remember that it is normal for all children to make occasional language errors while speaking. But frequent language errors, stemming from any one or a combination of the following conditions, could indicate that a child may run into trouble when beginning to learn to read.

Some of the spoken language difficulties may involve any one or more of the following (IDA, 2003; NAEYC, 1998; Shaywitz, 2003):

- *Delay in speaking.* Children generally say their first words at about 12 months of age and follow with phrases when between 18 and 24 months old. Because learning to read is closely linked to a child's phonologic skills in spoken language, delays in speaking may be an early indication of potential reading problems, espe-cially in a family that has a history of dyslexia.

- *Difficulties with pronunciation.* Children should have little difficulty pronouncing words correctly by 5 or 6 years of age. Difficulties in pronouncing words (sometimes referred to as "baby talk") may be an indication of future reading problems. Such trouble pronouncing long or complicated words could signal a snag in the parts of the brain that generate spoken language, causing a mix-up in the processing of the phonemes. Mispronunciations often involve mixing syllables within words (*aminal* for animal) and leaving off the beginning syllables (*luminum* for aluminum).

- *Difficulty in learning the letters of the alphabet.* Learning the names of the letters of the alphabet is an important, though not essential, step in learning to read. Marked difficulties in learning the letters could indicate a potential reading problem.

- *Recalling incorrect phonemes.* A child looks at a picture of a donkey and recalls the word *doggie,* a word similar in sound but not in meaning. This recall of incor-rect phonemes may cause a child to talk about a word without actually recalling it. The child may get frustrated because of the inability to say the word. As these children get older, they may resort more to vague words in order to mask their difficulties in retrieving specific words. They use general words like *things* and *stuff,* making their conversations hard to follow. It is important to remember that the problem here is not with their thinking, but with their ability to use expressive language, that is, to recall a word on command.

- *Insensitivity to rhyme.* Part of a young child's enjoyment of spoken language is playing with rhyme. Hearing and repeating rhyming sounds demonstrates how words can be separated into smaller segments of sound, and that different words may share the same sound. Children with good rhyming skills are showing their readiness for learning to read. Those with little sensitivity to rhyme, on the other hand, may have reading problems because they are unable to detect the consonant sound that changes the meaning of closely rhyming words.

- *Genetics.* Looking at the family tree for signs of dyslexia in close relatives is a clue because about 25 to 50 percent of the children born to a dyslexic parent will also be dyslexic (Kaminen et al., 2003; Londin et al., 2003; Shaywitz, 2003). Whether the child actually displays dyslexia depends somewhat on that child's environment. This revelation came from studies of identical twins. Because they share the same genes, if one twin has dyslexia, so should the other. But in reality, in 30 to 35 percent of the cases, one twin is dyslexic while the other is not (Fisher and DeFries, 2002). Apparently, even though these children had a genetic predisposition for dyslexia, differences in the home and school environments played important roles in determining how successful these children would be at reading.

Looking for Early Indicators of Reading Problems

Until the time that brain imaging becomes a standard diagnostic tool, researchers will continue to look for ways to accurately identify students with reading problems as early as possible. Multiple research studies have sought to find indicators of reading problems that are more valid than solely the professional judgment of the evaluating team. The obvious problem here is that the application of professional judgment is only as good as the training and competence of the team members. This approach can often lead to considerable variability in identification from district to district and even from state to state. Using more objective measures would reduce this variability. Research studies have found that letter fluency is a useful measure in kindergarten, while response to instruction can be a valuable measure in second grade.

Letter Fluency Tasks as Kindergarten Indicators

The earlier that children who are at risk for reading problems can be identified, the better. Trying to carry out such identification procedures in kindergarten is difficult because of the broad range of background experience these children bring to the classroom. Nonetheless, studies involving kindergarten children do seem to indicate that letter-name fluency and nonsense word fluency can be valid indicators of early reading skills, such as oral reading fluency (ORF).

One study (Speece and Mills, 2003) tested 39 kindergartners in the Spring in several language skill areas, including receptive vocabulary, phonological awareness, letter-name knowledge, letter-sound knowledge, letter-name fluency, and nonsense word fluency. These same children were again tested one year later in first grade in similar skills, plus oral reading fluency. Nonsense word fluency and letter-word fluency, respectively, were the highest predictors of oral reading fluency. In fact, the fluency measures were more accurate at predicting ORF than national normed measures of reading and phonological awareness, which identified only 33 percent of the poor readers in this study.

Using Response to Instruction as an Indicator in Second Grade

Another technique for avoiding the misidentification or nonidentification of students with reading problems is to place increased emphasis on measures of school performance. The response-to-treatment model identifies students based on low achievement, application of certain criteria for exclusion, and then response to interventions. Those who would be identified as having reading problems are children who did not respond to treatment and still display low achievement in reading, especially where the primary cause is not considered to be social and economic disadvantages, mental deficiency, or linguistic and cultural diversity.

Studies that tested this approach (Torgesen, 2001; Vellutino et al., 1996) provided children in primary grades with incremental periods of instruction and moved them out when they made adequate progress. One study (Vaughn, Linan-Thompson, and Hickman, 2003) of 45 second-grade, largely Hispanic students at risk for reading difficulties, sought to identify students by providing increments of supplemental instruction (10 weeks in length, 5 sessions per week, and about 35 minutes per session). The instruction included fast-paced lessons that focused on phonemic awareness, phonics, fluency, comprehension, and spelling, with correction and feedback and many opportunities for reading practice. Students were tested after each 10 weeks of supplemental instruction to determine if they met the exit criteria. Those who met the criteria were exited from the program and those who did not received another 10 weeks of supplemental instruction.

The exit tests included tests of oral reading fluency (ORF), word attack, passage comprehension, phonological processing, and general language proficiency. Ten students exited after the first 10 weeks of intervention, 14 after 20 weeks, and another 10 after 30 weeks. Even after 30 weeks of supplemental instruction, 11 students still did not meet the exit criteria, although most showed small improvements in reading fluency. The study showed that using a set of exit criteria linked to 30 weeks of supplemental instruction led to the identification of a distinct group of students who required substantial support and more explicit and intensive instruction, perhaps in special education. The researchers suggested that using response to treatment (1) provides supplemental instruction to a large number of at-risk students, (2) requires consistent monitoring of student progress, and (3) reduces the many biases inherent in the traditional referral systems that rely heavily on the interpretations and perceptions of classroom teachers.

Remember that all children make errors in spoken language and while reading. But the number of errors should decrease with time, and there should be clear evidence of growth in vocabulary and reading comprehension. Determining whether a child has consistent problems with reading requires careful and long-term observation of the child's fluency in speaking and reading. Most children display obvious improvements in their speaking and reading skills over time. Researchers, clinicians, and educators who study dyslexia and who work with poor readers look for certain clues that will show whether a child's reading ability is progressing normally.

The checklists that follow contain indications of reading problems commonly found in struggling readers, including people diagnosed with dyslexia. The indications have been gathered from several sources (Brady and Moats, 1997; IDA, 2003; NAEYC, 1998; Shaywitz, 2003; Stinson, 2003) and are separated into grade-level groupings. **The lists are not intended to be used for final diagnosis. Diagnosis of dyslexia or any other learning disorder can be made only by experienced clinicians.** However, the lists will help you to assess the degree of difficulty a child may be having in learning to read and to determine whether additional testing and consultations are required.

Use the following checklist to determine whether a child may be displaying problems. Circle the appropriate response to the right of each indicator. Those indicators marked "often" should be discussed among parents, teachers, and specialists in speech and language pathologies.

Preschool

Indicator (Inconsistent with the child's age or cognitive abilities) After the skills have been taught, the child . . .	Rating		
has difficulty pronouncing words	Rarely	Sometimes	Often
has difficulty with rhymes	Rarely	Sometimes	Often
is unable to recall the correct word	Rarely	Sometimes	Often
has difficulty in learning/remembering the names of letters	Rarely	Sometimes	Often
has difficulty following multi-step directions or routines	Rarely	Sometimes	Often
has difficulty telling/retelling a story in correct sequence	Rarely	Sometimes	Often
has trouble learning common nursery rhymes	Rarely	Sometimes	Often
has difficulty separating sounds in words	Rarely	Sometimes	Often

has difficulty blending sounds to make words	Rarely	Sometimes	Often
has difficulty listening to and discussing storybooks	Rarely	Sometimes	Often

Kindergarten and First Grade

Indicator (Inconsistent with the child's age or cognitive abilities) After the skills have been taught, the child . . .	Rating		
has difficulty recognizing that words can be separated into their basic sounds, such as *shoe* can be broken down into /sh/ and /oo/	Rarely	Sometimes	Often
has difficulty recognizing that words can be separated, such as *horseshoe* into *horse* and *shoe*	Rarely	Sometimes	Often
has trouble sounding out individual words in isolation	Rarely	Sometimes	Often
has difficulty using descriptive language	Rarely	Sometimes	Often
says that reading is difficult	Rarely	Sometimes	Often
has difficulty connecting letters to their sounds	Rarely	Sometimes	Often
says a word that is very different from its text, such as saying *house* when reading *giant*	Rarely	Sometimes	Often
has difficulty pronouncing the beginning sounds in words	Rarely	Sometimes	Often
has difficulty spelling high frequency short words	Rarely	Sometimes	Often
has difficulty reading orally with fluency	Rarely	Sometimes	Often
has difficulty using context to identify new words	Rarely	Sometimes	Often
has difficulty learning new vocabulary	Rarely	Sometimes	Often
has difficulty following simple directions, such as "Take out your notebook."	Rarely	Sometimes	Often
has difficulty retelling a story	Rarely	Sometimes	Often
has difficulty comprehending what was read	Rarely	Sometimes	Often

Second to Fourth Grade

Indicator (Inconsistent with the child's age or cognitive abilities) After the skills have been taught, the child . . .	Rating		
makes letter reversals, as *b* for *d* and *q* for *p*	Rarely	Sometimes	Often
makes letter inversions, as *n* for *u* and *w* for *m*	Rarely	Sometimes	Often
makes word reversals, as *pot* for *top*	Rarely	Sometimes	Often
confuses small words, as *and* for *said* and *goes* for *does*	Rarely	Sometimes	Often
has difficulty pronouncing long, unfamiliar words	Rarely	Sometimes	Often
confuses words that sound alike, as *left* for *felt* or *ocean* for *motion*	Rarely	Sometimes	Often
relies on guessing and context to decode new words rather than sounding them out	Rarely	Sometimes	Often
omits parts of words when sounding them out, as *enjble* for *enjoyable*	Rarely	Sometimes	Often
has difficulty breaking multisyllabic words into their component syllables	Rarely	Sometimes	Often
avoids reading aloud	Rarely	Sometimes	Often
pauses and hesitates during speech, lots of *ums*	Rarely	Sometimes	Often
has difficulty responding orally when questioned	Rarely	Sometimes	Often
relies heavily on memorizing instead of comprehending	Rarely	Sometimes	Often
has difficulty remembering facts	Rarely	Sometimes	Often
transposes number sequences	Rarely	Sometimes	Often
confuses arithmetic signs	Rarely	Sometimes	Often
has difficulty finishing written tests on time	Rarely	Sometimes	Often
has difficulty planning and organizing time and tasks	Rarely	Sometimes	Often
has difficulty representing the complete sound of a word when spelling	Rarely	Sometimes	Often

Fifth to Eighth Grade

Indicator (Inconsistent with the child's age or cognitive abilities) After the skills have been taught, the child . . .	Rating		
reverses letter sequences, as *soiled* for *solid*	Rarely	Sometimes	Often
has difficulty identifying and learning prefixes, suffixes, and root words	Rarely	Sometimes	Often
spells the same word differently on the same page	Rarely	Sometimes	Often
reads aloud slowly, laboriously, and without inflection	Rarely	Sometimes	Often
performs disproportionately poorly on multiple choice tests	Rarely	Sometimes	Often
avoids reading aloud	Rarely	Sometimes	Often
relies on guessing and context to decode new words rather than sounding them out individually	Rarely	Sometimes	Often
avoids writing	Rarely	Sometimes	Often
has difficulty with word problems in mathematics	Rarely	Sometimes	Often
has difficulty with comprehension when reading	Rarely	Sometimes	Often
has difficulty remembering facts (rote memory)	Rarely	Sometimes	Often
has difficulty responding orally when questioned	Rarely	Sometimes	Often
has difficulty with non-literal language, such as idioms, jokes, slang, and proverbs	Rarely	Sometimes	Often
avoids reading for pleasure	Rarely	Sometimes	Often
has difficulty planning and organizing time, materials, and tasks	Rarely	Sometimes	Often
has difficulty learning a foreign language	Rarely	Sometimes	Often
writes with difficulty with illegible handwriting	Rarely	Sometimes	Often

These lists can be useful tools in assessing whether a child (or adult) displays the symptoms common to those diagnosed with reading problems, including dyslexia. The symptoms must be persistent and not the occasional error. Persistence over a prolonged period of time is the key to determining the likelihood of dyslexia or any other physical condition that is interfering with the child's ability to read.

It is not unusual for struggling readers and dyslexic students to be depressed by their reading failures and self-conscious about their difficulties in the classroom. They often find the classroom a very stressful environment and are likely to exhibit behavior problems if they do not receive the special consideration that they need. Because dyslexia is a spectrum disorder ranging from mild to severe, children who are only mildly affected may exhibit one or a few of the problems mentioned in the checklists.

Remember the Strengths of Struggling Readers

Remember that struggling readers frequently have strengths in other areas, such as higher-order cognitive thinking that can help them manage or overcome their difficulties with reading. Many students with dyslexia are able to go on to higher education and be successful. But their phonologic deficits do not go away. Wilson and Lesaux (2001) studied the phonological processing skills of university students with dyslexia. Not surprisingly, the dyslexic students performed less well than the control group on measures of word recognition, word attack, reading vocabulary and comprehension, and spelling. However, the scores of the students with dyslexia in reading comprehension were not as low as expected. The researchers explained this finding by noting that there was no time limit for interpreting their reading, and that there were indications that the dyslexic students were using strategies different from typical university students in order to derive meaning from text. Apparently, these students were able to compensate for their persistent difficulties with phonological processing and become sufficiently competent readers to survive successfully in a university.

Growing scientific evidence continues to support the notion that most dyslexia is caused by deficits in phonological processing. It is important to recognize that dyslexia does not reflect an overall impairment in language, intelligence, or thinking skills. Many smart people are dyslexic. Rather, for most people it reflects an overall problem with the ability of a specific brain system, referred to earlier as the *phonologic module,* to put together the sounds of language to form words and to break words down into their basic sounds. This focus allows research to more closely examine the nature of these deficits and to explore methods for remediation. Other research evidence suggests that dyslexia may have multiple causes that require different forms of intervention. No doubt,

Famous dyslexics include:
Hans Christian Andersen
Winston Churchill
Tom Cruise
Leonardo da Vinci
Walt Disney
Albert Einstein
Jay Leno
Auguste Rodin
Steven Spielberg
W. B. Yeats

some individuals display dyslexic symptoms because of visual and auditory problems not directly associated with phonological processing, but their numbers are small.

Because reading does not come naturally to the human brain, children learning to read have to put much effort into associating their spoken language with the alphabet and with word recognition. To do this successfully, phonemic awareness is essential. In light of recent research, educators should have second thoughts about reading programs that delay phonemic awareness or that treat it as an ancillary skill to be learned in context with general reading.

> In light of recent research, educators should have second thoughts about reading programs that delay the teaching of phonemic awareness or treat it as an ancillary skill.

Educators should also become more aware of the scientific research into dyslexia and be able to recognize when students are having persistent reading problems. Early identification of struggling readers leads to early intervention. Researchers agree that a systematic, intensive, and comprehensive approach to early intervention can significantly reduce the number of students reading below the Basic level of proficiency.

A Note About "Cures" for Dyslexia

From time to time we read about a newly-discovered scientific "cure" for dyslexia. One recent claim from Britain was that dyslexia was caused by an underdeveloped cerebellum—the part of the brain responsible for motor coordination. Treatment involves stimulating the cerebellum by repeated physical activities and balancing exercises. According to the proponents, dyslexic students using this intervention showed improvement in reading and writing.

Another claim is that dyslexia is caused by a deficiency in the Omega-3 fatty acids that are essential for proper brain function. The "cure" involves administering very large doses of Omega-3 in capsule form. Here, too, proponents claim that dyslexic children have improved their reading skills.

Neither of the above claims is supported nor explained by current scientific knowledge or research. The scientific community is generally skeptical of any claims of curing developmental dyslexia. It is a life-long spectral disorder that can be overcome best through early and appropriate interventions that are systematic, sequential, and focused on developing phonological awareness.

Answer to Test Question # 7

Question: Dyslexic students often have problems in other cognitive areas.

Answer: *False.* Dyslexic students have had to construct extensive neural pathways and enhance specific neural regions when struggling to read. As a result, they often have strong capabilities in problem solving, reasoning, critical thinking, and concept formation.

What's Coming?

After recognizing that certain students are having reading problems, the next step is to select interventions that have been shown to be successful in helping struggling readers. All teachers are teachers of reading, and thus should have the training to strengthen the reading skills of students at every grade level. How to teach students with difficulties in reading is the focus of the next chapter.

CHAPTER 5
Overcoming Reading Problems

This chapter addresses several basic questions about overcoming reading problems. They include:

- *What are the basic ingredients of early intervention programs?*
- *What types of intervention programs are more successful with older students?*
- *How have some interventions actually rewired the dyslexic brain?*
- *What advice should be given to struggling readers and students with dyslexia and their parents?*

Many teachers work hard every day trying to help students with reading problems overcome their difficulties. Just how successful are these teachers? One study of fourth and fifth graders in special education classes showed virtually no change in their rate of reading growth when compared to their rate of growth in their regular education classes (Hanushuk, Kain, and Rivkin, 1998). Other studies have found that the reading programs being used in resource rooms lacked the effective interventions needed for learning the alphabetic principle and for developing skills in word recognition and text decoding (Vaughn, Moody, and Schumm, 1998). Even children taught in inclusion classrooms—where they receive special reading assistance within their regular classrooms—showed little change in their reading ability compared to their classmates (Zigmond and Jenkins, 1995). Conversely, the students receiving instruction in *scientifically-based programs* demonstrated rapid growth in reading achievement (Temple et al., 2003; Torgesen et al., 2001).

The secret to helping children overcome reading problems is early diagnosis. Chapter 4 dealt with the various clues that can alert parents and teachers to potential difficulties in learning to read. When there is sufficient evidence that a child is at risk for developing reading problems, quick intervention is essential. There are now several reading programs that are based on the more recent research and that have proven successful with struggling readers. The programs adhere to the notion that for children to become literate, they must break the reading code. Children with dyslexia may use different neural pathways and may have to work harder, but they still must master the skills of decoding printed text into recognizable sounds.

SOME CONSIDERATIONS FOR TEACHING STUDENTS WITH READING PROBLEMS

It is usually the regular classroom teacher who works the most with struggling readers and who helps them learn to read. The following thoughts may make the instructional process somewhat easier and more successful for all students (DITT, 2001).

General Considerations

✓ Make your classroom expectations clear.

✓ Ensure that classroom procedures are orderly, structured, and predictable.

✓ Remember that many struggling readers *can* learn to read. They just need different kinds of instructional strategies.

✓ Be constructive and positive. Labeling can often be disabling when you label the child rather than the behavior. Avoid labels and sarcasm that undermine the instructional environment and adversely affect the child's self-concept and performance.

✓ Recognize that struggling readers will take up to three times longer to complete work and will tire quickly.

✓ Avoid appeals to "try harder." The brains of struggling readers are already expending extra effort while decoding print, and these appeals will not improve performance. What is needed is slower speed with clearer comprehension.

✓ Determine and then complement these children's abilities, and teach through their strengths. Plan lessons so the students experience a sense of accomplishment rather than failure.

In the Elementary Classroom

✓ Get a complete explanation of the child's history of problems encountered when learning to read.

✓ Select scientifically-researched reading strategies and use a multi-sensory approach.

✓ Recognize the frustration that these students feel as they struggle to read.

✓ Show concern and understanding.

✓ Recognize that performance may be well below the child's potential.

✓ Remember that this child learns in different ways, but can learn.

✓ Realize that the child may have behavioral and self-esteem problems.

✓ Develop good student-teacher rapport.

✓ Maintain contact with the child's parents and give them periodic progress reports. Make suggestions of what they can do with the child at home to complement your classroom strategies.

✓ Ensure that other classmates understand the nature of dyslexia so that the child is not bullied or mocked.

✓ Assign a buddy to help the struggling reader in the class and school.

✓ Encourage the child to point out talents and strengths.

In the Secondary Classroom

✓ Get a complete explanation of the student's history of reading problems.

✓ Use a multi-sensory approach in classroom instruction.

✓ Recognize the compounded frustrations of a dyslexic teenager.

✓ Remember that dyslexic students learn in different ways, but they *can* learn.

✓ Realize that these teenagers may have problems with their self-esteem.

✓ Recognize that these students may have behavior or truancy problems.

✓ Realize that these students often have a significant gap between their performance and their potential.

✓ Show concern and understanding.

✓ Use diagrams and graphic organizers when teaching. Advanced organizers that contain important notes about the lesson are also very helpful and can help prevent failure.

✓ Develop good student-teacher rapport.

✓ Maintain contact with the student's parents and give them periodic progress reports. Make suggestions of what they can do with the student at home to complement your classroom strategies.

✓ Ensure that these students' legal rights are adhered to when taking tests.

✓ Mild dyslexics often develop coping strategies in elementary school. Be aware that these strategies may be inadequate for the complex and multi-faceted secondary curriculum.

✓ Ensure that any remedial materials are relevant to the maturity and not the academic level of the student.

✓ Be aware that struggling readers can have great difficulty reading an unseen text aloud in class. Asking them to do this can adversely affect their self-esteem.

BASIC INGREDIENTS OF EARLY INTERVENTION PROGRAMS

The National Reading Panel (NRP, 2000) has strongly recommended that beginning reading programs focus on systematic and explicit instruction in helping children master the alphabetic principle, especially for children at risk for reading difficulties. Dozens of reading programs flood the market every year. Deciding which program can best meet the needs of struggling readers is now easier thanks to our greater understanding of how the brain learns to read. Based on this understanding, a reading program is likely to be successful in helping children with reading difficulties if it includes explicit instruction in phonological awareness as well as word identification skills that lead to accurate, fluent reading and comprehension. Multiple research studies demonstrate the success of this approach (Chard and Dickson, 1999; Coyne, Kame'enui, and Simmons, 2001; Torgesen, 2002, 2004).

How Do I Develop Phonemic Awareness in Struggling Readers?

Training in phonemic awareness needs to be more intense for children with reading disabilities. Reading programs are filled with activities for separating words into phonemes, synthesizing phonemes into words, and deleting and substituting phonemes. Research suggests that the development of phonemic awareness is more likely to be successful if it follows these general principles (Chard and Osborn, 1998):

✓ *Continuous sounds before stop sounds.* Start with continuous sounds such as /s/, /m/, and /f/ that are easier to pronounce than the stop sounds of /b/, /k/, and /p/.

✓ *Modeling.* Be sure to model carefully and accurately each activity when it is first introduced.

✓ *Easy to complex tasks.* Move from easier tasks, such as rhyming, to more complex tasks, such as blending and segmenting.

✓ *Larger to smaller units.* Move from the larger units of words and onset-rimes to the smaller units of individual phonemes.

✓ *Additional strategies.* Use additional strategies to help struggling readers, such as concrete objects (e.g., bingo chips or blocks) to represent sounds.

We have already discussed how early awareness of phonemes is a strong indicator of later reading success. Further, the research on interventions clearly demonstrates the benefits of explicitly teaching phonemic awareness skills. No students benefit more from this instruction than those already burdened with reading problems. The development of phonemic awareness occurs over several years. It is the last step in a developmental continuum that begins with the brain's earliest awareness of rhyme. Figure 5.1 illustrates the continuum from rhyming to full phoneme manipulation (Chard and Dickson, 1999).

Figure 5.1 The development of phonemic awareness is a continuum that begins with simple rhyming and ends with the manipulation of individual phonemes.

General Guidelines

The first four steps in Figure 5.1, from rhyming to onset-rime blending, can occur during the preschool years in the appropriate environment. If the parent sings rhyming songs and reads to the child from rhyming books, the child's brain begins to recognize the sounds that comprise beginning language. However, many children begin school with a very weak phonological base. Teachers must then assess where students lie on the phonological continuum and select appropriate strategies to move them toward phonemic awareness. Edelen-Smith (1998) offers teachers the following guidelines to consider when selecting strategies to help students recognize and successfully manipulate phonemes.

- ✓ *Be specific.* Identify the specific phonemic awareness task and select the activities that are developmentally appropriate and that keep the students engaged in the task. Select words, phrases, and sentences from curricular materials to make this meaningful. Look for ways to make activities enjoyable so students see them as fun and not as monotonous drills.

- ✓ *Avoid letter names.* Use the phoneme sounds of the alphabet when doing activities, and avoid letter names. Letters sounded as they are named only confuse the learner. Keep in mind that one sound may be represented by two or more letters. Target specific sounds and practice beforehand so students can hear them clearly.

- ✓ *Treat continuant and stop sounds differently.* Continuant sounds are easier to manipulate and hear than the stop sounds. When introducing each type, treat them differently so students become aware of their differences. Exaggerate continuant sounds by holding on to them: *sssssssing* and *rrrrrrun*. Use rapid repetition with the stop consonants: */K/-/K/-/K/-/K/-/K/-/K/-athy.*

- ✓ *Emphasize how sounds vary with their position in a word.* Generally, the initial position in the word is the easiest sound. The final position is the next easiest and the middle position is the most difficult. Use lots of examples to make this clear, such as *mop, pin,* and *better.*

✓ *Be aware of the sequence for introducing combined sounds.* When introducing the combined sounds, a consonant-vowel pattern should come first, then a vowel-consonant pattern, and finally, the consonant-vowel-consonant pattern. For example: first *tie*, next *add,* and then *bed.*

Simple Phonemic Awareness

Young students are usually unaware that words are made of sounds that can be produced in isolation. This leaves it up to the teacher to find ways to emphasize the concept of speech sounds through *systematic* and *direct* instruction. An effective reading program should include activities that help children manipulate phonemes. Here are some ways to do this (Edelen-Smith, 1998):

✓ *Recognizing isolated sounds.* Associate certain speech sounds with an animal or action that is familiar to the students. For example, the buzzing sound of a bee or snoring in sleep is *zzzzzzzz–*, the hissing of a snake, *sssssssss–*, the sound of asking for quiet, *shhhhhhhh–*, or the sound of a motor scooter or motor boat, *pppppppp–*. Alliteration also helps with this task. Talking about Peter Piper picking a peck of peppers affords the valuable combination of sound recognition, story telling, and literary context. It also provides self-correcting cues for initial-sound isolation and for sound-to-word matching.

✓ *Counting words, syllables, and phonemes.* It is easier for a child's brain to perceive words and syllables than individual phonemes. Thus word and syllable counting is a valuable exercise for sound recognition that can lead later to more accurate identification of phonemes. Start with a sentence from the curriculum and say it aloud. Do not write it out because the students should focus on listening. Ask the students to count the number of words they think are in the sentence. They can use markers or tokens to indicate the word number. Then show or write the sentence and have the students compare the number of words to their own count. Syllable counting can be done in many ways. Students can count syllables in the same way they identified the word count. Also, they can march around the room while saying the syllables, they can clap hands, tap pencils, or do any other overt activity that indicates counting.

✓ *Synthesizing sounds.* Sound synthesis is an essential yet easily performed skill for phonemic awareness. Start with using the initial sound and then saying the remainder of the word. For example, the teacher says, "It starts with *b* and ends with *-and,* put it together and it says *band.*" The students take turns using the same phrasing to make up their own words. Variations include limiting the context to objects in the classroom or in the school, or to a particular story that the class has recently read.

Guessing games can also be productive and fun activities for playing with sounds. One game involves hiding an object in a bag or some other place and then giving clues to its name sound-by-sound or syllable-by-syllable. When a student guesses the word correctly, you reveal the object. Songs can also be used. Blending the music with the sounds of words increases the chances that the phonemes will be remembered.

✓ *Matching sounds to words.* This activity asks the learner to identify the initial sound of a word, an important skill for sound segmentation. Show the student a picture of a kite and ask, "Is this a *dddd-ite,* or a *llll-ite,* or a *kkkk-ite?*" You could also ask, "Is there a *k* in *kite?*," or "Which sound does *kite* start with?" This allows the students to try three onsets with three rimes and to mix and match until they get it correct. Consonants make a good beginning because they are easier to emphasize and prolong during pronunciation. Have students try other words in threes. Be sure to use the phoneme sound when referring to a letter, not the letter name.

✓ *Identifying the position of sounds.* Segmenting whole words into their components is an important part of phonemic awareness. This ability is enhanced when learners recognize that sounds occur in different positions in words: initial, medial, and final. Edelen-Smith (1998) suggests explaining that words have beginning, middle, and end sounds just like a train has a beginning (engine), middle (passenger car), and end (caboose). Slowly articulate a consonant-vowel-consonant (CVC) word at this time, such as *c-a-t,* and point to the appropriate train part as you sound out each phoneme. Then have the students sound out other CVC words from a list or recent story, pointing to each train part as they say the parts of the word.

> One of the more difficult phonemic tasks for children is to separately pronounce each sound of a spoken word in order.

✓ *Segmenting sounds.* One of the more difficult phonemic tasks for children is to separately pronounce each sound of a spoken word in order. This process is called sound segmentation. Developing this skill should start with isolating the initial phonemes. The previous activities —matching sounds to words and identifying the position of sounds—help the learner identify and recognize initial phonemes. Visual cues can also play an important part in segmenting sounds. Select words that are familiar to the students (or have the students select the words) so that they can use contextual clues for meaning. After sufficient practice, eliminate the cards so that students can perform the sound segmenting task without visual cues.

✓ *Associating sounds with letters.* For the reading process to be successful, the brain must associate the sounds that it has heard during the pre-reading years of spoken language with the written letters that represent them. This is particularly difficult for students with disabilities that hamper the learning of reading. Consequently, extensive practice is essential. Nearly all of the activities mentioned above —especially those involving visual cues—can be modified to include associations between sounds and letters. As the students master individual sounds, their corresponding letter names can then be introduced. A type of bingo game can also be used to practice sound-with-letter association. Each student gets a card with letters placed into a bingo grid. Draw a letter from a container and call out the phoneme. Students place tokens on the letter that corresponds to the phoneme. The student who first gets "phoneme bingo" names the letters aloud. Teachers can devise all types of variations to this bingo game to maintain the practice while keeping the task interesting and fun.

Compound Phonemic Awareness

In compound phonemic awareness, the learner must hold one sound in memory while matching it to a second sound. For example, "Do *dog* and *deer* begin with the same sound?" The two activities that develop compound phonemic awareness involve matching one word to a second word and the deleting of sounds in a word.

✓ *Matching one word to another word.* Byrne (1991) has suggested three games to develop phonemic word matching skills. The words and pictures used in each of these games should relate to themes and readings done in the classroom. One involves making a set of dominoes that have two objects pictured on each tile. The students have to join the tiles that share the same beginning or ending sounds.

A second game uses picture cards that are placed face down in a pile. Each student draws a card from the pile and places it face up. Students continue to draw cards and place them in the face-up pile. The first student to match the beginning or ending sound of a drawn card with the top card on the face-up pile says the match aloud and collects the pile.

The third game is a variation of bingo. Each bingo card contains pictures, which the students mark when their picture has the same beginning or ending sounds as the word said by the caller (student or teacher).

✓ *Deleting sounds.* Deleting sounds from words and manipulating phonemes within words are more difficult tasks for the young brain to accomplish. Studies show that most children must attain the mental age of seven years before this task can be accomplished adequately (Cole and Mengler, 1994). Furthermore, segmentation skills and letter names must be mastered before sound deletion tasks can be successfully learned.

Three tasks seem to be particularly important to mastering this skill: deleting parts of a compound word, identifying a missing sound, and deleting a single sound from a word.

1. *Deleting parts of a compound word.* To illustrate deleting parts of a compound word, point to a picture or an object that is a compound word and demonstrate how each word can be said with one part missing. For example, "This is a classroom. I can say *class* without the *room*. And this is a farmhouse (or greenhouse). I can say *farm* (*green*) without *house*. Now you try it. This is a playground." Use other common examples, such as *lighthouse, airplane, grandmother, seashore, sandbox, toothpaste,* and *nightlight.*

2. *Identifying the missing sound.* In this task, focus on deleting the initial and final sounds instead of the medial sounds, which is the first step to master for the young brain. Take word pairs, such as *ate-late,* and ask "What's missing in *ate* that you hear in *late*?" Other examples are *ask-mask, able-table,* and *right-bright.* After a few trials, have the students make up their own word pairs, preferably from lesson material.

3. *Deleting a single sound from a word.* This task should begin with segmentation practice. First, separate the sound for deletion. For example, separate *g* from *glove.* "Glove. It starts with *g* and ends with *love.* Take the first sound away and it says *love.*" Use words for which a sound deletion results in another real word. Other examples are *spot-pot, train-rain, scare-care,* and *snap-nap.* After practicing this skill, say a word aloud and ask students to say the word with the initial sound missing: "Say *mother* without the *m.*" Visual clues can help those who have difficulty saying a word with the deleted sound.

Onset and Rime

The young brain's awareness of onsets, rimes, and syllables develops before an awareness of phonemes. Onsets are the initial consonants that change the meaning of a word; rimes are the vowel-consonant combinations that stay constant in a series. For example, in *bend, lend,* and *send,* the onsets are *b, l,* and *s;* the rime is *-end.* Using literature, word families, and direct instruction are strategies that focus on word play designed to enhance onset and rime recognition (Edelen-Smith, 1998).

> The young brain's awareness of onsets, rimes, and syllables develops before an awareness of phonemes.

✓ *Literature.* Books with rhyming patterns (like many books by Dr. Seuss) are easily recalled through repeated exposure. Almost any literary source that plays with word sounds is valuable. Books that particularly develop awareness of sound patterns associated with onset and rime are those using alliteration (the repetition of an initial consonant across several words, e.g., *Peter Piper picked a peck of peppers*) and assonance (the repetition of vowel sounds within words, e.g., *The rain in Spain stays mainly on the plain*).

✓ *Word families charts.* Using words from a story or book, construct a chart that places a different beginning letter in front of a rime. For example, start with the rime *-at* and add *f, h, b,* and *s* to form *fat, hat, bat,* and *sat.* Have the students make up a story line whenever the word changes (e.g., *The fat cat chased a hat*). Encourage the students to make their own charts with different rimes and to keep them for future reference.

✓ *Direct instruction.* Students who have difficulties distinguishing the sounds among rhyming words need more direct instruction. Model rhyming pairs (e.g., *sun-fun* and *hand-band*) using flash cards so students match what they see with what they hear. Be sure they repeat each rhyming pair several times to reinforce auditory input. Another activity includes three cards, only two of which have rhyming words. Ask students to pick out and say the two that rhyme, or the one that doesn't. Later, change the rhyming words to two rhyming pictures out of three (e.g., a nose, a rose, and a horse).

Successful Early Intervention Programs

Several early intervention programs have been consistently successful for years and deserve to be mentioned here. Two notable ones are Reading Recover and Success for All.

Reading Recovery

Started in 1984, Reading Recovery has served more than one million children. This program is designed for the lowest-achieving readers in first grade. Specially trained teachers meet with the children individually for 30 minutes daily for 12 to 20 weeks. Instruction focuses on developing phonemic awareness, practice learning letter-sound relationships through phonics, strategies to enhance text comprehension, and teaching for fluency and phrasing. The children are tested before entering the program, at the end of the Reading Recovery instruction, and at the end of first grade. Their scores are compared with a random sample of their peers. A Spanish version is available.

Numerous studies and research reports over the last 15 years document the effectiveness of Reading Recovery for the lowest-performing first graders. Cumulative 17-year results show that 81 percent of children who have the full series of lessons can read at the class average. Furthermore, most of these children maintain and improve their gains in later grades (Reading Recovery Council, 2002).

Success for All — Reading First

Based on the widely-used Success for All comprehensive reform model introduced in 1987, this adaptation is a core reading program for grades K to 3 designed to strengthen the students' phonemic awareness, phonics, vocabulary, fluency, and comprehension. Students have a 90-minute reading period daily with specially trained teachers. The program uses proven instructional strategies, such as cooperative learning, partner reading, a rapid pace of instruction, frequent standards-based assessments, and effective classroom management techniques to engage each student. Also included are activities that build around existing textbooks to emphasize comprehension of narrative and expository texts, metacognitive comprehension strategies, writing, study skills, and home reading. Children are assessed every eight weeks in decoding, reading comprehension, and fluency. Based on these assessments, teachers regroup the children across grade lines so that each teacher can work with children at one reading level. This program is also available in Spanish.

Since the inception of the basic program, Success for All has been evaluated in grades K to 3 through several major experimental studies. The studies found that, in comparison to matched control schools, students in Success for All schools read significantly better, are promoted regularly from grade to grade, are less often referred to special education, and attend school more regularly (Weiler, 1998).

PROGRAMS FOR OLDER STUDENTS

How Do I Develop Fluency and Comprehension in Older Struggling Readers?

Older struggling readers are able to develop strong reading capabilities when provided with effective instructional conditions (Lyon, 2002). To be effective, reading programs must include activities that promote reading fluency. Shaywitz (2003) strongly supports the notion of short, intense daily practice sessions in reading in order to develop fluency. The children's practice continues over weeks and months as they reread passages until they attain high accuracy. Intense practice helps children build fluency because decoding becomes automatic, the same way that practice assists athletes and musicians perform motor skills almost without thinking (Shaywitz calls this *overlearning,* the ability to perform something without attention or conscious thought).

Fluency comes through repetition of words and sentences. Such repetition increases the chances that words and common phrases will be stored in long-term memory, allowing for faster word recognition during subsequent encounters. The National Reading Panel (NRP, 2000) recommended reading programs that emphasize repeated oral reading accompanied by teacher feedback and guidance, a strategy referred to as *guided repeated oral reading.* The feedback is necessary because it gives children the opportunities to modify their pronunciation so that the stored representation of the word in their mental lexicon continues to approach its correct pronunciation and spelling. Whenever readers mispronounce words, it means that they do not have accurate mental representations of those words in their brains and will thus have difficulty storing or retrieving information related to that word. Guided repeated oral reading is an especially effective technique for helping readers practice aloud unfamiliar vocabulary. Such practice builds accurate neural representations of the vocabulary and enhances comprehension.

What Strategies Teach Fluency and Comprehension to Struggling Readers?

Studies have shown that children with reading problems are able to master the learning strategies that improve reading comprehension skills. For students with learning problems, learning to use questioning strategies is especially important because these students do not often spontaneously self-question or monitor their own reading comprehension.

Here are three strategies that researchers and teachers have found particularly effective. Some of the strategies have been around for over 20 years, but their fundamental premises have been reaffirmed by recent research.

Questioning and Paraphrasing: Reciprocal Teaching

Reciprocal teaching is a strategic approach that fosters student interaction with the text being read (Palincsar and Brown, 1984). In reciprocal teaching, students interact deeply with the text through the strategies of questioning, summarizing, clarifying, and predicting.

> Reciprocal
> teaching involves
> – Questioning
> – Summarizing
> – Clarifying
> – Predicting

Organized in the form of a discussion, the approach involves one leader (students and teacher take turns being the leader) who, after a portion of the text is read, first frames a question to which the group responds. Second, participants share their own questions. Third, the leader then summarizes the gist of the text, and participants comment or elaborate upon that summary. At any point in the discussion, either the leader or participants may identify aspects of the text or discussion that need to be clarified, and the group joins together to clarify the confusion. Finally, the leader indicates that it is time to move on and solicits predictions about what might come up next in the text.

The value of paraphrasing, self-questioning, and finding the main idea are well researched strategies. Students divide reading passages into smaller parts, such as sections, subsections, or paragraphs. After reading a segment, students are cued to use a self-questioning strategy to identify main ideas and details. The strategy requires a high level of attention to reading tasks because students must alternate their use of questioning and paraphrasing after reading each section, subsection, or paragraph.

Reciprocal teaching is an effective strategy because it requires the brain to integrate prior knowledge with new learning, to make inferences, to maintain focus, and to use auditory rehearsal to enhance retention of learning. Research studies support the value of reciprocal teaching. One study of 50 at-risk post-secondary students enrolled in a community college showed that the reciprocal teaching group performed significantly better than the comparison group on reading comprehension and strategy acquisition. There were no differences on perception of study skills. Poorer readers in the reciprocal teaching group outperformed poorer readers in the comparison group on both reading comprehension and strategy acquisition measures (Hart and Speece, 1998). See more about reciprocal teaching in Chapter 6.

Questioning to Find the Main Idea

This self-questioning strategy focuses primarily on identifying and questioning the main idea or summary of a paragraph. Here's how it works. Students are first taught the concept of a main idea and how to do self-questioning. Students then practice, asking themselves questions aloud about each paragraph's main idea. They can use a cue card for assistance. Following the practice, the teacher provides immediate feedback. Eventually, following successful comprehension of these short paragraphs, students are presented with more lengthy passages, and the cue cards are removed. Continuing to give corrective feedback, the teacher finishes each lesson with a discussion of students' progress and of the strategy's usefulness. Studies show that students with learning disabilities who were trained in a self-questioning strategy performed significantly higher (i.e., demonstrated greater comprehension of what was read) than untrained students (Idol, 1987; Sousa, 2001b).

Story Map

```
                    ┌──────────┐
                    │  Title   │
                    └──────────┘
              ┌───────────┴───────────┐
      ┌──────────────┐        ┌──────────────┐
      │  Main Idea   │        │  Main Idea   │
      └──────────────┘        └──────────────┘
       ┌─────┴─────┐            ┌─────┴─────┐
    ┌─────┐     ┌─────┐      ┌─────┐     ┌─────┐
```

S u p p o r t i n g   I n f o r m a t i o n

Figure 5.2 This is just one example of a story map. It helps students discover the author's main ideas and to search out information to support them (Sousa, 2001a).

Story-Mapping

In this strategy, students read a story, generate a map of its events and ideas, and then answer questions. (Figure 5.2 is one example of a story map.) In order to fill in the map, students have to identify the setting, characters, time, and place of the story; the problem, the goal, and the action that took place; and the outcome. The teacher models for students how to fill in the map, then gives them many opportunities to practice the mapping technique for themselves and receive corrective feedback. The map is an effective visual tool that provides a framework for understanding, conceptualizing, and remembering important story events. The reading comprehension of students can improve significantly when the teacher gives direct instruction on the use of the strategy, expects frequent use of the strategy, and encourages students to use the strategy independently.

Focusing on Comprehension: The PASS Process

Students with reading disorders often have difficulty deriving meaning from what they read. If little or no meaning comes from reading, students lose motivation to read. Furthermore, meaning is essential for long-term retention of what they have read. Strategies designed to improve reading comprehension have been shown to improve students' interest in reading and their success.

The PASS Process. One such successful strategy, suggested by Deshler, Ellis, and Lenz (1996), is a four-step process called by the acronym PASS (Preview, Ask, Summarize, and Synthesize). The teacher guides the students through the four steps, ensuring that they respond orally or in writing to the activities associated with each step. Grouping formats, such as cooperative learning, can be used to encourage active student participation and reduce anxiety over the correctness of each student's response.

1. **P**review, Review, and Predict:
   - Preview by reading the heading and one or two sentences.
   - Review what you already know about this topic.
   - Predict what you think the text or story will be about.

2. **A**sk and Answer Questions:
   - Content-focused questions:
   - Who? What? Why? Where?
   - How does this relate to what I already know?
   - Monitoring questions:
     Does this make sense?
     Is my prediction correct?
     How is this different from what I thought it was going to be about?
   - Problem-solving questions:
     Is it important that it make sense?
     Do I need to reread part of it?
     Can I visualize the information?
     Does it have too many unknown words?
     Should I get help?

3. **S**ummarize:
   - Explain what the short passage you read was all about.

4. **S**ynthesize:
   - Explain how the short passage fits in with the whole passage.
   - Explain how what you learned fits in with what you knew.

If students have difficulty with any particular step, they can go back to the previous step to determine what information they need in order to proceed.

Collaborative Strategic Reading

Another excellent technique for helping students comprehend what they read and build vocabulary is called Collaborative Strategic Reading (CSR). It is particularly effective in classrooms where students have many different reading abilities and learning capabilities. The strategy is compatible with all types of reading programs.

> Collaborative Strategic Reading is particularly effective in classrooms where students have many different reading abilities and learning capabilities.

CSR uses direct teaching and the collaborative power of cooperative learning groups to accomplish two phases designed to improve reading comprehension (Klingner, Vaughn, and Schumm, 1998). The first phase is a teacher-led component that takes students through four parts of a reading plan: Preview, Click and Clunk, Get the Gist, and Wrap-Up. The second phase involves using cooperative learning groups to provide an interactive environment where students can practice and perfect their reading comprehension skills.

PHASE ONE
Teacher-Led Activities

✓ *Preview the reading.* Students know that previews in movies give some information about coming events. Use this as a hook to the new reading. The learners preview the entire reading passage in order to get as much as they can about the passage in just a few minutes time. The purpose here is to activate their prior knowledge about the topic and to give them an opportunity to predict what they will learn.

Refer to student experiences about a movie, television program, or prior book that might contain information relevant to the new reading. Also, give clues to look for when previewing. For example, pictures, graphs, tables, or call-out quotes provide information to help predict what students already know about the topic and what they will learn.

✓ *Click and clunk.* Students with reading problems often fail to monitor their understanding while they read. Clicks and clunks are devices to help students with this monitoring. Clicks are parts of the reading that make sense; clunks are parts or words that don't.

Ask students to identify clunks as they go along. Then the class works with the teacher to develop strategies to clarify the clunks, such as

- Rereading the sentences while looking for key words that can help extract meaning from the context
- Rereading previous and following sentences to get additional context clues
- Looking for a prefix or suffix in the word that could help with meaning
- Breaking the word apart to see if smaller words are present that provide meaning

✓ *Get the gist.* The goal of this phase is twofold. First, ask the readers to state in their own words the most important person, place, or thing in the passage. Second, get them to tell in as few words as possible (i.e., leaving out the details) the most important idea about that person, place, or thing. Because writing often improves memory, occasionally ask the students to write down their gists. Students can then read their gists aloud and invite comments from the group about ways to improve the gist. This process can be done so that all students benefit by enhancing their skills.

✓ *Wrap-up.* Wrap-up is a closure activity that allows students to review in their mind what has been learned to ensure that it makes sense and has meaning. Focus students on the new learning by asking them to generate questions whose answers would show what they learned from the passage. They should also review key ideas.

Start with questions that focus on the explicit material in the passage, such as who, what, where, and when. Afterward, move to questions that stimulate higher-order thinking, such as, "What might have happened if . . .?" and "What could be another way to solve this problem?" Writing down the response will help students sort out and remember the important ideas.

PHASE TWO
Cooperative Learning Groups

This phase puts the students into cooperative learning groups to practice CSR in an interactive environment. True cooperative learning groups are usually made up of about five students of mixed ability levels who learn and perform certain roles in the group to ensure completion of the learning task (Johnson and Johnson, 1989). The roles rotate among the group members so that every student gets the opportunity to be the leader and use the various skills needed to perform each task. Although there are many roles that students can perform, here are the most common (assuming five members per group):

- **Leader.** Leads the group through CSR by saying what to read next and what strategy to use.
- **Clunk expert.** Reminds the group what strategies to use when encountering a difficult word or phrase.
- **Announcer.** Calls on different group members to make certain that everyone participates and that only one person talks at a time.
- **Encourager.** Gives the group feedback on behaviors that are to be praised and those that need improvement.

- **Reporter.** Takes notes and reports to the whole class the main idea that the group has learned and shares a question that the group generated during its wrap-up.

Here are suggestions for using the cooperative learning groups with this strategy:

✓ *Cue sheets.* Giving all group members a cue sheet to guide them through the CSR provides a structure and focus for the group. The cue sheet should be specific for each role. For example, the leader's sheet contains statements that steer the group through each step of CSR (e.g., "Today's topic is . . ." "Let's predict what we might learn from this." "Let's think of some questions to see if we really understand what we learned.") and also direct other group members to carry out their role (e.g., "Announcer, please call on others to share their ideas." "Encourager, tell us what we did well and what we need to do better next time.").

✓ *CSR learning logs.* Recording in logs helps students to keep track of what was learned. Students can keep separate logs for each subject. The log serves as a reminder for follow-up activities and can be used to document a student's progress as required by the individualized education plan.

✓ *Reading materials.* CSR was originally designed for expository text, but has also been used successfully with narrative text. For the strategy to be successful, select reading passages that are rich in clues, that have just one main idea per paragraph, and that provide a context to help students connect and associate details into larger ideas.

Additional Strategies

Some of the models for teaching reading discussed in Chapter 3 that involve repeated oral reading are appropriate to use with older struggling readers. Paired (or partner) reading and readers' theatre are particularly effective classroom strategies. Reading aloud helps students of all ages gain confidence in their developing reading skills. This is especially important around the fourth grade where there is a large increase in vocabulary words with irregular pronunciations. Struggling readers need considerable practice with these words to develop fluency and avoid the well-known drop in reading performance that occurs in fourth grade. Two of the main sources of irregular pronunciation problems are:

1. Words that contain the same root but are pronounced differently. Examples are *bough, cough, dough* and *rough; have* and *gave;* or *bead* and *dead.*

2. Words where the same letters get different pronunciations, as in the following pairs: *electric–electricity, grade–gradual, nation–national, muscle–muscular,* and *sign–signature.*

These words must be learned and overlearned by repeated practice as part of the fluency exercises given in class.

Attention Therapy to Improve Comprehension

Successful reading requires sustained attention to the printed text. Researchers now recognize that attention is a complex process that requires the brain to focus, shift, sustain, and encode relevant stimuli while simultaneously impeding the processing of irrelevant stimuli (Mirsky, 1996). In reading, visual attention (the eyes scanning the page) must be sustained long enough for the visual processing system (in the rear of the brain) to perceive the text so that the cognitive processing system (frontal lobe) can comprehend the text. Visual attention, therefore, is the catalyst that links perception to comprehension.

Students with attention deficits often have reading difficulties as well. Because visual attention is a learned skill, the research question here is: Can giving students with reading difficulties attention therapy that improves visual attention lead to better reading comprehension? In a recent study (Solan, Shelley-Tremblay, Ficarra, Silverman, and Larson, 2003), 30 grade 6 students with reading problems were split into two groups. One group received 12 one-hour sessions of individually monitored, computer-based attention therapy programs. The second group served as the control and was given no therapy during the 12-week period. The therapy program consisted of computer-based activities designed to improve perceptual accuracy, visual efficiency, visual search, visual scan, and visual span. Each session was followed with paper-and-pencil exercises for additional practice. The program also emphasized improving visual memory.

After completing the program, the mean reading comprehension scores improved significantly, from the 23rd to the 35th percentile, and a grade equivalent increase from 4.1 to 5.2. Because this improvement is well over one standard deviation, it is unlikely that the results can be attributed to the practice that occurred as part of the program. This study is significant because it showed that (1) attention skills are malleable and measurable, (2) attention therapy improves attention duration, and (3) students who receive attention therapy score better in tests of reading comprehension than controls.

Although the sample in this study was small, the results were intriguing. If further studies support these findings, then computer-based attention therapy programs may someday become another tool that teachers of remedial reading may consider in their efforts to improve their students' reading comprehension.

Answer to Test Question # 8

Question: Many poor readers have attention problems that schools are not equipped to handle.

Answer: *False.* Many poor readers expend a great deal of effort at first trying to decode text, but their struggle leads to frustration and eventually to inattentiveness.

Tutoring in Reading for Fluency

Tutoring can be a significant enhancement to fluency in reading (Snow et al., 1998). Tutors can be volunteers, older students, or parents. Essentially, tutors provide individual guided practice and corrective feedback to a student while the student reads aloud from meaningful text at a suitable level of difficulty. To be effective, it is important that the tutors have a specific approach to the tutoring session. All tutors should be provided training in basic tutoring techniques and in the selection of appropriate materials. These materials should be closely related to the reading materials that the students are using in their classes.

Parker, Hasbrouck, and Denton (2002a) suggest three types of tutoring interventions: (1) repeated reading with a model, (2) oral reading with monitoring and feedback, and (3) error monitoring and reading practice.

Repeated Reading With a Model

Simultaneous, repeated reading with a tutor is an effective method for improving the fluency of reluctant readers. By carefully adjusting the timing and control of the repeated readings, the tutor helps the student foster independent reading skills. Here are the three steps to this approach.

✓ *Step One: Introduction*
- Start with a passage that will take 3 to 5 minutes for the student to read aloud.
- Read the title.
- Give a general description of the topic.
- Ask if the student knows anything about the topic.
- Give a reason or purpose for reading the topic.
- Explain that the passage may be difficult so you will read it together.

✓ *Step Two: Simultaneous reading*
- Read the passage with the student, sitting slightly behind so as not to be a visual distraction.
- Read slowly in a clear, soft voice as the student reads aloud at the same time.
- Regulate your speed of reading to allow the student to keep up.
- The student and you should move your fingers under the printed text as you read.
- Listen carefully as to whether the student is following, with, or leading your reading of difficult words. Most students will initially follow the tutor. But with greater confidence, they will read more nearly with the tutor, and eventually will lead.
- As the student comes closer to your reading speed, soften your voice. As the student leads more, soften your voice further and slow your pace slightly to allow the student to lead even more.

✓ *Step Three: Simultaneous repeated readings*
- After a short break, begin rereading. From two to five readings will be beneficial, depending on the student's motivation and age.
- With each rereading, maintain a smooth pace and encourage the student to read with you and to lead by softening your voice and slowing your pace slightly.

Oral Reading With Monitoring and Feedback

This process uses a text that the student can read with 90 to 95 percent oral reading accuracy, and at a moderate level of difficulty. The tutor provides direct feedback on difficult words encountered in the text. The aim here is for the student to avoid long pauses while attempting to decode unfamiliar words and to build fluency and confidence in reading. Here are the two steps in this process.

✓ *Introduction*
- Ask the student to read the passage aloud as smoothly, quickly, and accurately as possible.
- Reassure the student that, although you do not want to interrupt the reading, you will help with words that are unfamiliar or misread.
- Show the student how to use a finger or marker to pace the reading and to keep on track.

✓ *Providing feedback*
- Sit slightly behind the student so as not be a visual distraction.

- Immediately pronounce correctly any mispronounced word, and have the student quickly repeat it without breaking stride in reading.
- Strive for minimal interruption, but immediately correct each error. If the student is making more than one error every 10 words or so, then the passage is too difficult.
- Have the student use a finger or marker to pace the reading.
- Take note of any pattern in the student's errors, such as any specific words that are missed with high frequency, missing specific letter or sound patterns, and violations of phonics rules. This is an advanced tutoring skill and should only be done by tutors who have a good knowledge of phonics and word structure.

Error Monitoring and Reading Practice

This approach gives students the opportunity to practice difficult words not connected to text. Students practice reading word patterns, words, and sentences from flashcards. The flashcard practice proceeds rapidly, without interruption, for 15 to 25 cards, or 3 to 5 minutes, depending on the student's age. If the student gets stuck on a word, wait only 1 to 3 seconds before saying it. Stick the more difficult words back in the deck toward the front so the student has more practice with them. Here are three different variations of this reading practice.

✓ *Word patterns*
- Write the words to be practiced on index cards. The student can help make the cards, if appropriate.
- Consider writing the word on both sides of the card to make it easier for you to see it.
- Group flashcards with similar error patterns for later, focused practice.

✓ *Word practice*
- As the student is reading a passage aloud, mark any word reading errors with a pencil check or underline them on a separate copy.
- Allow the reading to continue until the student has made 5 to 15 errors. Stop the reading at the end of a sentence or paragraph.
- Prepare flashcards with selected missed words on them. Avoid the names of characters, places, or vocabulary specific to the story as well as unusual or rarely used words. Select words that are commonly used by the student and that reflect useful phonemic and structural patterns.

✓ *Sentence practice (in context)*
- As the student is reading a passage aloud, mark on a separate copy any word reading errors with a pencil check or underline.

- Allow the reading to continue until the student has made 5 to 15 errors. Stop the reading at the end of a sentence or paragraph.
- Point out the student's first error and ask, "What is this word?" If the student cannot read it, identify the word.
- Have the student read the entire sentence again until it can be done without hesitation or error. Continue this process with all the original errors.
- When completed, have the student continue reading the passage until another 5 to 15 errors are made. Repeat the above steps.

Evaluating the Effectiveness of Tutoring

Effective tutoring should enable the student to read meaningful, connected text at that student's instructional reading level. Reading performance can be evaluated by three indexes: oral reading accuracy (ORA), oral reading fluency (ORF), and through questions on comprehension presented after the student has read a passage. These evaluations should be carried out periodically to provide feedback to the tutor.

Oral Reading Accuracy (ORA). This is calculated by a simple formula in which the number of word errors (not counting repetitions or self-corrected errors) is subtracted from the total number of words read, and then dividing that result by the total number of words. The resulting decimal is multiplied by 100 to yield a percentage.

Have the student read a previously practiced passage without the tutor and calculate the student's ORA. For example, if the student reads a passage of 150 words and makes 15 errors while reading all the words, the calculation would be 150 minus 15, which is 135, divided by 150. The result is 0.9, which is then multiplied by 100 to yield 90 percent. The goal is for a 95 percent ORA. If the goal is not met, the student continues to practice on that passage with the tutor, attempting to reach the goal.

$$\frac{\text{(Total Number of Words Read)} - \text{(Number of Word Errors)}}{\text{(Total Number of Words)}} \times 100 = \%\ \text{Oral Reading Accuracy}$$

Oral Reading Fluency (ORF). Because time is involved, this is also known as the student's *reading rate,* and is the same as the calculation of words correct per minute (WCPM) discussed in Chapter 3 (see Table 3.1).

For example, a third-grade student reads a passage of 150 words with 17 errors in one-and-a-half minutes. Subtracting the 17 errors from the 150 words yields a total of 133 words that were correctly read in 1.5 minutes. Dividing the 1.5 minutes into 133 words yields a

WCPM of 89. Comparing the 89 to the average reading rates listed in Table 3.2 shows that this student is reading at the lower end of the range for third grade.

First calculate the ORF for an unpracticed reading and compare that to the ORF after the student has practiced with the passage. The change in ORF values will be a measure of the student's progress toward fluency. It is also helpful to compare the student's ORF with a chart of average reading rates for students in grades 2 through 12 (see Table 3.2).

Both the ORA and the ORF can be charted on a bar or line graph to provide additional motivation for the student (see Figure 3.7). Having the students participate in creating the chart will also increase their sense of accomplishment.

Tutoring in Reading for Comprehension

Poor readers often fail to comprehend what they have read. This may occur because they failed to comprehend key words or sentences, or how the sentences related to each other, or simply because they did not maintain concentration or interest. It is also possible that the readers lack the background knowledge necessary to comprehend the text. Tutoring in reading comprehension starts with carefully selecting reading materials and with improving understanding and motivation. Here are some suggestions for how to accomplish this (Parker, Hasbrouck, Denton, 2002b).

✓ *Selecting reading passages or books*
- To select readable text, ask the student to read a 100-word segment of the selected text and calculate the student's oral reading accuracy (ORA), as explained earlier. An ORA score of 80 or less means that the text is too frustrating for the reader. Scores of 85 to 90 percent are acceptable when the tutoring involves close monitoring and feedback from the tutor and multiple practices with the same text. An ORA score of 90 to 95 percent is considered best for closely monitored tutoring. A text with ORA scores of 95 percent and higher can be used with little tutor guidance and should be considered for independent reading practice by the student.
- To select comprehensible text, ask the student to read a passage. Then ask three or four brief open-ended questions that cannot be answered by common knowledge alone. The questions should cover most of the content of the passage and should not rely on trivial details. For example, "Why did that happen?" "What did he mean when...?" "What do you think will happen if...?" If the student can answer two or three questions correctly, the text can be used in tutoring. On the other hand, if the student can answer none or just one question, the text is not appropriate for tutoring.

✓ *Improving understanding*

- What did it say? Recognize that comprehension problems are often caused by problems with fluency. In their attempt to read smoothly and accurately, students lose the meaning at the sentence level and beyond. Sit beside the student with a 4" x 6" card. After the student reads one or two sentences, cover them and ask, "What did that say?" The student should paraphrase the meaning of what was just read. Praise the student's response and either elaborate on the response or offer a model summary, such as "I would add..." or "I would say..." Ensure the student that many different responses are acceptable.

  Move on to the next few sentences and repeat the process. As the student develops summarizing skills, ask the student to summarize longer selections of three or four sentences or a full paragraph. With this approach, the student's comprehension progresses from single sentence, to multisentence, to paragraph, and on to several paragraphs. As the text selection gets longer, remind the student to keep the oral summary to just one or two sentences.

- Read to find out. This approach for improving understanding requires you to read the text and prepare ahead of time. Ask the student to read a certain amount of text (depending on the reader's skill level) and to find out a certain amount of information. The answer should not be found through common knowledge alone and should not rely on trivial details. The student can refer back to the text to substantiate the answer. Listen to the student's response, provide supportive feedback, and augment the student's response or offer a model one of your own, if necessary.

✓ *Improving motivation*

- Students become motivated when they see achievement and greater understanding as a result of their efforts. By teaching students how to learn, rather than just specific skills, you help them apply a set of skills to solve tasks more effectively and efficiently in school as well as in nonacademic settings.

- Students are also motivated when you give them a reason to read. Most students really want to succeed in school. Knowing how to read fluently and with understanding can be a powerful motivator for reading more and for pleasure.

The READ 180 Program

Among the commercial programs available to help older struggling readers, the READ 180 program, now published by Scholastic, Inc., has yielded some impressive results. The research behind this program began in 1985 at Vanderbilt University where computer software was developed that used student performance data to adjust and differentiate the path of reading instruction. The software program continued to be revised and was eventually field-tested with more than 10,000 students in the Orange County, Florida schools from 1994 through 1997. Designed for low-achieving readers in grades 4 and above, the software program emphasizes direct, explicit, and systematic instruction in word analysis, phonics, spelling, reading comprehension, and writing.

Because of its success in raising the reading scores of older struggling readers in Orange County, the Council of Great City Schools piloted the program during 1998-1999 in the Department of Defense schools and in some of its largest urban schools, including Boston, Columbus, Dallas, Houston, and Los Angeles. Most students in the pilot schools who participated in the program showed significant improvements in reading and overall school performance as well as the development of more positive attitudes and behaviors. See the **Resources** section for more information on READ 180.

REWIRING THE BRAINS OF STRUGGLING READERS

Can the human brain be rewired for certain tasks? If so, is it possible to reroute the auxiliary circuits used by struggling readers to utilize the left posterior regions that are predisposed to rapid and automatic reading? Perhaps the most exciting news from neuroscience about reading has been the studies to determine whether such rewiring can occur as a result of using reading interventions. These imaging studies looked at children with difficult reading problems before and after they were subjected to an extensive phonologically-based reading program.

In Chapter 4, Figure 4.7 shows the fMRI images before the interventions. Note the activation in the frontal areas of the brain typical of dyslexic readers. In a study sponsored by Syracuse University, specially-trained teachers provided second-grade and third-grade struggling readers with 50 minutes of individualized tutoring daily in activities related to the alphabetic principle. The tutoring, which lasted eight months (105 hours) was in addition to the students' regular reading instruction. At the end of the year-long intervention, all of the children improved their reading in varying degrees. The fMRI images taken immediately after the program showed the emergence of primary processing systems on the left side of the brain (like those used by good readers) in addition to the auxiliary pathways on the right side common to dyslexic and struggling readers. Furthermore, one year after the program intervention, fMRIs indicated there was additional development of the primary neural systems on the left rear side of the brain while the right front areas were less prominent (Figure 5.3). In other words, the program intervention appeared to have rewired the brains of struggling readers to more closely approximate the reading circuitry in the brains of typical readers, resulting in accurate and *fluent* readers (Shaywitz, 2003; Shaywitz et al., 2003).

Changes in Brains of Struggling Readers

Before Reading Interventions   **After Reading Interventions**

Figure 5.3 These representative scans show the changes evident in the brains of struggling readers about one year after their involvement with effective reading interventions. Note that the interventions have helped the children develop reading areas (shown in white) that more closely resemble the areas used by typical readers, as shown in Figure 4.3 (Shaywitz et al., 2003).

A University of Washington fMRI study of shorter duration used a program based on phoneme and morpheme mapping with 10 dyslexic children and 11 normal readers. After 28 hours of instruction, the fMRI scans showed changes in the brain functions of the dyslexic children that closely resembled the neural processing characteristics of typical readers (Aylward et al., 2003).

Another study addressed the question of how much time the auditory system needs to correctly process the onset (or beginning) phoneme in a word. The only way to hear the difference between the words *bear* and *pear* is in the first 40 milliseconds of the onset of those sounds. You will recall from Chapter 4 that if the visual and auditory processing systems are not synchronized during reading, a child will have difficulty correctly matching phonemes to the letters that represent them. As a result, other brain regions are called into play in an effort to decode the words. Dyslexic students are thus required to use a more labor-intensive set of neural pathways to recognize, decode, and comprehend the words they are reading.

The study involved 20 dyslexic children aged 8 to 12 years (Temple et al., 2003). Their brains were scanned with functional MRIs before and after participating in a eight-week training program that focused on developing the alphabetic principle and phonemic practice. A control group of 12 students with normal reading abilities also had their brain scanned but did not participate in the training.

The pretraining scans were taken while the children were asked to identify letters that rhymed. During this exercise, children with typical reading abilities showed activity in the left temporal area (Broca's area) as well as in the occipito-temporal region typical of skilled readers. Dyslexics, however, struggled with the task and showed activation mainly in the left and right frontal areas, similar to those shown for the dyslexic reader in Figure 4.7.

The dyslexic students then used a computer program called *Fast ForWord* for 100 minutes a day, five days a week. The program was designed to help students recognize the differences between onset sounds, especially those in words that rhyme. For example, the computer would show a picture of a boy and a toy. The computer voice would ask the student to point to the boy. At first, the computer voice asked the questions in a slow, exaggerated manner to help the student hear the differences in the /b/ and /t/ onset sounds. As the student progressed, the speed of the computer voice slowly increased.

After eight weeks of training, the dyslexic children were again given fMRIs while performing the rhyming activities. Their brain scans showed increased activity after remediation in the same areas that were activated in the typical reading children performing this task. As in other similar studies, the intense training in phonological awareness stimulated areas in the dyslexic brain that were not activated while reading prior to the training. There was also increased activity in right frontal brain regions not used by typical reading children. Apparently, the recovery of a more typical pathway also reactivated frontal areas that are used in dyslexic children to compensate for their decoding difficulties. The researchers speculate that this activation pattern in the right frontal area might continue to change over time and come closer to that of typical readers (Habib, 2003).

The dyslexic children were retested after the training in several reading and language skills. In Figure 5.4, it is evident that the posttraining scores of the dyslexic children went up in the three reading areas tested by the Woodcock-Johnson Reading Mastery Test, namely, word identification, word attack, and passage comprehension.

> Studies using fMRI indicate that intensive research-based interventions can change the brain functions of struggling readers to more closely match that of typical readers.

These and subsequent studies seem to indicate that research-based reading programs that use computers to help students build phonemic awareness can substantially—and perhaps permanently—benefit struggling readers. The changes due to remediation brought the brain function of dyslexic children closer to that seen in children without reading problems. Apparently, the commonly observed dysfunction in the brains of dyslexic children can be at least partially improved through programs that focus on auditory processing and oral language training, resulting in improved language and reading ability. Three effective computer programs are *Earobics* by Cognitive Concepts, Inc., *Fast ForWord* by the Scientific Learning Corporation, and the *Lindamood Phoneme Sequencing Program (LiPS)* by the Lindamood-Bell Learning Processes Company. See the **Resources** section for more information.

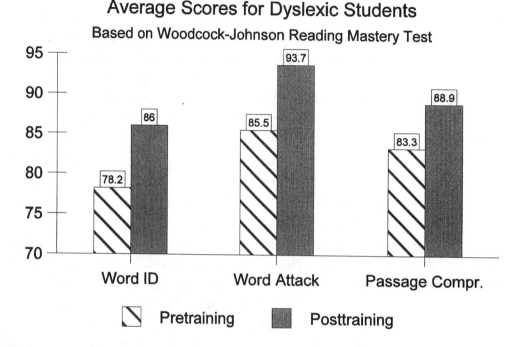

Figure 5.4 The graph shows the pretraining and posttraining average scores of the dyslexic students on the word identification, word attack, and reading comprehension sections of the Woodcock-Johnson Mastery Test (Temple et al., 2003).

READING PROBLEMS AND TAKING TESTS

Tests are a difficult undertaking for students with reading problems, regardless of age. Teachers and schools, however, can make appropriate allowances and modifications that allow these students to show what they really know. Here are some accommodations to consider. Tailor the accommodations to meet the specific needs and age level of each student (Sams, 2003).

✓ When designing a test for these students, stick to a large simple type font (e.g., Arial), put key words in boldface, and provide plenty of space for answers.

✓ Make the purpose of the test clear to the student. If appropriate, also note that spelling, grammatical errors, and handwriting will not affect the test grade.

✓ Make sure you give clear and concise instructions.

✓ Allow additional time so that the test is a measure of what they know, not of the speed of their reading or writing.

✓ For essay exams, provide a model answer that shows the layout, paraphrasing, and conclusions expected in the answer. This helps students understand what is expected of them.

✓ Read out the questions, if needed, in areas such as mathematics and science since those are the areas being tested, not reading.

✓ For some children, have an adult record the child's answers thereby allowing the child to focus on responses rather than on writing.

✓ Consider allowing the student to use a word processor to record answers.

✓ Use visual aids where appropriate since many struggling readers and dyslexic students often have strong visual-spatial skills.

✓ Test in a location where students can work without being self-conscious about their work pace, rest breaks, or additional time.

✓ Consider alternative testing formats, such as an oral examination, PowerPoint presentations, or allowing the student to submit an audiotape with responses.

ADVICE TO STUDENTS WITH READING PROBLEMS

Here are some suggestions that parents and teachers can give to students with reading problems that can help them overcome many of the difficulties associated with this condition. Note that some of the advice is more appropriate for older children in that it relates to at-home situations where poor readers and dyslexic students need practice in organizing and managing their affairs (DITT, 2001; Shaywitz, 2003).

At home
● Pack your school bag before you go to bed, assuring a calm start to the next day.
● Put copies of your school schedule around the house, especially in the area where you do your homework. Make extra copies in case you lose them.
● Write down important information, such as class assignments, due dates for class work, tests, extra-curricular activities, and other appointments.
● Know your body's rhythm. Avoid doing homework when you are hungry, tired, or feeling low.

- Keep the telephone numbers of at least two classmates who can tell you the homework assignment if you failed to record it accurately.
- When doing long assignments, break them down into smaller chunks and take frequent breaks to maintain your interest. Recognize that it will take you longer to read a passage than other students because your brain uses a pathway that is slower. But take the time you need and use your intellect and reasoning to understand the material fully and accurately.
- Do your homework in an area that is quiet and free from distractions.

In school

- Avoid taking too many courses that include a large amount of reading.
- Sit in the front of the class and away from windows to avoid being distracted.
- Develop your own shorthand so you can take notes during class to help you remember important information.
- If possible, tape-record your classes and listen to the recording when you are more relaxed and can absorb more.
- Many textbooks are now available on audiotape from Recording for the Blind and Dyslexic. Check out their book list at www.rfbd.org.
- Get extra help from your teacher to develop your study skills, especially before tests.
- Ask your teacher if you can take a short essay test in place of a multiple-choice test. Multiple-choice tests do not give you enough context to decode unfamiliar words. Also, short essay responses give you a better opportunity to show what you have learned.
- Visualizing images probably comes easily to you. Whenever possible, design concept maps and use other types of graphic organizers to help you organize your work.
- Do not be afraid to tell your teacher that you do not understand something. Other students are likely to be in the same situation.
- Giving oral responses in the class may be difficult for you. Share this with your teachers to determine if there are other ways you can demonstrate your knowledge.
- Work on your computer skills because typing is a lot easier than writing. Be sure to proof-read and spell-check your work.
- Being dyslexic may make your school work seem hard, but it is no excuse for not putting forth the effort. Many dyslexics are successful.
- Use the Internet to find out more about dyslexia and to get ideas on how to develop your study skills.

ADVICE FOR PARENTS OF CHILDREN WITH READING PROBLEMS

Parents who learn that their child has reading problems, such as dyslexia, often experience blame, denial, guilt, fear, isolation, and anger. But by accepting that their child has a specific learning difficulty, they will be able to work on those strategies needed to allow their child to reach full potential. Here are some thoughts for parents of a child with reading problems to consider (DITT, 2001; Shaywitz, 2003):

- You know your child better than anyone else. If you suspect a reading problem, there probably is.
- Get professional help as soon as possible. Knowing exactly what is wrong will help you decide the best course of action for your child. Remember that not all struggling readers have dyslexia.
- Make your home an encouraging and safe place. To a child with reading problems, school can be a disheartening experience.
- Do not discuss your children's learning problems in front of them without including them in the discussion.
- Even if diagnosed with dyslexia, remember that your child is more normal than different. Explain to the child that dyslexia means having a hard time learning to read. Emphasize that this has nothing to do with intelligence. Many people with this condition have learned to read and have become successful students and adults. With effort and practice, the child will learn to read.
- Tell the child that struggling readers and people with dyslexia often have trouble hearing all the sounds in a word. They may only hear two sounds in a three syllable word. Reassure the child that other children have this problem and that it can be overcome with proper instruction.
- You might even explain about the different pathways that normal and dyslexic brains take when learning to read (see Chapter 4). Dyslexic children will learn to read, but it will take longer.
- Encourage the child to pursue areas of strength, such as music or sports, to experience the feelings of success in other areas of life.
- Teach your child how to pack the school bag for each day.
- Give your child the opportunity to tell you in a calm environment what happened in school and during the day. Sharing problems and concerns with a sympathetic listener can make them much less burdensome.
- Keep a record of how long it takes your child to do homework. Share this information with teachers who may be unaware of how much time your child needs to complete these tasks.

- Get in touch with the school periodically to discuss what strategies are being used to help your child. Use similar strategies at home when reading with your child.
- Read assigned books and other materials to or with your child, explaining the meaning of new words and checking if your child understands what has been read.
- If the child asks questions about grammar or spelling when writing, give the answer so the child can move on. Dyslexic children often have problems with short-term memory, so supply the answer if they know the process.
- Seek out support groups for families with dyslexic children. They often can provide a lot of useful information about how to deal with learning difficulties.

What's Coming?

The strategies and considerations presented in this chapter are designed to teach poor readers how to overcome their difficulties and become better readers. Such progress is particularly important as students in elementary school move up to middle and high school where reading of the course content becomes a vital part of successful learning. The strategies and techniques that teachers can use to help all students cope with the vast amount of reading required in secondary school content areas are the focus of the next chapter.

CHAPTER 6
Reading in the Content Areas

This chapter addresses several basic questions about improving reading in the content areas. They include:

- *What are some successful strategies for helping students comprehend content material?*
- *In what sequence should these strategies be used?*
- *What are some patterns that exist in the organization of content in different subject areas?*

Students entering the intermediate grades, middle school, and high school are faced with an increased amount of reading and the expectation that they are able to comprehend the content in their texts. Yet, little effort is made to determine either the reading ability of the students entering the class or the difficulty of the reading materials. Consequently, some students are doomed to failure from the start because they cannot read the course material, and they end up frustrated at both the teacher and the subject.

Many secondary teachers express concern about the reading and reading-related problems of their struggling students. Yet, except in English and Language Arts, most content area teachers do not view themselves as reading teachers, and they often express doubts about their ability to provide effective instruction in reading strategies. Studies show, however, that when content area teachers take the time to teach and use reading strategies regularly, student achievement in the content area rises, especially in middle schools (Bryant, Linan-Thompson, Ugel, Hamff, and Hougen, 2001).

In their earlier years, students were taught developmental reading through the use of multilevel texts. However, content teachers usually teach from a single text written at a certain reading level. Furthermore, developmental reading emphasizes the process (learning to read) while content area reading emphasizes application (reading to learn). In any particular class, the range of reading achievement among students often spans several grade levels. The challenge for the teacher, then, is to determine what strategies will help students acquire the content knowledge while trying to manage the wide range of differences in reading achievement.

> The challenge for the content area teacher is to determine what strategies will help students acquire the content knowledge while managing the wide range of differences in reading achievement.

For some students, the text itself is intimidating. High school science and history texts can easily run over 1,000 pages. Content teachers often assume that students come to their classes with the reading skills necessary to use the required text successfully. Moreover, these teachers may not recognize three major differences between the developmental reading that students had in earlier grades with the expository reading required for their course. The first difference is in learning new vocabulary. In developmental reading, vocabulary is taught in context, meaning is clarified, and words are rehearsed and practiced at a pace that most children can accomplish. In content courses, the vocabulary used in basic texts is highly specialized and technical, and often presented so quickly that students have little time to fully comprehend its meaning.

The second difference lies in the way concepts are introduced and explored. In developmental reading, teachers present concepts that are familiar, and they cover them at a pace that is appropriate for most children. In content courses, teachers present concepts that are unfamiliar and complex, usually at a rapid pace because there is so much to cover. The third difference is in the specialized type of reading that is needed for some courses, such as the ability to read charts, tables, graphs, maps, globes, and technical instruments (Baer and Nourie, 1993). Table 6.1 summarizes the main differences between developmental reading and reading in content areas.

It is important for content area teachers to determine the level of reading difficulty in their course materials and the ability of their students to read them. By making some accommodations in materials and selecting appropriate strategies, all teachers can help more students succeed in learning the course content.

STRATEGIES FOR HELPING STUDENTS READ CONTENT MATERIAL

The strategies described here are compiled from a variety of sources (Baer and Nourie, 1993; NIFL, 2001; OPS, 2003; Slavin, 1995) and are intended to help students acquire course content successfully through reading and other methods. They are not intended to imply that

Table 6.1 Differences Between Developmental and Content Area Reading		
	Developmental	**Content Area**
Texts	Several multilevel texts	Usually a single text at a fixed reading level
Teaching Approach	Learning the process of reading (learning to read)	Learning to apply what has been read (reading to learn)
Range of Reading Abilities	Usually limited to a span of one or two grade levels	Can span five or more grade levels
Vocabulary Acquisition	Mostly general in nature. Presented at modest pace so students have time to practice words, clarify meanings, and reinforce comprehension.	Highly specific and technical. Presented quickly, so students have little time to practice words and develop meaning.
Presentation of Concepts	Concepts are usually familiar and presented at a modest pace.	Concepts are unfamiliar and complex, and presented at rapid pace with little time for thorough processing.
Specialized Reading	Limited mostly to printed text.	Can include reading charts, tables, graphs, maps, globes, and technical instruments.

Source: Baer and Nourie, 1993

the school can abdicate its ongoing responsibility to help students improve their reading skills at all grade levels. To some extent, every content teacher is also a teacher of reading, not of developmental reading, but by virtue of using a variety of techniques that allow students with reading problems to learn content. The strategies are:

- Using direct instruction
- Conquering vocabulary
- Helping with comprehension
- Rewriting content material
- Incorporating supplemental textbooks
- Establishing in-class vertical files
- Using audiovisual aids
- Promoting cooperative learning groups

Using Direct Instruction

Students who have reading problems usually rely heavily on teacher explanations to grasp concepts and to identify what is essential to learn. Therefore, direct instruction can be a critical factor in their achievement. During direct instruction

✓ Clearly identify important concepts

✓ Explain why we are learning them

✓ Present the concepts in an organized manner

✓ Define and use unusual vocabulary words in context

✓ Recommend a limited and specific reading textbook assignment that covers your presentation

✓ Ask students to summarize orally the main points you presented in the direct instruction segment

✓ Consider asking the students to write out the summary as well

✓ Suggest other print sources (of a lower reading level) that also explain the content

Conquering Vocabulary

Technical, unfamiliar, and unusual words are often stumbling blocks for students when reading course content. Familiar words used in a specialized context can also cause problems. Students encountering such words can learn them in any of four different ways (NIFL, 2001)..

✓ *Learning a new meaning for a known word.* The student recognizes the word but is learning a new meaning for it. For example, the student knows what a tree *branch* is, but is learning that the word can also describe a *branch* of government or *branch* of a river.

✓ *Learning the meaning of a new word to describe a known concept.* The student knows the concept but not this particular word to describe it. For example, the student has had experience with globes and baseballs but does not know they are examples of *spheres*.

✓ *Learning the meaning of a new word for an unknown concept.* The student is not familiar with the concept or the word that describes it, and must learn both. For example, the student is not be familiar with the process or the word *osmosis.*

✓ *Clarifying and enriching the meaning of a known word.* The student is learning finer distinctions or connotations in the usage of what may seem like similar words. For example, understanding the distinctions among *dashing, jogging, running, sprinting,* and *trotting.*

All these types of learning vary in difficulty. The third type, learning the meaning of a new word for an unknown concept, is one of the most common, yet challenging. Much learning in the content areas involves this type of word learning. As students learn about *photosynthesis, secants,* and *oligarchies,* they may be learning new concepts as well as new words. Learning concepts and words in mathematics, social studies, and science may be even more difficult because each major concept is often linked to other new concepts. For example, the concept *oligarchy* can be associated with other unfamiliar concepts, such as *monarchy, plutocracy,* and *dictatorship. Photosynthesis* can be associated with *phototropism* and *osmosis.*

Identify these types of words in advance of assigning the reading. Work to develop students' word consciousness by calling their attention to the way writers choose words to convey meaning. Help them research a word's origin or history and to see if they can find examples of that word's usage in their everyday lives.

Decoding New Words

Older students acquire more than half of the approximately 3,000 new words they learn each year through reading (Stahl, 2000). For English language learners, vocabulary knowledge is one of the most critical factors affecting their achievement in the content areas. Teachers cannot assume that English language learners possess the vocabulary needed to decode and comprehend the numerous word meanings they encounter in the course materials. Even though these students may possess proficient listening and speaking skills in English, it takes time and rereading to understand the formal aspects of English as used in secondary level texts. Because knowledge of vocabulary is so closely linked to reading comprehension, students need to learn strategies for decoding new words that they encounter in the content texts. These strategies include decoding multisyllabic words and getting the meaning of unfamiliar words from context (OPS, 2003).

Decoding Multisyllabic Words. One strategy for decoding multisyllabic words takes just six steps. The teacher guides the student through the steps. Using a worksheet to analyze the word facilitates the process. Figure 6.1 illustrates one possible worksheet format with an example.

<table>
<tr><td colspan="2" align="center">**Learning New Words**</td></tr>
<tr><td>1. Write it down</td><td align="center">transcontinental
_____
WORD</td></tr>
<tr><td>2. Split it up, if possible</td><td align="center">_____   X   _____   X   _____</td></tr>
<tr><td>3. Find prefixes and suffixes</td><td align="center">trans   continent   al
___ ___   _____   ___ ___
PREFIXES   **ROOT WORD**   **SUFFIXES**</td></tr>
<tr><td>4. Find the syllables in the root word and all write down all word parts</td><td align="center">trans con ti nent al
___ ___ ___ ___ ___ ___ ___ ___
SYLLABLES</td></tr>
<tr><td>5. Write the whole word again and blend the sounds</td><td align="center">transcontinental
_____
WORD</td></tr>
<tr><td>6. Use the word in a sentence</td><td align="center">The transcontinental railroad connected the
_____
eastern and western parts of the United States.</td></tr>
</table>

Figure 6.1 This chart helps students to decode new words through a six-step process. The word "transcontinental" is used here as an example (Adapted from OPS, 2003).

1. The student first writes the whole word down, *transcontinental*.
2. If it is a compound word, such as *butterfingers,* the student writes down each word part, *butter* and *fingers*.
3. If it is not a compound word, the student puts an "x" on these lines and moves to the nest step which is to write down the root word and any prefixes and suffixes so that *transcontinental* becomes *trans, continent, al*.
4. Next, the student breaks down the root word into its syllables (*continent = con, ti, nent*) and writes down all the word parts, *trans, con, ti, nent, al*.
5. Now the student writes the whole word again while saying it aloud and blending the syllable sounds, *transcontinental*.
6. Finally, the student uses the new word in a sentence, *The transcontinental railroad connected the eastern and western parts of the United States.*

Using Context Clues. The context in which an unfamiliar word is used can often give hints as to its meaning. Help students use context clues by doing the following:

✓ Select an authentic text passage containing the unfamiliar words that can be defined through context. Ensure that the students have enough prior knowledge that they can reasonably determine the words' meanings.

✓ Model the process of using context clues to determine meaning by going through the steps of the Context Clues Strategy (See box).

✓ Think aloud as you use the strategy so that students can follow your reasoning.

✓ Explain how you used the clues to arrive at the meaning of the word.

✓ Identify the key words surrounding the target word that helped you decide on its meaning.

✓ Verify the word's meaning in the dictionary.

✓ Have students practice the model by giving them a page of text with three unknown words highlighted.

Context Clues Strategy

1. When you come to a word you don't know, continue reading to a good stopping place.
2. Use the context to figure out the meaning of the new word.
3. Guess what the meaning might be.
4. Test your guess by asking if the meaning:
    Looks right
    Sounds right
    Makes sense
5. Check your guess in the dictionary.

Helping With Comprehension

Students who are struggling readers often have difficulty comprehending what they are reading. Strategies that help students to relate the content to their prior knowledge, to practice mental imagery, and to locate the main idea can be very effective aids to comprehension. Here is some general advice you can give students to help them with comprehension.

✓ Look over what you will be reading, noting words and phrases that are in bold face or italics. Look also for any charts, graphs, and pictures. Review any chapter summaries and related questions that are useful to guide your reading. Not everything in the text is equally important, so read to capture the main ideas.

✓ Take notes or draw diagrams while reading to help you remember main phrases and ideas. Use graphic organizers and mind maps, too.

✓ Read the text more than once.

✓ When you encounter an unknown word, try to guess its meaning by looking at the context. The sentences immediately before and after can give you good clues to determine meaning.

✓ Try to make connections between main ideas and their supporting details.

✓ Each time you finish a paragraph, stop and try to summarize it in your own words.

✓ Discuss what you have read with others who have read the same text.

Narrative and Expository Text. Some strategies need to be modified depending on the nature of the text. Narrative text is commonly associated with literature instruction and focuses on settings, characters, plots, conflicts, conflict resolution, and themes. Expository text is more commonly found in science and social studies texts and focuses on acquiring and processing information related to comparisons, cause and effect, and sequencing. In mathematics, expository text relates to the semantic and linguistics structures necessary to translate word problems into mathematical expressions.

Using Prior Knowledge

Students bring with them a wide range of knowledge and experiences about many topics. Prior knowledge significantly influences a reader's comprehension of new topics, concepts, and vocabulary found in content area texts. Comprehension of those texts relies heavily on the students' prior knowledge and their ability to apply it to the topics being covered in the content area. Reading difficult content text can be made easier if students can relate the reading to what they already know. Before assigning a difficult text selection,

✓ Preview the text with them

✓ Ask them what they already know about the content of the selection (a concept, time period, or topic)

✓ Discuss and explain any unusual or technical words

✓ Use visual aids whenever possible

Using Mental Imagery

Readers often form mental images or pictures while reading. These visualizations help them remember and understand what they have read. Encourage students to form visual images of what they are reading by urging them to picture a character, setting, a model in motion, or an event described in the text.

Imagery runs the gamut from simple concrete pictures to complex motor learning and multistep procedures. Because imagery is still not a common instructional strategy, it should be implemented early and gradually. These guidelines are adapted from Parrott (1986) and West, Farmer, and Wolff (1991) for using imagery as a powerful aid to understanding text and retention.

✓ *Prompting.* Use prompts for telling students to form mental images of the content being learned. They can be as simple as "form a picture in your mind of ..." to more complex directions. Prompts should be specific to the content or task and should be accompanied by relevant photographs, charts, or arrays, especially for younger children.

✓ *Modeling.* Model imagery by describing your own image to the class and explaining how that image helps your recall and use of the current learning. Also, model a procedure and have the students mentally practice the steps.

✓ *Interaction.* Strive for rich, vivid images where items interact. The richer the image, the more information it can include. If there are two or more items in the images, they should be visualized as acting on each other. If the recall is a ball and a bat, for example, imagine the bat hitting the ball.

✓ *Reinforcement.* Have students talk about the images they formed and get feedback from others on the accuracy, vividness, and interaction of the images. Talk provides mental rehearsal and helps students to remember the image for an extended period of time.

✓ *Add context.* Whenever possible, add context to the interaction to increase retention and recall. For example, if the task is to recall prefixes and suffixes, the context could be a parade with the prefixes in front urging the suffixes in the rear to catch up.

✓ *Avoid overloading the image.* Although good images are complete representations of what is to be remembered, they should not overload the working memory's capacity in older students of about seven items.

Locating the Main Idea

Help students develop a strategy for locating the main idea in fiction and nonfiction passages (OPS, 2003).

✓ Model the procedure used in the Strategy for Locating the Main Idea (see box on the next page).

✓ After modeling, lead the students through guided, then independent practice.

✓ Use graphic organizers that are appropriate for the passage.

✓ The paragraph summaries can take several forms, depending on whether you are using narrative or expository text. Have students identify which type of text they are reading, since they are different in form and intent.

✓ Narrative text:
Start by giving them some sentence fragments, such as
"This story takes place _____."
"_____ is a character who_____."
"A problem occurs when_____."
"The problem is finally solved when _____."
"At the end of the story _____."

✓ Expository text:
Main idea/Topic: _____.
   Subtopic: _____.
      Detail 1 _____.
      Detail 2 _____.
   Subtopic: _____.
      Detail 1 _____.
      Detail 2 _____.

✓ Consider using cooperative learning for this activity, because it gives students opportunities to share and critique their summaries. This oral rehearsal aids in retention of important ideas, concepts, and details.

✓ If students have difficulty, provide summaries that are partially filled in and let the students furnish the missing details.

Strategy for Locating the Main Idea

1. Look at the title, headings, and picture. What do you already know about this topic?
2. Predict what the author might say about this topic.
3. Read the passage to find out the significant details or facts. Reread the passage to clarify any questions.
4. Modify your thoughts about the main idea as you review each detail.
5. Think about what the details or facts have in common.
6. Decide on the main idea.
7. Write a summary paragraph that includes the author's essential points and supporting details.

(Adapted from OPS, 2003)

Paraphrasing for Comprehension

Paraphrasing is commonly thought of as copying information from a text source and changing a few words. That process rarely results in retention of learning because the copying act can be done almost automatically and without much conscious thought. If the purpose of paraphrasing is to give students opportunities to get a deeper understanding of the text, to make connections to what they already know, and to enhance remembering, then a much more systematic process must be followed.

Effective paraphrasing incorporates reading, writing, listening, and speaking, thereby activating the brain's frontal lobe and leading to a fuller comprehension of the course material. It can be used in all content areas and with students in the upper elementary grades and beyond, and it can help students learn from many different types of texts, including fiction and nonfiction.

The process encourages active student participation, provides for mental, oral, and written rehearsal of newly-learned material, and enhances comprehension and retention. At the same time, it develops reading, communication, and creative skills (Fisk and Hurst, 2003). See the box on the next page for the guidelines and steps for using paraphrasing successfully in the classroom.

Paraphrasing for Comprehension

Guidelines:

This strategy is appropriate for upper elementary grades and beyond. It can be used in all content areas and with all types of texts, including fiction and nonfiction. It is effective because it uses all modes of communication: reading, writing, listening, and speaking. The process encourages active student participation, provides for mental, oral, and written rehearsal of newly-learned material, and enhances comprehension and retention. At the same time, it develops reading, communication, and creative skills.

A good paraphrase must convey the original meaning of the author but in the student's own words and phrasing. The voice of the author also should be maintained. If the original work is humorous, satirical, sarcastic, or melancholy, the paraphrase should be also. Students should therefore identify the author's meaning and voice before they start writing.

The teacher should explain the purpose and benefits of paraphrasing. Students already do some paraphrasing when they take notes in class, write a book report, or give a speech. Outside examples can include telling someone about a trip taken, or a news reporter summarizing an interview.

Steps:

This general scheme has four steps. Modify the steps as appropriate for the age level of the students and the nature of the material being read.

1. *First reading and discussion.* Read aloud the text to be paraphrased while students follow along in their own texts. Have the students suggest possible definiitions for any unfamiliar words. After clarifying the vocabulary, ask the students to identify the main idea and the author's tone.
2. *Second reading and note-taking.* Students read the text on their own and take detailed notes when they finish a paragraph. The notes should capture the main idea and supporting details, but should be in the student's own words. Students may want to use a thesaurus to help them with difficult or technical words.
3. *Written paraphrase.* When finished with the note-taking, the students put the original text away so it will not to influence the next step. Using only their notes, the students write their paraphrased version that communicates the main ideas with the same voice of the original text.
4. *Sharing paraphrases.* When the paraphrases are completed, the students form pairs and compare the similarities and differences between their respective paraphrases. They are also asked to decide how the author's voice is communicated in their versions.

(Adapted from Fisk and Hurst, 2003)

Reading Aloud to the Class

Consider reading certain parts of the text to the class, especially those parts that use difficult or highly technical words or describe complex situations. Remember that many students can understand something when they hear it even though they may not be able to read about it themselves. Reading aloud can also be used to make connections between texts, to develop background information, or for enjoyment. Where appropriate, the oral reading can be done by other students, school volunteers, or parents. Another option is for you or a student to record certain text sections on audiotapes and have them available for student use in the school's media center.

Rewriting Content Material

Consider the possibility of rewriting some of the course materials that may have a particularly high level of reading difficulty. Rewriting the material at a reading level closer to that of the students who are having problems, allows those students to gain confidence in their ability to understand the content despite their reading difficulties. Another possibility is to have students who do understand the course material rewrite it for their classmates. This approach reinforces both reading and writing skills.

Incorporating Supplemental Textbooks

Identify textbooks that cover the same material as the course text but are written at a lower reading level. This may require using several books because it is unlikely that one book will cover all the course content. Trade books are another possibility. They also present concepts covered in the primary textbook but are generally at a lower reading level. Furthermore, trade books help students recognize that the study of content subjects is not limited to school textbooks. By presenting concepts in many different ways, supplemental texts enhance student learning.

Establishing In-Class Vertical Files

Students will often read a magazine or newspaper article about a subject more readily than a textbook. Establish and maintain a file of such articles that relate to the course content. Update the file periodically and encourage students to contribute to the file when they come across an appropriate article.

Using Audiovisual Aids

Audiovisual aids are a great help to students with reading problems. Many students today have grown up in and become acclimated to a multimedia environment. Whenever possible, use videotapes, audiotapes, television, computer programs, overhead transparencies, and other technology to supplement and accompany direct instruction. All students benefit from the use of these materials.

Promoting Cooperative Learning Groups

Cooperative learning (Johnson and Johnson, 1989) is a particularly effective strategy in classes that have a wide range of student abilities, including reading. This approach allows students to work in teams and to be assigned tasks that match their ability and that contribute to the whole group effort. As the team members interact, students have opportunities to share and learn the concepts being studied.

SEQUENCING THE READING STRATEGIES

Now that we have discussed some of the strategies content area teachers can use to help their students comprehend course materials, the next step is to look at the sequence in which the strategies should be presented for maximum effect on student comprehension. The sequence can be divided into three phases: activities before, during, and after reading the content text (Cibrowski,1993; Paterno, 2001).

Phase 1: Before Reading

The purpose of these activities is to activate prior knowledge and to stimulate the brain's memory recall and imagery systems to spark curiosity, to motivate, and to facilitate retention of learning. Deciding which strategies to use depends on the material to be read and the background knowledge of the students.

> ✓ *Questions to ask.* Using questions to engage students in a dialogue about something they are about to read can clarify their thinking and help them determine what to expect from reading the material.
>   • Make connections between the learner's background knowledge and the read-ing. "This passage is about_____. What do you already know about this?"

State a purpose for reading the passage. "This section is about_____. What are some things we could learn about this?"

- Make predictions. "This passage is about_____. What do you think this could be about? What might happen to you if you_____?"

✓ *Select core vocabulary.* Choose the words that are likely to be unfamiliar and difficult and present them on the board or on paper. Ask students to write a definition, even if it is only a guess. Collect and return the papers at the end of Phase 3 to complete by filling in the correct definitions.

✓ *Write out the predictions.* Have students write out what they think the passage will be about and what they might learn from it.

✓ *Analogies and visual images.* Relate the material in the new reading to knowledge the students already possess. Ask them to think about what they know that is similar to what they think will be in the passage.

✓ *Concept maps.* Concept maps used before reading help students identify important concepts and ideas and how they are related to each other. By understanding these relationships in advance, students are more likely to comprehend their text readings.

Phase 2: During Reading

These strategies are designed to address two difficulties that poor readers have with content area texts: (1) The students spend far more time struggling with individual words than in constructing meaning from text. (2) The texts often have main ideas deeply embedded in text and too many concepts are superficially presented at once.

✓ *Questions to ask.* These questions help students review what they are learning while reading, confirm or change their predictions, and make connections to prior readings.
- Clarify and review what has happened so far. "What are some things you have already learned about_____?"
- Confirm or create new predictions. "Now that you have learned_____, will you keep or change your predictions?"
- Make connections to other readings.

✓ *Reciprocal teaching techniques.* As explained earlier, this is a powerful technique because students assume a dominant role in their own learning. It includes the four strategies of questioning, clarifying, summarizing, and predicting. Teachers and students become partners in improving the students' understanding of the content material and their ability to monitor their own comprehension. Although the technique was developed more than 20 years ago, it is not part of the common practice of secondary content area teachers. When it is used, however, research studies have demonstrated that students who worked with reciprocal teaching increased their group participation and use of the strategies taught, learned from the passages studied, and increased their learning when reading independently. Furthermore, the studies showed that the technique could be used in various settings and that the students maintained the reading gains they achieved (Slater and Horstman, 2002).

The technique takes about 10 days to teach, during which time the teacher is doing a lot of modeling. Eventually, the teacher increasingly hands over responsibility to the students who take assume the roles of teacher/leader and lead the discussions with the other students. The teacher monitors the group and intervenes to keep the students on task and to facilitate the discussion. See the box on the next page for an explanation of the steps and procedures involved in reciprocal teaching.

✓ *Summary notes.* Students write down a summary of each section of the passage as soon as they finish it. The summary should include the main idea and supporting details. Concept maps can help.

Phase 3: After Reading

The strategies here are to help students rehearse, analyze, and extend their reading to increase the chances they will remember what they have read. Questioning and vocabulary prediction are important parts of this process.

✓ *Questions to ask.* These questions foster retention of learning by reinforcing the concepts in the reading and encouraging critical thinking and personal response.
  • Reinforce the concept. "Have you had any of the experiences mentioned in the passage? If so, how did you feel about them?"
  • Model ways of thinking through the information they have read. "What events are described in this passage? What caused them? How do you know that?"
  • Encourage critical thinking and personal response. "What do you think might have happened if ___? Why did the author ___?"

Reciprocal Teaching

Guidelines:

The teacher explains the four supporting strategies used in this technique: *Questioning* focuses the students' attention on main ideas and provides a means for checking their understanding of what they are reading. *Clarifying* requires students to work on understanding confusing and ambiguous sections of text. *Summarizing* requires students to determine what is important in the text and what is not. *Predicting* requires students to rehearse what they have learned and to begin the next section of text with some expectation of what is to come.

The teacher models the sequence of strategies. Eventually, the teacher increasingly hands over responsibility to the students who now assume leadership roles in the discussion. The teacher monitors the group to keep students on task and to facilitate the discussion.

Specific Steps:

1. The leader reads aloud a short segment of text.
2. Questioning: The leader or other group members generate several questions related to the passage just read, and group members answer the questions. Ex: What was the problem here? What was the cause? What was the solution? What was the chain of events?
3. Clarifying: The leader and group members clarify any problems or misunderstandings. Ex: What does the word____mean? What did the author mean when he said_____?
4. Summarizing: After all problems have been clarified, the leader and group members summarize the text segment.
5. Predicting: Based on the discussion and the reading thus far, the leader and group members make predictions about the contents of the upcoming text.
6. This sequence is repeated with subsequent sections of the text. With daily practice, struggling readers will master the four supporting strategies and will use them for all their independent reading in other content area courses.
7. Some cautions:
   Start with simple questions at the beginning. But as students gain more practice, model open ended questions that are thought-provoking:
   Explain why ___.
   Explain how ___.
   What is a new example of ___?
   What conclusions can you draw from ___?
   What do you think causes ___? Why?
   What evidence do you have to support your answer?
   What are the strengths and weaknesses of ___?
   Compare ___ and ___ with regard to ___.
   Do not hesitate to provide more modeling and direct explanation, when needed, throughout the reciprocal teaching process.

(Adapted from Cibrowski, 1993; Slater and Horstman, 2002)

- Build awareness of common themes. "What else have we read that is similar to this? What parts are the same and what parts are different?"

✓ *Vocabulary prediction.* Redistribute the vocabulary prediction forms from Phase 1 and have the students write in the definitions based on their reading. Ask them to discuss what they learned about the meaning and use of the vocabulary words.

✓ *Analyze good and bad examples of writing.* Have the students view, analyze, and discuss good and bad examples of chapter summaries. Ask them to explain the characteristics of good and bad summaries and to write their own, using the criteria for the good summaries.

✓ *Other readings related to the course text.* Suggest other resources for the students to read that relate to the text. Trade books or magazines at the appropriate reading level should be available in class or at the school's library media center.

GRAPHIC ORGANIZERS AND COMPREHENSION OF CONTENT AREA READING

Graphic organizers have been mentioned in previous chapters as valuable tools for organizing and representing knowledge and for illustrating relationships between concepts. Even though graphic organizers have been mentioned in pedagogical literature for over 30 years, content area teachers have been slow to incorporate them as a routine instructional tool. Yet, research studies have shown them to be particularly effective in helping students with reading problems and other learning disabilities to learn content area material. The studies also have found that reading assignments that require students to complete graphic organizers in lieu of answering traditional study guide questions can significantly increase reading comprehension as well (Chmielewski and Dansereau, 1998; Katayama and Robinson, 2000). With this evidence in mind, let's spend some time discussing the reasons why graphic organizers can be effective and present some different types of organizers for consideration.

Graphic organizers are effective because they (Ellis, 1998)

- Show the organization or structure of concepts as well as relationships between concepts
- Make it more clear to students what they are expected to do and allow students to focus on what is important
- Provide a mental framework for helping students to organize knowledge and build the framework piece by piece, linking it to other learned frameworks

- Show how each item on the graphic can serve as a link to remembering related information discussed in class
- Reduce the cognitive demands on the learner by showing (as opposed to just telling) students how the information is structured, allowing the teacher to present information at more sophisticated and complex levels
- Develop literacy and thinking skills because the quality of the students' writing improves not only in the organization of ideas, but also in fluency and in other areas such as writing mechanics (punctuation, spelling, capitalization, etc.)
- Encourage students to use information processing and higher-order thinking skills, such as using cues to recognize important information, making decisions about what is important or essential, consolidating information, identifying main ideas and supporting details, and making decisions about the best way to structure the information
- Stimulate students who have constructed different organizers to discuss their diagrams and debate the importance of various points, draw conclusions, make connections to other ideas, and form inferences, predictions, or forecasts
- Result in an almost immediate improvement in performance on classroom tests for many students, whereas increased scores on standardized achievement tests occur more gradually as students gain skills using graphic organizers strategically

Some teachers resist using graphic organizers because they believe it takes too much class time to draw them. But now there are inexpensive computer programs (e.g., Inspiration Software) that help students construct and print different types of organizers in just minutes.

Types of Organizers

Graphic organizers come in several different forms, depending on the nature of the associated material to be learned. Among the most common types of graphic organizers are the following:

- Concept mapping
- Flowchart
- Matrix
- Webbing

Concept Mapping

One of the first types of graphic organizers to be developed, concept maps were originally used in the late 1970s to help students learn complex concepts in science. As research studies revealed how much more science children learned through using concept maps, they spread slowly to other subject areas (Novak and Musonda, 1991). More recent studies show that concept mapping also improves content area text comprehension and summarization for intermediate, middle, and high school students (Chang, Sung, and Chen, 2002; Chmielewski and Dansereau, 1998). Concept maps are now becoming more popular. There are multiple Internet sites that offer numerous examples of concept maps in all subject areas.

Concept maps are used to

- Develop an understanding of a body of knowledge
- Explore new information and relationships
- Access prior knowledge.
- Gather new knowledge and information.
- Share knowledge and information generated.

Share the guidelines included in the box on tips for making concept maps. Computer programs that build graphic organizers would be more efficient than paper-and-pencil versions, but both are equally effective at improving learning. Cooperative learning teams find Post-its

---

Tips for Making a Concept Map

Before students get started with their concept map, they should answer the following questions:

- What is the central word, concept, research question, or problem around which to build the map?
- What are the concepts, items, descriptive words, or important questions that one can associate with the concept, topic, research question, or problem?

Here are some suggestions that will help them construct the map:

✓ Consider using a computer program, such as *Inspiration,* to construct the map. If that is not available, Post-its are handy and allow you to move the concepts around a board easily.
✓ Use either a top-down approach, working from general to specific, or use a free association approach by brainstorming items and then develop the links and explain the relationships.
✓ If possible, use different colors and shapes for items and links to identify different types of information.
✓ Use different colored items to identify prior and new information.
✓ Experiment with a variety of different layouts until you find one that is compelling, understandable, and attractive .
✓ Be prepared to revise the map several times. This is another reason why computer software is helpful.

are very useful because they allow items to be moved around on a board or chart until the team is satisfied that they have the best arrangement. The Post-its also make revisions easy.

Before getting started on their concept maps, the students should get their research materials, class notes, and related articles together to use as their database for constructing the map. They should also ask themselves questions about the learning, such as:

- What is the central word, concept, research question, or problem around which to build the map?
- What are the concepts, items, descriptive words, or important questions that I can associate with the concept, topic, research question, or problem?

Procedure. Classroom instruction about the major topic usually takes place first. Armed with their new knowledge, the students gather their resources. Working independently, in teams, or as a whole class, the students start selecting the items, identifying the relationships, and choosing the descriptive words that will describe the relationships. After making the first chart, they review it to determine if the relationships are correctly labeled, and whether some other arrangement would make the map clearer or more attractive. Remember, there is rarely only one way to do a concept map. Later, students with different maps can discuss their variations and debate their differences. Figure 6.2 shows a concept map built around the process of photosynthesis. All the basic steps are included. The map can be made more attractive with pictures of plants, a sun, or a glass of water placed near the appropriate item.

Flowchart

A flowchart is used typically to depict a sequence of events, stages, phases, actions and outcomes. This version is good to use with young children and as a first step in developing linear relationships. The questions to ask before completing the chart are:

- What is the name of the event, procedure, or person that will be described?
- What are the specific stages, steps, phases, or events?
- Are the events in the correct sequence?
- How do the stages, steps, phases, or events relate to one another?
- What is the final outcome?

After the important steps have been identified, the students fill in the flowchart in the proper sequence. In some situations the flowchart can represent a part of a cycle, as in the case of the example on the left side of Figure 6.3. The flowchart shows the five steps in reciprocal teaching for a passage of text read aloud. After completing the steps in the first passage, the process is repeated for the second passage, and so on.

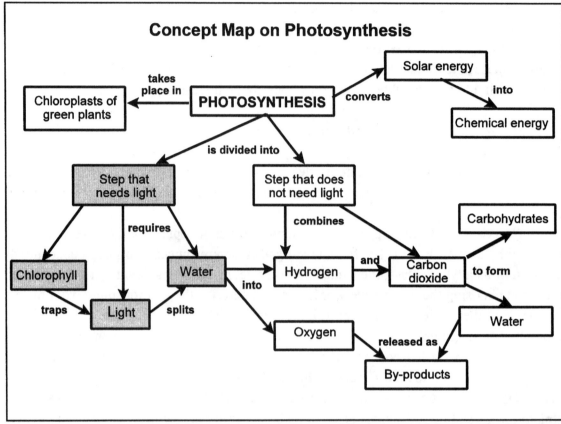

Figure 6.2 This is an example of a concept map built around the process of photosynthesis. As long as the basic steps are included, there are many different configurations that this map could take. It is important that the student write the relationship between any two items near the arrow that links them.

Venn Diagrams

John Venn first used these diagrams in the late 1800s to show relationships in mathematics. They are now used across many content areas to compare and contrast the qualities of two or three items, such as people, places, events, stories, ideas, situations, and things. Use a double Venn diagram to work with two items and a triple Venn diagram for three items. The questions to ask when preparing to use a Venn diagram are:

- What items do you want to compare?
- What characteristics do the items have in common (intersecting portions)?
- What characteristics do the items not have in common (nonintersecting portions)?

The Venn diagram on the right in Figure 6.3 compares some of the similarities and differences between fish and whales. Characteristics that are common to both fish and whales are shown in the area where the two circles overlap.

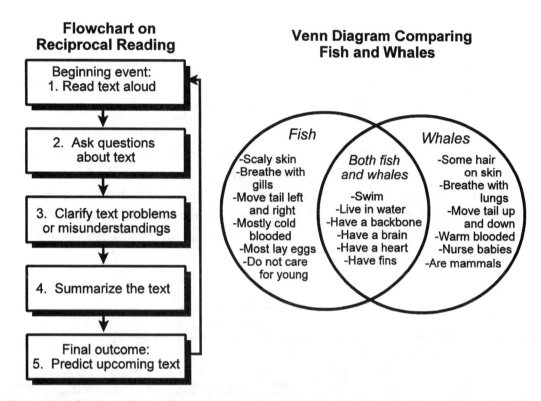

Figure 6.3 On the left is a flowchart organizer depicting the steps in the reciprocal reading process. The arrow from Step 5 to Step 1 shows the process is repeated for each passage of text. On the right is a Venn diagram comparing characteristics of fish and whales. Common characteristics are in the area where the circles overlap.

Matrixes

When comparing the characteristics of more than three items, Venn diagrams become too difficult to construct. In this instance, the matrix is a much easier organizer to use and it can be adapted to a variety of learning activities. Among the most common types are the following three:

- Comparison matrix
- K-W-H-L hart
- Content grids

Comparison Matrix. This matrix is used to describe and compare attributes and characteristics of two or more items, such as people, places, events, stories, ideas, situations, and things. One distinct advantage of this matrix is that there is no limit to the number of items or characteristics that can be included.

The questions to ask when preparing the matrix chart are:

- What items do you want to compare?
- What characteristics do you want to compare?
- How are the items similar or different based on these characteristics?

In constructing the matrix, the student generally places the items to be compared down the left column and the characteristics across the top row. After defining the specific characteristic, the student places an "X" in the box to indicate if that item possesses the characteristic. For example, if we wanted to expand the fish and whale comparisons used in the Venn diagram in Figure 6.3 to include other animals, such as humans and dogs, the matrix pictured in Figure 6.4 is one possibility.

Animal	Characteristics							
	Swim	Breathe air with lungs	Have fins	Have a brain	Have a backbone	Warm blooded	Most lay eggs	Are mammals
Fish	X		X	X	X		X	
Whales	X	X	X	X	X	X		X
Humans	X	X		X	X	X		X
Dogs	X	X		X	X	X		X

Figure 6.4 A comparison matrix of different characteristics belonging to several types of animals.

K-W-H-L Chart. This is an expansion of the more familiar K-W-L matrix in that it includes a step whereby the students identify how they plan to find out the needed information. The K-W-H-L chart's familiarity does not detract from its usefulness. Although it is more commonly used in elementary schools, it is an effective memory device at all grade levels (Figure 6.5). With this matrix, students plan and gather initial information on a topic or theme, identify primary and secondary resources they need to access, develop a plan for accessing resources, and identify the attributes and characteristics they will need to research.

The questions to ask when preparing to use a K-W-H-L chart are:

- What do we already know?
- What do we want to find out?
- How are we going to find out? What primary and secondary resources can we access?

- What attributes or characteristic should we focus on?
- What have we learned?

After reading the text and learning the material, the students go back to the "K" column to determine if any of their prior knowledge was inaccurate. They should note any of the statements that are inaccurate, according to the text, and rewrite them so that they are correct. Then they go to the "W" column and check any of their questions that the text did not answer. Students should be prepared to bring these unanswered questions up in class, or tell how they will find answers to them and where they will look to get the answers.

K	W	H	L
What do we **K**now?	What do we **W**ant to find out?	**H**ow can we find out what we need to learn?	What did we **L**earn?
Plants are living things.	What do plants need to live?	Biology books	Plants need sunlight, water, and nutrients to survive.
Many plants are green.	Why are plants green?	Biology books Internet search	Plants are green because they contain chlorophyll.
Some plants grow tall.	What are some plants that grow tall?	Internet search Field trips	Sunflowers and corn are plants that grow tall.
Some animals eat plants.	What do we call animals that eat just plants?	Biology books Encyclopedia	Animals that eat only plants are called herbivores.
Attributes we need to use: plant size, color, location			

Figure 6.5 This type of matrix takes advantage of the students' prior knowledge and encourages them to monitor their own learning. This example is a lesson on the characteristics of plants. (Adapted from Bender and Larkin, 2003)

Content Grids. This type of matrix helps students to think about and evaluate certain characteristics of people, places, events, and things. It may include making a decision about who was the bravest person in recent history, the best type of computer to buy, or the greatest environmental threat of the 21st century. Before beginning, the class should decide on the items to be included as well as the set of criteria that will be used to determine their decisions. Then they write in each block their judgment and rationale about how well or how poorly each item (person, place, thing, etc.) meets each criterion. Students can complete this matrix alone first and discuss their decisions later in groups, or they can complete the matrix together as part of a cooperative learning activity. Either way, the process leads students to higher-order thinking in that they must analyze and judge competing items against the same set of criteria. Figure 6.6 shows examples of different types of course content matrices.

Who Was the Bravest Leader in Recent History?				
	Fought against evil	Improved people's lives	Persistent	Trustworthy
Mahatma Ghandi				
Winston Churchill				
Franklin Roosevelt				

What Is the Greatest Environmental Threat of the 21st Century?				
	Economic impact	Number of people affected	Degree of danger	Length of danger
Ozone layer depletion				
Dumping toxic chemicals in the ground				
Global warming				
Acid rain				

Figure 6.6 These are two examples of content grids. The class must first decide on the items and criteria before filling in the matrix with their judgments and rationale.

Webs

Webs come in many varieties but they are generally used for brainstorming ideas about something that has been read and for solving problems in content areas. They are effective memory devices because they translate printed words into vivid visual images of relationships between items that the slower reader may not detect in the text. Brainstorming webs integrate the language components of the brain's left hemisphere with the visual and spatial talents of the right hemisphere—a "whole brain" approach that is important in learning and remembering. Creativity is also an essential component here because the brain's frontal lobe makes free associations and begins to build a holistic picture from seemingly isolated items. As the process continues, the brain reorganizes concepts into images that can be communicated to others. Thus, brainstorming webs are excellent discussion tools that stimulate higher-order thinking and processing.

Although brainstorming webs involve free associations, they are not unguided activities that just consume time, as some teachers think. Rather, the brainstorming process is always guided by specific questions, such as

- What is the topic to be brainstormed?
- Is the process of brainstorming clear?
- What should be the final product?

Brainstorming webs are usually made individually when a student is mapping out relationships that appear in the content reading. When working individually, students produce a wider range of ideas and patterns than when working in the group. They do not have to worry about other people's opinions and can therefore be more creative.

For problem solving, brainstorming in cooperative learning groups is very effective because it uses the brain power and experiences of everyone in the group. When individual members reach their limit on an idea, another member's background knowledge or experience may take the idea to another stage. In this manner, group brainstorming tends to produce web diagrams that include more subtle and deeper relationships. Figure 6.7 is an example of a web developed by a cooperative learning group based on some of the characteristics of vertebrates.

READING PATTERNS IN CONTENT AREAS

Recall from earlier chapters that the human brain seeks patterns in order to interpret its environment. This same pattern-seeking trait applies to reading content area material. As the brain reads content area text, such as science or social studies, it looks for patterns of thought that can be connected with past experience and comprehended. Each content areas is comprised of unique patterns of organized knowledge that the reader must identify in order to successfully understand that particular subject. When content area teachers clearly identify the types of patterns that students should be looking for when they read the subject text, they help their students establish the mind-set their brains need to make sense of the printed text. Here

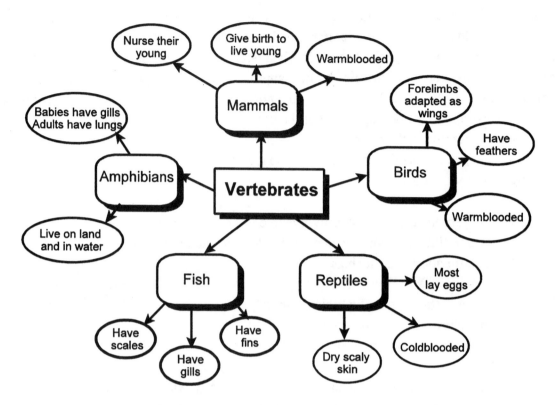

Figure 6.7 This web diagram depicts some of the characteristics of vertebrates. The web could be expanded by adding more characteristics and giving specific examples of each type.

are some of the patterns of organized knowledge that comprise some of the school's curriculum areas.

Art/Music/Drama
- Dialogue that describes, visualizes, and portrays actions
- Interpreting language through movement
- Readers' theatre to link oral and written language
- Role-playing to practice and interpret dialogue
- Understanding the perspective of the artist, composer, or writer

Literature
- Describing and visualizing the setting
- Character development of main and supporting characters, their authenticity and their relationships
- Distinguishing plot and episodes
- Understanding the literary piece's genre
- Discovering the moral, theme, or message

Mathematics
- Patterns and key words for solving word problems
- Symbolic relationships and operators
- Searching for evidence and reasoning
- Understanding graphic relationships

Science
- Types of classification
- Experimental procedures
- Cause and effect
- Steps in problem solving
- Definitions and explanations, with or without diagrams

Social Studies
- Definitions and explanations
- Cause and effect
- Chronological or sequential events
- Comparing and contrasting
- Distinguishing fact and opinion

Studies indicate that a large number of students of all ethnic backgrounds are functioning below grade level in their reading. This is a particularly difficult problem for students reading in the content areas where they are reading to acquire knowledge and skills in subjects such as mathematics, health, science, and social studies. In these subjects, the vocabulary used in the texts is often technical and written at a more difficult readability level. In this chapter, I have offered numerous tested strategies that could be used to aid these students in acquiring and understanding vocabulary, and in gaining a more accurate and deeper comprehension of the content they read. My hope is that teachers willing and determined to make "reading to learn" a successful experience for their students will consider adding these strategies to their repertoire.

Answer to Test Question # 9

Question: There is little that secondary school content area teachers can do to improve the comprehension skills of their students who are poor readers.

Answer: *False.* Content area teachers can use numerous tested strategies that aid poor readers in understanding vocabulary and in gaining a more accurate and deeper comprehension of the content they read.

What's Coming?

The next and last chapter looks at the basic components of a successful reading program. It summarizes what students need to know as they learn to read and what teachers need to do to make that process more successful for all students. The chapter also suggests professional development activities for teachers and school principals, presents some ways of closing the reading achievement gap, and discusses the importance of implementing action research in schools and classrooms.

CHAPTER 7

Putting It All Together

This chapter addresses several basic questions about what parents and educators can do to help more children learn to read successfully. They include:

- *What are the basics of a successful reading program?*
- *What do beginning readers need to learn?*
- *What do teachers need to know about teaching reading?*

THE BASICS OF A SUCCESSFUL READING PROGRAM

Surely by now it is clear that learning to read is no easy task. Unlike spoken language, there are no areas of the brain prewired for reading. Thus, there is no reason to consider reading to be a natural ability like speaking. Human beings have been talking for thousands of years, while reading is a relatively recent and quite artificial accomplishment. Toddlers seem to be preprogrammed to talk, and they usually learn to do so without formal instruction. On the other hand, the fact that large numbers of adults never do learn to read suggests that this ability is not in the same category.

Of course, some children learn to read with minimal instruction. These children, however, do not as a result read stories in a qualitatively different way from children taught via systematic phonics. The only difference seems to be that they have managed to crack the phonetic code on their own, without much teaching. How they learned the letter-sound correspondences seems to make no difference to the end result. Children who have become good readers though the whole-language approach have no advantage over children who have become good readers through systematic phonics. There is no harm in some children learning to read on their own. The problem is that the vast majority do not. Consequently, one of the major long-term goals of schools is to graduate students who are lifelong and highly competent readers.

Successfully achieving that long-term goal is not easy, because some barriers need to be overcome. These include teachers uninformed about the new understandings of how the brain learns to read, outdated materials for teaching reading, outdated methods for teaching reading, and the overemphasis on test scores. Moreover, to accomplish a long-term goal, short-term goals must first be achieved. I offer here some suggested short-term goals that I hope educators will consider. They are based on the current state of research on how we learn to read and on studies of effective instruction in reading.

Expose Teachers to Current Scientific Knowledge About How the Brain Learns to Read

During the past 10 years, research developments in neuroscience and cognitive psychology have added greatly to our understanding of how the brain learns to read and the nature of the problems that can arise during that process. We now know enough from this research to put many myths about reading to rest. We have a better idea which instructional strategies will increase the likelihood that more children can learn to read successfully. The research supports the continued use of some strategies while doubting the effectiveness of others. Armed with this knowledge, teachers can make better choices in reading programs and in their own instructional methods. That is the good news. The bad news is that the implications of this research for our practice are not getting to many classroom teachers fast enough. Nevertheless, teachers of early reading are aware that there is a growing body of newer research on reading, so word is slowly getting out.

One recent survey of nearly 550 kindergarten and first-grade teachers (Bursuck, Munk, Nelson, and Curran, 2002) was designed to examine their attitudes toward, and knowledge of, beginning reading practices that are research supported. Most teachers believed that many reading problems could be prevented with early intervention. On the other hand, teachers rated themselves low on their knowledge of effective literacy practices and on their ability to identify at-risk readers. Teachers are listening to the research but apparently need to be more involved in those teacher-training efforts that translate the research into effective classroom practices.

Teachers of reading must have access to the summaries of findings from a broad base of research on reading-related topics. They also need to recognize different types of studies. For example:

- *Experimental studies* provide generalizations that offer sound advice based on trends.
- *Correlational studies* usually provide reasoned hypotheses about how two variables can affect each other.
- *Case studies* help teachers consider new methods for instruction and assessment.

The responsibility of the school district is to engage teachers in ongoing study of the changing knowledge base produced by discoveries in scientific research on the reading process. Teachers need to be a vital part of the decision-making process in schools because it is through their work that children learn to read. With this approach, teachers recognize that teaching

> Teaching is not just an art form anymore; it is now a science and an art form.

is not just an art form anymore; it is now a *science* and an art form. By staying abreast of scientific developments, they can make informed decisions and contribute to locally developed, scientifically-based programs of instruction and assessment in reading.

Develop a Scientifically-Based Reading Program and Stick With It

The scientific evidence is clear: Learning to read successfully requires the ability to manipulate sounds into words, to break down words into their component sounds, and to match sounds with the letters that represent them. A scientifically-based reading program, therefore, will focus on developing phonological awareness, and then on to the more sophisticated phonemic awareness. Children need to know and recognize the alphabet in print and be able to match those letters with the sounds they represent. Mastering the alphabetic principle is essential to becoming a proficient reader, and instructional methods that explicitly teach this principle are more effective than those that do not. Learning phonics is especially important for children who are at risk for not learning to read. In addition to phonics instruction, using whole-language activities as a *supplement* helps to make reading enjoyable and meaningful. The reading program should emphasize vocabulary building, and the rules of grammar and syntax, and include activities that lead to reading fluency and comprehension.

Reading programs that overemphasize extensive and repetitive drills in phonics will bore students, and programs that overemphasize guessing how words sound and what they mean will be a source of frustration for students, especially those at risk of not learning to read. Phonological awareness, phonemic awareness, and the alphabetical principle should be taught in interesting and innovative ways, using a variety of materials. Usually, the program begins with coded texts to reinforce letter-sound correspondences. But teachers should select other high-interest sources of reading that maintain student attention and demonstrate that learning to read can be enjoyable.

> Concerns about whether the technologically-centered toys that children play with today, including computers, will lessen their motivation to read are unfounded.

Concerns abound about whether the technologically-centered toys that children play with today, including computers, will lessen their motivation to read. The concerns are unfounded, because a major portion of computer interactions still involves reading and writing, and that will continue to be the case for the near future. Parents and teachers need to find ways of using the attraction of the technology to lure children into working with programs that will help them learn to read.

Once a program with these components has been developed or selected, stick with it. Too much energy, teacher good will, and resources are wasted when districts leap from one reading program to another, based on the latest political favorite or on which publisher has made the greatest offer. Consistency is essential if we expect the program to have a lasting impact on developing the reading skills of students in the early grades.

What Skills Should Be in Place by Grade 3?

Most researchers agree that reading skills have to be in place by the end of third grade if the student is to cope successfully with the increasing reading requirements of the ensuing grades. What reading skills should our students have acquired at that time to demonstrate that they can continue to progress as successful readers? Calfee and Norman (1998) suggest that by the end of third grade, students should acquire critical literacy, which includes the skill and will to use language in all its forms as well as to solve problems and communicate effectively. To do so, children need to

- Master the alphabetic principle
- Read fluently
- Understand what they are reading
- Have strategies to sound out unfamiliar words
- Be confident in spelling
- Read almost any book in the elementary school library
- Write almost anything that falls within the child's knowledge and experience
- Have an appetite for reading and writing

Offer Ongoing Professional Development That Includes Teaching Strategies Based on the New Research

Because all reading programs are not the same, teachers must be educated in how to evaluate the different programs to determine which ones are based on strong evidence. Preservice and inservice programs need to provide teachers with the training necessary to select, develop, and implement the most appropriate reading program. Systematic phonics instruction is a necessary and vital component of learning to read, but it is not the only component. A total reading program should include instruction in phonemic awareness, vocabulary development, fluency, and comprehension (NRP, 2000).

Beginning teachers are in extra need of inservice support. Too often their preservice courses did not provide them with sufficient knowledge and skills to help all children become successful readers. Studies of teacher preparation programs show that too little time is allocated to the teaching of reading and that there is wide variance in the content of these programs (NRP, 2000; Snow et al., 1998).

Every day teachers try to help students learn to read. For some children, learning to read comes quickly, usually because of exposure to frequent language experiences during the preschool years. But for other children, learning to read is a struggle, and this is when teachers really *do* make a difference. Recent studies bear this out. Torgesen and his colleagues (2001) conducted two separate studies of children with reading disabilities using the same instructional methods. However, the researchers found that the outcomes were different. The students in the study that used highly skilled and knowledgeable teachers with considerable experience in teaching showed the greater improvement in reading achievement compared to the other study that had largely inexperienced teachers with little understanding of scientifically-based methods.

> Teachers make a difference. Students of experienced teachers with knowledge of scientifically-based methods had higher reading achievement scores that students of inexperienced teachers.

When early literacy teachers do participate in training to learn about research-based practices, the results can be impressive. For example, Abbott and her colleagues implemented a three-year project designed to train kindergarten and first-grade teachers in phonemic

What Beginning Readers Need to Learn

- *Phonological awareness:* Rhyming, alliteration, deleting, and substituting sounds, sound patterns
- *Phonemic awareness:* Segmenting words into individual sounds, manipulating phonemes
- *Visual perception of letters:* Understanding the names of the letters of the alphabet and recognizing them in print
- *Alphabetic principle:* Correlating letter-sound patterns with specific text
- *Word recognition:* Learning words that occur most often in language and that are needed in writing
- *Orthographic awareness:* Understanding spelling rules and writing conventions
- *Syntax:* Understanding rules affecting the word order in phrases and sentences
- *Fluency in oral reading:* Rereading texts to develop fluency

awareness concepts (Abbott, Walton, and Greenwood, 2002). The training for kindergarten teachers included onset fluency, rapid letter naming, and phonemic segmentation fluency. For first-grade teachers, the training expanded on phonemic segmentation. Research procedures were translated into step-by-step classroom procedures with teacher input. Students of the kindergarten teachers trained in the research-into-practice program scored remarkably well on all three areas tested. These same students also made impressive gains in phoneme segmentation the following year in first grade.

Children who come to school with phonics skills already developed and who can apply them correctly do not need the same intensity and level of phonics instruction as children who are just beginning to learn to read. Professional development should help teachers assess the needs of individual children and tailor instruction to meet these needs.

Remember the Content Area Teachers

To some degree, all teachers are teachers of reading. Yet, we often overlook content area teachers when designing professional development programs to enhance reading instruction. Districts should provide meaningful training to content area teachers that includes simple yet effective strategies they can use to help their students better comprehend their content material (see Chapter 6 for suggested strategies).

Even modest training times can be effective. Ten middle school content area teachers participated in a four-month professional development program to enhance the reading outcomes of the struggling readers in their classrooms (Bryant et al., 2001). The professional development program examined the teachers' knowledge of reading instruction and reading difficulties, and the training helped the teachers integrate three reading strategies (word identification, fluency, and comprehension) into their content area instruction. At the conclusion of the study, three findings emerged:

1. Content area teachers were not cognizant of the reading difficulties their students had and were overwhelmed by these challenges.
2. The content area teachers welcomed the inservice training on the comprehension strategies, insisted on substantial modeling, engaged in biweekly support meetings, and took time in class to implement the strategies.
3. Teachers saw positive effects from the strategies through improvements in vocabulary decoding and use, reading comprehension, and graph interpretations.

Middle school is the last chance for struggling readers to get the support they need in reading to learn. Content area teachers at this level who are knowledgeable in how to use research-based interventions can have a major impact on the reading success of their students.

Teach Reading Through the Students' Strengths

Difficulties with reading frequently mask a student's strengths in other cognitive areas. Because struggling readers have problems with their phonologic module's ability to interpret the meaning of individual words, they will miss details in the text. Furthermore, they have difficulty remembering extended lists of unfamiliar words long enough to comprehend complex sentences. You will recall from Chapter 3 that dyslexics deal with this situation by calling upon their brain's right frontal lobe during reading to interpret the overall meaning of a passage. Consequently, the dyslexic students' reliance on the right frontal lobe develops other cognitive strengths, such as creativity, problem solving, critical thinking, concept formation, and reasoning (Shaywitz, 2003).

> Difficulties with reading frequently mask a student's strengths in other cognitive areas.

Although overall cognitive ability may not influence the acquisition of phonemic awareness or of understanding phonics, reasoning and verbal skills can help dyslexic children and other struggling readers comprehend what they are reading. By using their bank of vocabulary words, personal experiences, and other knowledge, these students can use their cognitive skills to identify unfamiliar words in text. Teachers can work with these students to

---

What Teachers Need to Know About Teaching Reading

- How the brain learns to read
- The relationship between spoken language and reading
- How to provide direct instruction in phonics
- How to provide direct instruction in the alphabetic principle
- The relationship between phonology and morphology in relation to spelling
- How to diagnose spelling and reading skills
- How to use strategies that help students gain fluency
- How to help students understand the rules of syntax
- The dependence of reading comprehension on other aspects of reading and on language skills
- Procedures for ongoing in-class assessment of children's reading abilities
- How to modify instructional strategies based on in-class assessments
- Understanding the needs of students with disabilities and those with limited English proficiency
- How to use a variety of reading intervention strategies to address different learning styles and cultures
- How to apply research judiciously to their practice and how to update their knowledge base

expose them to opportunities that bolster their strengths through enhancing their vocabularies, expanding their storehouse of knowledge, and enriching their worldly experiences. This approach allows students with reading difficulties to use their other strengths to overcome their phonological weakness.

Offer Professional Development in Reading to Building Principals

Principals are the instructional leaders of their school. They need to become familiar with the latest scientific research on reading. Learning to read is far too important a goal to be left to discretionary programs and individual teacher decisions about what approach to take. The challenge for the principal is to maintain consistency of instruction while still encouraging the unique contributions of teachers. In the end, however, principals must insist that the district select a scientifically-based reading program, ensure that all teachers of beginning reading follow it, and stress the development of phonological awareness.

Effective reading instruction in kindergarten and the primary grades should be one of the principal's top priorities. Below is a brief survey that may help principals and teachers determine the extent to which the school's reading program is meeting the needs of all children. (For a much more comprehensive program evaluation survey, see Simmons and Kame'enui, 2003.)

Component	Little or None 1	Some 2	Significant 3
Components of Our Reading Program			
Directions: Circle the number that most closely describes the extent to which a component is present in your school's reading program. When finished, connect the circles with straight lines to get a profile of your reading program. Add up the values of the circled numbers (highest score is 63). Discuss the importance of any individual component that receives a score of 1.			
Program is research based	1	2	3
Teachers have been trained in research-based strategies related to the program	1	2	3
Emphasis on phonemic awareness	1	2	3
Systematic instruction and practice in phonics	1	2	3
Systematic instruction in the alphabetic principle	1	2	3
Activities and practice to enhance word decoding	1	2	3

Component	Little or None 1	Some 2	Significant 3
Activities and practice on word recognition	1	2	3
Activities and practice on semantics	1	2	3
Activities and practice on syntax	1	2	3
Writing activities are coordinated with reading instruction	1	2	3
Activities for building vocabulary growth	1	2	3
Strategies that use morphology to build spelling skills and enhance vocabulary growth	1	2	3
Instructional practices develop the children's ability to monitor their reading comprehension	1	2	3
Activities for improving reading fluency	1	2	3
Activities for improving reading comprehension	1	2	3
Strategies for improving content area reading	1	2	3
Inservice opportunities connected to the program	1	2	3
Other literature sources are integrated into the program	1	2	3
Instructional practices in middle grades build on reading and literacy growth in the primary grades	1	2	3
Interventions for helping teachers diagnose and address reading difficulties	1	2	3
Constructive communication about the program is maintained with parents	1	2	3

When you have completed the chart, add up the values of the circled numbers to get a total score. The highest possible score is 63. Take a close look at any component with a score of 1. Why is that the case? What can you do about it?

Working With Parents and Students

Principals provide a great community service when they talk to parents of newborns and alert them to the importance of the early preschool years in developing a child's literacy. Given the evidence that the brain's ability to acquire spoken language is at its peak in the early years, parents should create a rich environment that includes lots of communication activities, such as talking, singing, and reading aloud. In schools, this means addressing any language-learning problems quickly to take advantage of the brain's ability to rewire improper connections during this important period of growth. It also means that parents and teachers should not assume that children with language-learning problems are going to be limited in cognitive thought processes as well.

Principals can also ensure that the school's reading program will help students associate reading with pleasure. For readers having difficulties, principals can develop a library of specially recorded books that have a slow pace, clear phrasing, and small amounts of material per tape side. Struggling readers need to listen to the audiotape and to follow along.

Close the Achievement Gap in Reading

We hear a lot these days about closing the achievement gap between low-income and minority children, and other students. Despite the continuing concern, money, and effort, the gap in reading scores refuses to narrow. What causes this unfortunate situation depends on who you ask. Adults often say these students achieve poorly because they don't eat breakfast, they are too poor, their parents don't care, and they don't have any books at home. This focuses blame on the children and their families. But talking with students often produces different reasons. They talk about teachers who are not qualified in what they are teaching, about counselors who underestimate their potential, about principals who dismiss their concerns, and of a curriculum that is boring and irrelevant to their needs.

No one argues that issues like poverty, family stability, and home environment do not matter, because clearly they do. But if educators assume that unfortunate social and economic conditions will affect how *much* a child learns, then we end up not challenging the child. As a result, these students become the object of a self-fulfilling prophesy: We expect less of them, so we give them less, and they produce less in return.

Educators are not usually able to change what happens to children outside of school, but they can ensure that what happens *in school* really matters. Closing the achievement gap, in my opinion, requires concerted effort in four areas.

- *Establish and maintain high standards, and expect all students to meet them.* People rise and fall to the level of expectations we set for them. Too often in high-poverty schools there is little expectation that students can meet the reading standards. We misinterpret their lack of literacy as an inability to acquire literacy. Schools must be clearly committed to the notion that standards are for everyone and that everyone *can* reach them with appropriate instruction and, if needed, systematic interventions.

- *Design a challenging reading curriculum that is aligned with the standards.* Assume that all students can learn phonemic awareness and the alphabetic principle, although some students may take longer. Keep the practice consistent and challenging and introduce interesting literature as appropriate to enhance comprehension.

- *Provide systematic research-based additional help for struggling readers.* Many schools have programs, such as Title 1, designed to offer additional help in reading and mathematics. But these sessions can subject the students to more of the same outdated strategies that did not work in their regular classrooms. For some children, the school day just does not provide enough time to include the activities they need to catch up. More effort should be made to provide help through an extended school day, on weekends, before school, during vacation periods, and in the summer. Districts that have implemented these extended instructional times for struggling readers are reporting significant improvements in reading achievement.

- *Ensure that teachers thoroughly know the subjects they are teaching.* In many states, more than 20 percent of middle school and high school teachers are teaching outside their areas of college study (NCES, 2002). That number increases dramatically in high-poverty schools because fully-qualified teachers often find those positions less desirable and succeed in avoiding them. Numerous research studies over decades have shown that the classroom teacher remains the single greatest factor that determines most students' success in learning. As I have stated in my earlier books, the quality of learning rarely exceeds the quality of teaching. When we have fully-qualified teachers with high expectations and an updated knowledge base of how to teach reading, we can make great headway in closing the reading achievement gap.

> The quality of learning rarely exceeds the quality of teaching.

Encourage Teachers to Be Researchers

Teachers cannot be mere consumers of the knowledge emerging from scientific research. They must position themselves as active participants in the research community. One way to do this is through action research. Action research gives the practitioner a chance to be a researcher and to investigate specific problems that affect teaching and learning. Unlike traditional education research, where teachers are studied by outsiders, action research is conducted by teachers themselves to study their own classroom practices. It is a systematic investigation into some aspect of the school pursued by educators out of a desire to improve what they do. Action research expands the role of a teacher as an inquirer into teaching and learning through systematic classroom research.

> Action research expands the role of the teacher as an inquirer into teaching and learning through systematic research.

Teachers of reading can test whether a particular strategy they want to use is effective by trying it with some students and not with others. By setting up a small research project in the classroom, teachers can determine how well the students using the strategy (test group) learned compared with those that did not use the strategy (control group).

Action research is well suited to schools because of its democratic methodology, inclusiveness, flexibility of approach, and potential for changing practice. Action research uses a solution-oriented approach that is characterized by cycles (Figure 7.1) of

- Identifying the problem ("Will this strategy be more effective than other ones I have used?")
- Systematically collecting data ("How will I know if it worked?")
- Analyzing the data ("Did it improve their learning? How?")
- Taking action on the data ("What changes should I make?")
- Redefining the problem, if necessary ("Is there something else I should try?")
- Sharing the results with colleagues

Figure 7.1 The diagram illustrates the six steps in the action research cycle, starting with identifying or redefining the problem.

Because the teacher who is responsible for implementing changes also does the research, a real fit is created between the needs of a specific learner and the action taken. Teachers of reading should understand that their own honing of proven instructional strategies through reflection and systematic monitoring of their students' progress is a critical component of a scientifically-based reading program. Action research provides a means to that end.

Action research also provides teachers with opportunities to gain knowledge and skills in research methods and applications and to become more aware of the possibilities and options for change. Teachers using action research are likely to be receptive and supportive of systemic changes that school leaders may be seeking. We teach our students that inquiry is a tool of scientists. By engaging in action research, teachers extend their knowledge of reading instruction through inquiry. They carefully observe, generate and test hypotheses, collect data, and draw conclusions based on evidence that are shared with other reading teachers and researchers.

CONCLUSION

One point I have made in this book is that teaching children to read is not an easy task. This is especially true in the typical primary classroom where teachers welcome children from an ever-increasing variety of home situations, cultures, and native languages. Given these variables, successful teachers of reading are flexible rather than rigid in their approach, and they know through experience what they need to do to make learning to read exciting and meaningful. They also acknowledge that the findings of scientific studies are clear: explicit instruction in phonemic awareness is essential because it helps the beginning reader understand the alphabetic principle and apply it to reading and writing. Enriched text complements this process to provide relevant and enjoyable reading experiences.

This balanced approach avoids the seemingly endless reading wars and recognizes that learning to read and write are complex activities requiring at least seven levels of brain processing that must eventually be integrated:

- Phonological - knowing the sound system of language, phonemic awareness, and sound-letter correspondences
- Graphic - visually perceiving letters and symbols
- Lexical - recognizing words and their component parts, such as prefixes and suffixes
- Syntactic - understanding rules of grammar and discourse
- Semantic - comprehending meaning and detecting thematic structures
- Communicative - expressing purposes and intentions
- Cultural - communicating shared beliefs and knowledge

Effective reading programs and reading teachers should address all these levels of processing because each level supports the others. At the same time, children must be encouraged to use all the resources available to them in their efforts to decode, comprehend, and compose text. During this process, teachers need to have the skills to quickly recognize reading problems that arise and be able to select tested strategies to help students overcome those problems. Studies show that effective classroom instruction alone can reduce reading failure to about 6 percent (Foorman et al., 1998).

Researchers recently reported that effective classroom instruction coupled with targeted small-group instruction reduced the proportion of students with IQs of 77 to122 who were performing below the 30th percentile in early reading skills to less than 2 percent (Denton and Mathes, 2003; Torgesen, 2002, 2004). The importance of quality professional development became clear when studies of nearly 4,900 children in high-poverty schools found reading improvement to be significantly related to professional development within a coaching and mentoring model in the classroom, irrespective of the reading method used (Foorman and Moats, 2004; Moats and Foorman, 2003). There is little doubt that the knowledge, strength, and sophistication of the teacher is what really matters in helping children learn to read successfully. It is to that end that this book was written, and it is my hope that teachers and parents who read it will feel more empowered to help their children gain the literacy skills they need to be productive citizens of the world.

> There is little doubt that the knowledge, strength, and sophistication of the teacher is what really matters in helping children learn to read successfully.

Glossary

Acoustic analysis. The process that separates relevant word sounds from background noise, decodes the phonemes of the word, and translates them into a phonological code that can be recognized by the mental lexicon.

Affix. Letters attached to the beginning (prefix) or end (suffix) of a word.

Alphabetic principle. The understanding that spoken words can be broken down into phonemes, and that written letters represent the phonemes of spoken language.

Aphasia. The impairment or loss of language abilities following damage to the brain.

Automaticity. The instant decoding of letters (and other stimuli), such that the brain processing involved in the decoding process is automatic.

Balanced approach. An approach that advocates the incorporation of both phonics instruction and enriched text to teach beginning readers.

Blending. Combining the phonemes of a spoken word into a whole word, as in blending /d/ /o/ /g/ into *dog*.

Blocking. A linguistic principle that prevents a rule from applying to a word that already has an irregular form, such as the existence of *stood* blocks a rule from adding *-ed* to *stand,* thus preempting *standed.*

Broca's area. A region of the brain located behind the left temple that is associated with speech production, including vocabulary, syntax, and grammar.

Chunking. The ability of the brain to perceive a coherent group of items as a single item or chunk.

Collaborative strategic reading (CSR). A technique to improve reading comprehension by using heterogeneous groups in multilevel classes.

Comprehension. The ability to understand and attribute meaning to what is heard or read.

Content area reading. Reading in curriculum areas where students learn course content, such as facts and concepts, rather than learning skills.

Corpus callosum. The bridge of nerve fibers that connects the left and right cerebral hemispheres and allows communication between them.

Decoding. The ability to use the alphabetic principle to sound out a word by recognizing which phonemes are represented by the letters, and then blending those phonemes into a legitimate word.

Deep orthography. A language writing system, such as English, which does not have a one-to-one correspondence between the spoken phonemes and the letters that represent them. The same phoneme can be represented by different letters in words.

Digraph. A phoneme consisting of two successive letters that is pronounced as a single sound, as the *-ea* in *clean,* the *ch-* in *child,* or the *-ng* in *song.*

Dyslexia. A persistent developmental problem in learning to read. In 2002, the International Dyslexia Association adopted the following definition: "Dyslexia is a specific learning disability that is neurobiological in origin. It is characterized by difficulties with accurate and/or fluent word recognition and by poor spelling and decoding abilities. These difficulties typically result from a deficit in the phonological component of language that is often unexpected in relation to other cognitive abilities and the provision of effective classroom instruction. Secondary consequences may include problems in reading comprehension and reduced reading experience that can impede growth of vocabulary and background knowledge."

Event-related potential (ERP). An electrical signal emitted by the brain in response to a stimulus such as a picture or a word. The signals are detected by electrodes pasted to the scalp.

Fixation. The period of time when our eyes stop after making rapid movements across the page during reading. It is during these fixations of about 200 to 250 milliseconds that the eyes actually acquire information from the text.

Frontal lobe. The front part of the brain that monitors higher-order thinking, directs problem solving, and regulates the excesses of the emotional system.

Functional magnetic resonance imaging (fMRI). A process that measures blood flow to the brain to record areas of high and low neural activity.

Gist. An interpretation and mental representation of the meaning of a phrase, sentence, paragraph, passage, and so on.

Grapheme. The smallest part of written language that represents a single phoneme in the spelling of a word. A grapheme may be just one letter, such as *b, d, g,* and *s,* or several letters, as in *ck, sh, igh,* and *th.*

Immediate memory. A temporary memory where information is processed briefly (in seconds) and subconsciously, then either blocked or passed on to working memory.

Invented spelling. The creation of plausible spellings of real words using one's knowledge of letter names and sounds.

Lexicon. A person's mental dictionary consisting of words and their meanings.

Long-term storage. The areas of the brain where memories are stored permanently.

Millisecond (ms). A unit of time that represents one one-thousandth of a second.

Morpheme. The smallest units into which words can be cut that have meaning, as in *un-in-habit-able* (four morphemes).

Morphology. The component of grammar that studies how words are built from pieces called morphemes, and that affixes change the meaning of words in predictable ways.

Magnetic resonance imaging(MRI). A process that uses radio waves to disturb the alignment of the body's atoms in a magnetic field to produce computer-processed, high-contrast images of internal structures.

Nonword. A string of letters that cannot be pronounced and that have no meaning, such as *ndwsb* or *tgzaq*.

Occipito-temporal area. The area of the brain that overlaps portions of the occipital and temporal lobes where all the important information about a word is stored, including its spelling, pronunciation, and meaning.

Onset. The initial consonant sound of a syllable, such as the *t-* sound in *tag,* or the *sw-* sound in *swim.*

Oral reading accuracy. This is calculated by subtracting the number of word errors during reading (not counting repetitions or self-corrected errors) from the total number of words read, and dividing that result by the total number of words. The resulting decimal is multiplied by 100 to yield a percentage.

Oral reading fluency. Also known as **words correct per minute,** this measure is calculated by subtracting the number of word errors during one minute of reading (not counting repetitions or self-corrected errors) from the total number of words read.

Orthography. The written system that describes a spoken language. Spelling and punctuation represent the orthographic features of written English.

Overlearning. The ability to perform a task with little attention or conscious thought.

Parieto-temporal area. The area of the brain that overlaps portions of the parietal and temporal lobes where word analysis is thought to occur during reading.

Positron emission tomography (PET). A process that traces the metabolism of radioactively-tagged sugar in brain tissue, producing a color image of cell activity.

Phoneme. The smallest units of sound that make up a spoken language. For example, the word *go* has two phonemes, *guh* and *oh.* The English language has about 44 phonemes. Some phonemes are represented by more than one letter.

Phonemic awareness. The ability to hear, identify, and manipulate phonemes in spoken syllables and words.

Phonics. The understanding that there is a predictable relationship between the sounds of *spoken* language (phonemes) and the letters that represent those sound in *written* language (graphemes).

Phonologic memory. The ability to retain verbal bits of information (phonemes) in working memory.

Phonological awareness. In addition to phonemic awareness, it includes the ability to recognize that sentences are comprised of words, words are comprised of syllables, and syllables are comprised of onsets and rimes that can be broken down into phonemes.

Phonology. The component of grammar that studies the sound patterns of a language, including how phonemes are combined to form words, as well as patterns of timing, stress, and intonation.

Prosody. The rhythm, cadence, accent patterns, and pitch of a language.

Pseudoword. A string of letters that can be pronounced but has no meaning (also called nonsense or invented words), such as *gebin* or *splor*.

Regression. The movement of the eyes backwards over a written line to re-read text.

Rehearsal. The reprocessing of information in working memory.

Rime. A part of a syllable that contains the vowel and all that follows it, as the *-ag* sound in *tag* or the *-im* sound in *swim*.

Schema theory. This theory suggests that mental structures resulting from our experiences help us interpret and predict new situations.

Semantics. The study of how meaning is derived from words and other text forms.

Shallow orthography. A language writing system, such as Spanish or Finnish, that has a consistent correspondence between the spoken phonemes and the letters that represent those phonemes in writing.

Silent sustained reading (SSR). A strategy in which students are assigned to do silent reading for a specified number of minutes each day. Its effectiveness has not been proved.

Syllable. A word part that contains a vowel or vowel sound pronounced as a unit: *speak-er, a-lone.*

Syntax. The rules and conventions that govern the order of words in phrases, clauses, and sentences.

Wernicke's area. The region of the brain, usually located in the left hemisphere, thought to be responsible for sense and meaning in one's native language.

Whole-language. An approach to reading instruction that emphasizes the recognition of words as wholes and de-emphasizes letter-sound relationships.

Word-blindness. The inability to read words even when a person's eyes are optically normal.

Word form. The neural model that encompasses the spelling, pronunciation, and meaning of a word.

Working memory. The temporary memory of limited capacity where information is processed consciously.

References

Abbott, M., Walton, C., and Greenwood, C. R. (2002). Phonemic awareness in kindergarten and first grade. *Teaching Exceptional Children, 34,* 20-26.

Ahmed, S. T., and Lombardino, L. J. (2000). Invented spelling: An assessment and intervention protocol for kindergarten children. *Communication Disorders Quarterly, 22,* 19-28.

Allington, R. L., and Woodside-Jiron, H. (1998). Decodable text in beginning reading: Are mandates and policy based on research? *ERS Spectrum, 16,* 3-11.

Amitay, S., Ben-Yehudah, G., Banai, K., and Ahissar, M. (2002). Disabled readers suffer from visual and auditory impairments but not from a specific magnocellular deficit. *Brain, 125,* 2272-2285.

Anglin, J. M. (1993). Vocabulary development: A morphological analysis. *Monographs of the Society for Research in Child Development, 58,* 10.

Armbruster, B. (1996). Schema theory and the design of content-area textbooks. *Educational Psychologist, 21,* 253-276.

Aylward, E., Richards, T., Berninger, V., Nagy, W., Field, K., Grimme, A., Richards, A., Thomson, J., and Cramer, S. C. (2003). *Instructional treatment associated with changes in brain activation in children with dyslexia.* Paper presented at the conference of the Organization for Human Brain Mapping, June, 2003, New York, NY.

Baer, G. T., and Nourie, B. L. (1993). Strategies for teaching reading in the content areas. *The Clearing House, 67,* 121-122.

Bailey, G. (1993). A perspective on African-American English. In D. Preston (Ed.), *American dialect research* (pp. 287-318). Philadelphia: Benjamins.

Beaton, A. (1997). The relation of planum temporale asymmetry and morphology of the corpus callosum to handedness, gender, and dyslexia: A review of the evidence. *Brain and Language, 60,* 255-322.

Beatty, J. (2001). *The human brain: Essentials of behavioral neuroscience.* Thousand Oaks, CA: Sage Publications.

Bender, W. N., and Larkin, M. J. (2003). *Reading strategies for elementary students with learning difficulties.* Thousand Oaks, CA: Corwin Press.

Berninger, V. W., Vaughan, K., Abbott, R., Abbott, S., Rogan, L., Brooks, A., et al. (1997). Treatment of handwriting problems in beginning writers: Transfer from handwriting to composition. *Journal of Educational Psychology, 89,* 652-666.

Bischoff-Grethe, A., Proper, S. M., Mao, H., Daniels, K. A., and Berns, G. S. (2000). Conscious and unconscious processing of nonverbal predictability in Wernicke's area. *Journal of Neuroscience, 20,* 1975-81.

Bolton, F., and Snowball, D. (1993). *Ideas for spelling.* Portsmouth, NH: Heinemann.

Brady, S., and Moats, L. (1997). *Informed instruction for reading success: Foundations for teacher preparation.* Baltimore, MD: International Dyslexia Association.

Brady, S. and Moats, L. (1998). Buy books, teach reading. *The California Reader, 31,* 6-10.

Brown, R., Pressley, M., Van Meter, P., and Schuder, T. (1996). A quasi-experimental validation of transactional strategies instruction with low-achieving second grade readers. *Journal of Educational Psychology, 88,* 18-37.

Brown, W. E., Eliez, S., Menon, V., Rumsey, J. M., White, C. D., and Reiss, A. L. (2001). Preliminary evidence of widespread morphological variations of the brain in dyslexia. *Neurology, 27,* 781-783.

Brun, M., Bouvard, M., Chateil, J., Bénichou, G., Bordessoules, M., and Allard, M. (2003). *Phonological treatment in dyslexic children: Neural network in fMRI.* Paper presented at the conference of the Organization for Human Brain Mapping, June, 2003, New York, NY.

Bryant, D. P., Linan-Thompson, S., Ugel, N., Hamff, A., and Hougen, M. (2001). The effects of professional development for middle school general and special education teachers on implementation of reading strategies in inclusive content area classes. *Learning Disabilities Quarterly, 24,* 251-264.

Burdette, J. H., Hairston, W. D., Flowers, D. L., and Wallace, M. T. (2003). *Cross-modal temporal integration in developmental dyslexia.* Paper presented at the Annual Conference of the Society for Neuroscience, November 8, 2003, New Orleans, LA.

Burnham, D., Kitamura, C., and Vollmer-Conna, U. (2002). What's new pussycat? On talking to babies and animals. *Science, 296,* 1435.

Bursuck, W. D., Munk, D. D., Nelson, C., and Curran, M. (2002, Fall). Research on the prevention of reading problems: Are kindergarten and first grade teachers listening? *Preventing School Failure,47,* 4-9.

Byrne, B. (1991). Experimental analysis of the child's discovery of the alphabetic principle. In L. Riehen and C. Perfetti (Eds.), *Learning to read: Basic research and its implications* (pp. 75-84). Hillsdale, NJ: Erlbaum.

Calderón, M., Hertz-Lazarowitz, R., and Slavin, R. (1998). Effects of Bilingual Cooperative Integrated Reading and Composition on students making the transition from Spanish to English reading. *The Elementary School Journal, 99,* 153-166.

Calderón, M., and Minaya-Rowe, L. (2003). *Designing and implementing two-way bilingual programs.* Thousand Oaks, CA: Corwin Press.

Calfee, R. C., and Norman, K. A. (1998). Psychological perspectives on the early reading wars: The case of phonological awareness. *Teachers College Record, 100,* 242-274.

Camilli, G., and Wolfe, P. (2004, March). Research on reading: A cautionary tale. *Educational Leadership, 61,* 26-29.

Carbo, M. (2003, September). How principals can do it all in reading — Part III. *TEPSA Instructional Leader, 16,* 1-3.

Carnine, D. W., Silbert, J., and Kame'enui, E. J. (1997). *Direct instruction reading.* Upper Saddle River, NJ: Prentice Hall.

Chang, K., Sung, Y., and Chen, I. (2002). The effect of concept mapping to enhance text comprehension and summarization. *Journal of Experimental Education, 71,* 5-23.

Chard, D. J., and Dickson, S.V. (1999, May). Phonological awareness: Instructional and assessment guidelines. *Intervention in School and Clinic, 34,* 261-270.

Chard, D. J., and Osborn, J. (1998). *Suggestions for examining phonics and decoding instruction in supplementary reading programs.* Austin, TX: Texas Education Agency.

Cheour, M., Ceponiene, R., Lehtokoski, A., Luuk, A., Allik, J., Alho, K., & Näätänen, R. (1998, September). Development of language-specific phoneme representations in the infant brain. *Nature Neuroscience, 1,* 351–353.

Chmielewski, T., and Dansereau, D. F. (1998). Enhancing the recall of text: Knowledge mapping training promotes implicit transfer. *Journal of Educational Psychology, 90,* 407-413.

Chomsky, C. (1979). Approaching reading through invented spelling. In L. Resnick and P. Weaver (Eds.), *Theory and practice of early reading* (Vol. 2, pp. 43-65). Hillsdale, NJ: Erlbaum.

Cibrowski, J. (1993). *Textbooks and students who can't read them.* Cambridge, MA: Brookline Books.

Cole, P. G., and Mengler, E. D. (1994). Phonemic processing of children with language deficits: Which tasks best discriminate children with learning disabilities from average readers? *Reading Psychology, 15,* 223-243.

Coles, G. (2004). Danger in the classroom: "Brain glitch" research and learning to read. *Phi Delta Kappan, 85,* 344-351.

Collins, A. M. and Loftus, E. F. (1975). A spreading-activation theory of semantic processing. *Psychological Review, 82,* 407-428.

Cooper, G. (Ed.) (1987). *Red tape holds up bridge, and more flubs from the nation's press.* New York: Perigee Books.

Coyne, M. D., Kame'enui, E. J., and Simmons, D. C. (2001). Prevention and intervention in beginning reading: Two complex systems. *Learning Disabilities Research and Practice, 16,* 62-73.

Cunningham, A. E., and Stanovich, K. E. (1997). Early reading acquisition and its relation to reading experience and ability. *Developmental Psychology, 33,* 934-945.

Cunningham, A. E., and Stanovich, K. E. (1998, Spring/Summer). What reading does for the mind. *American Educator,* pp. 8-17.

Damasio, H., Grabowski, T. J., Tranel, D., Hichwa, R. D., and Damasio, A. (1996). A neural basis for lexical retrieval. *Nature, 380,* 499-505.

Dapretto, M., and Bookheimer, S. Y. (1999). Form and content: Dissociating syntax and semantics in sentence comprehension. *Neuron, 2,* 427.

Dehaene-Lambertz, G. (2000). Cerebral specialization for speech and non-speech stimuli in infants. *Journal of Cognitive Neuroscience, 12,* 449-460.

Demb, J. B., Boynton, G. M., and Heeger, D. J. (1998). Functional magnetic resonance imaging of early visual pathways in dyslexia. *Journal of Neuroscience, 18,* 6939-6951.

Denton, C. A., and Mathes, P. G. (2003). Intervention for struggling readers: Possibilities and challenges. In B. Foorman (Ed.), *Preventing and remediating reading difficulties.* Baltimore, MD: York Press.

Deshler, D.D., Ellis, E.S., and Lenz, B.K. (1996). *Teaching adolescents with learning disabilities: Strategies and methods.* Denver, CO: Love Publishing.

Driscoll, M. (1994). *Psychology of learning for instruction.* Boston: Allyn and Bacon.

Dyslexia International – Tools and Technology (DITT). (2001). *Language shock – Dyslexia across cultures.* Brussels: Author.

Eckert, M. M., Leonard, C. M., Richards, T. L., Aylward, E. H., Thomson, J., and Berninger, V. W. (2003). Anatomical correlates of dyslexia: Frontal and cerebellar findings. *Brain, 126,* 482-494.

Edelen-Smith, P.J. (1998). How now brown cow: Phoneme awareness activities for collaborative classrooms. *Intervention in School and Clinic, 33,* 103-111.

Ehri, L. (1998). Grapheme-phoneme knowledge is essential for learning to read words in English. In J. Metsala and L. Ehri (Eds.), *Word recognition in beginning literacy* (pp. 3-40). Mahwah, NJ: Erlbaum.

Ehri, L., Shanahan, T., and Nunes, S. (2002). Response to Krashen. *Reading Research Quarterly, 37,* 128-129.

Ellis, E. S. (1998). *The framing routine.* Tuscaloosa, AL: Masterminds.

Escamilla, K. (1994). Descubriendo la Lectura: An early intervention literacy program in Spanish. *Literacy, Teaching, and Learning, 1,* 57-70.

Fisher, S. E., and DeFries, J. C. (2002). Developmental dyslexia: Genetic dissection of a complex cognitive trait. *Nature Reviews Neuroscience, 30,* 767-780.

Fisk, C., and Hurst, B. (2003). Paraphrasing for comprehension. *The Reading Teacher, 57,* 182-185.

Fitzgerald, J., and Noblit, G. (2000). Balance in the making: Learning to read in an ethically diverse first-grade classroom. *Journal of Educational Psychology, 92,* 3-22.

Foorman, B. R., Francis, D. J., Fletcher, J. M., Schatschneider, C., and Mehta, P. (1998). The role of instruction in learning to read: Preventing reading failure in at-risk children. *Journal of Educational Psychology, 90,* 37-55.

Foorman, B. R., and Moats, L. C. (2004). Conditions for sustaining research-based practices in early reading instruction. *Remedial and Special Education, 25,* 51-60.

Francis, N., and Kucera, H. (1982). *Frequency analysis of English usage: Lexicon and grammar.* Boston: Houghton Mifflin.

Galuske, R. A. W., Schlote, W., Bratzke, H., and Singer, W. (2000). Interhemispheric asymmetries of the modular structure in human temporal cortex. *Science, 289,* 1946-1949.

Gazzaniga, M. S. (1998). *The mind's past.* Berkeley, CA: University of California Press.

Gazzaniga, M. S., Ivry, R. B., and Mangun, G. R. (2002). *Cognitive neuroscience: The biology of the mind* (2nd ed.). New York: Norton.

Gernsbacher, M. A. (1990). *Language comprehension as structure building.* Hillsdale, NJ: Erlbaum.

Goldberg, E. (2001). *The executive brain: Frontal lobes and the civilized mind.* New York: Oxford University Press.

Gough, P. B., and Juel, C. (1991). The first stages of word recognition. In L. Rieben and C. A. Perfetti (Eds.), *Learning to read: Basic research and its implications* (pp. 47-56). Hillsdale, NJ: Erlbaum.

Graham, S., Harris, K. R., and Fink, B. (2000). Is handwriting causally related to learning to write? Treatment of handwriting problems in beginning writers. *Journal of Educational Psychology, 92,* 620-633.

Gunn, B., Biglan, A., Smolkowski, K., and Ary, D. (2000). The efficacy of supplemental instruction in decoding skills for Hispanic and non-Hispanic students in early elementary school. *The Journal of Special Education, 34,* 90-103.

Habib, M. (2003). Rewiring the dyslexic brain. *Trends in Cognitive Science, 7,* 330-333.

Hanushuk, E. A., Kain, J. F., and Rivkin, S. G. (1998). Does special education raise academic achievement for students with disabilities? *National Bureau of Economic Research,* Working Paper No. 6690, Cambridge, MA.

Harm, M. W., and Seidenberg, M. S. (1999). Phonology, reading acquisition, and dyslexia: Insights from connectionist models. *Psychological Review, 106,* 491-528.

Hart, B, and Risley, T. R. (2003). The early catastrophe: The 30 million word gap by age 3. *American Educator, 27,* 4-9.

Hart, E. R. and Speece, D. L. (1998). Reciprocal teaching goes to college: Effects of postsecondary students at risk for academic failure. *Journal of Educational Psychology, 90,* 670.

Hasbrouck, J. E., and Tindal, G. (1992). Curriculum-based oral reading frequency norms for students in grades 2 through 5. *Teaching Exceptional Children, 24,* 41-44.

Helenius, P., Salmelin, R., Richardson, U., Leinonen, S., and Lyytinen, H. (2002). Abnormal auditory cortical activation in dyslexia 100 msec after speech onset. *Journal of Cognitive Neuroscience, 14,* 603-617.

Howes, N., Bigler, E. D., Burlingame, G. M., and Lawson, J. S. (2003). Memory performance of children with dyslexia: A comparative analysis of theoretical perspectives. *Journal of Learning Disabilities, 36,* 230-246.

Idol, L. (1987). Group story mapping.: A comprehensive strategy for both skilled and unskilled readers. *Journal of Learning Disabilities, 20,* 196-205.

Indefrey, P., Kleinschmidt, A., Merboldt, K. D., Kruger, G., Brown, C., Hagoot, P., and Frahm, J. (1997). Equivalent responses to lexical and nonlexical visual stimuli in occipital cortex: A functional magnetic resonance imaging study. *NeuroImage, 5,* 78-81.

International Dyslexia Association (IDA). (2003). *Common signs of dyslexia.* Baltimore, MD: Author.

Johnson, D.W., and Johnson, R.T. (1989). Cooperative learning: What special educators need to know. *The Pointer, 33,* 5-10.

Joseph, J., Noble, K., and Eden, G. (2001). The neurobiological basis of reading. *Journal of Learning Disabilities, 34,* 566-579.

Kaminen, N., Hannula-Jouppi, K., Kestila, M., Lahermo, P., Muller, K., Kaaranen, M., Myllylouma, B., Voutilainen, A., Lyytinen, H., Nopola-Hemmi, J., and Kere, J. (2003, May). A genome scan for developmental dyslexia confirms linkage to chromosome 2pll and suggests a new locus on 7q32. *Journal of Medical Genetics, 40,* 340-345.

Katayama, A. D., and Robinson, D. H. (2000). Getting students partially involved in note-taking using graphic organizers. *Journal of Experimental Education, 68,* 119-133.

Kim, K. H. S., Relkin, N. R., Lee, K. M., and Hirsch, J. (1997). Distinct cortical areas associated with native and second languages. *Nature, 388,* 171-174.

Klingner, J. K., Vaughn, S., and Schumm, J. S. (1998). Collaborative strategic reading during social studies in heterogeneous fourth grade classrooms. *Elementary School Journal, 99,* 3-22.

Krashen, S. (2001). More smoke and mirrors: A critique of the National Reading Panel report on fluency. *Phi Delta Kappan, 83,* 119-123.

Krashen, S. (2002). Phonemic awareness training necessary? *Reading Research Quarterly, 37,* 128.

Labov, W. (2003). When ordinary children fail to read. *Reading Research Quarterly, 38,* 128-131.

Lai, C. S., Fisher, S. E., Hurst, J. A., Vargha-Khadem, F., and Monaco, A. P. (2001). A forkhead-domain gene is mutated in a severe speech and language disorder. *Nature, 413,* 519-523.

Leonard, C. M. (2001). Imaging brain structure in children: Differentiating language disability and reading disability. *Learning Disability Quarterly, 24,* 158-176.

Londin, E. R., Meng, H., and Gruen, J. R. (2003). A transcription map of the 6p22.3 reading disability locus identifying candidate genes. *BMC Genomics, 4.* Available online at http://www.biomedcentral.com/1471-2164/4/25.

Lyon, G. R. (2002). Reading development, reading difficulties, and reading instruction: Educational and public health issues. *Journal of School Psychology, 40,* 3-6.

Mahony, D., Singson, M., and Mann, V. A. (2000). Reading ability and sensitivity to morphophonological situations. *Reading and Writing: An Interdisciplinary Journal, 12:3/4,* 191-218.

Mann, V. A. (2000). Introduction to special issue on morphology and the acquisition of alphabetic writing systems. *Reading and Writing: An Interdisciplinary Journal, 12:3/4,* 143-147.

Martinez, M., Roser, N., and Strecker, S. (1999). "I never thought I could be a star": A readers' theatre ticket to fluency. *The Reading Teacher, 52,* 326-334.

Mather, N. and Goldstein, S. (2001). *Learning disabilities and challenging behaviors: A guide to intervention and classroom management.* Baltimore, MD: Brookes.

McCandliss, B. D., Cohen, L., and Dehaene, S. (2003, July). The visual word form area: Expertise for reading in the fusiform gyrus. *Trends in Cognitive Sciences, 7,* 293-299.

Michigan Department of Elementary and Secondary Education (MDESE). (2003). *Missouri parents as teachers graphs.* Available online at http://dese.mo.gov/divimprove/fedprog/earlychild/ECDA/PAT%20FACT%20Sheet.pdf.

Mirsky, A. F. (1996). Disorders of attention: A neuropsychological perspective. In G. R. Lyon and N. A. Krasnegor (Eds.), *Attention, memory, and executive function* (pp. 71-95. Baltimore, MD: Brookes.

Moats, L. C., and Foorman, B. R. (2003). Measuring teachers' content knowledge of language and reading. *Annals of Dyslexia, 53,* 23-45.

Moats, L. C., Furry, A. R., and Brownell, N. (1998). *Learning to read: Components of beginning reading instruction.* Sacramento, CA: Comprehensive Reading Leadership Center.

Morris, D., Bloodgood, J. W., Lomax, R. G., and Perney, J. (2003). Developmental steps in learning to read: A longitudinal study in kindergarten and first grade. *Reading Research Quarterly, 38,* 302-328.

Munakata, Y., McClelland, J. L., Johnson, M. H., and Siegler, R. S. (1997). Rethinking infant knowledge: Toward and adaptive process account of success and failures in object permanence tasks. *Psychological Review, 104,* 686-713.

Nandy, R., Cordes, D., Berninger, V., Richards, T., Aylward, E., Stanberry, L., Richards, A., and Maravilla, K. (2003). *An fMRI approach to the diagnosis of dyslexia using CCA and a phoneme matching task.* Paper presented at the conference of the Organization for Human Brain Mapping, June, 2003, New York.

National Assessment of Educational Progress (NAEP). (2003). *The nation's report card: Reading 2003.* Washington, DC: Author.

National Association for the Education of Young Children (NAEYC). (1998). *Learning to read and write: Developmentally appropriate practices for young children.* Available online at http://www.naeyc.org/resources/position_statements/psread4.htm.

National Center for Educational Statistics (NCES). (2002). *Qualifications of the public school teacher workforce: Prevalence of out-of-field teaching 1987-88 to 1999-2000.* Available online at http://nces.ed.gov/programs/coe/2003/section4/indicator28.asp.

National Institute for Literacy (NIFL). (2001). *Put reading first: The research building block for teaching children to read.* Jessup, MD: Author.

National Reading Panel (NRP). (2000). *Teaching children to read: An evidence-based assessment of the scientific research literature and its implications for reading instruction.* Washington, DC: National Institute of Child Health and Human Development.

Nicolson, R. I., Fawcett, A. J., and Dean, P. (2001, September). Developmental dyslexia: The cerebellar deficit hypothesis. *Trends in Neuroscience, 24,* 508-511.

Novak, J. D., and Musonda, D. (1991). A twelve-year longitudinal study of science concept learning. *American Educational Research Journal, 28,* 117-153.

O'Connor, R. E., and Jenkins, J. R. (1995). Improving the generalization of sound/symbol knowledge: Teaching spelling to kindergarten children with disabilities. *The Journal of Special Education, 29,* 255-275.

Omaha Public Schools (OPS). (2003). *Reading tips: Secondary content teachers.* Available online at www.ops.org/reading.

Palincsar, A. S., and Brown, A. L. (1984). The reciprocal teaching of comprehension-fostering and comprehension-monitoring activities. *Cognition and Instruction, 1,* 117-175.

Parker, R., Hasbrouck, J. E., and Denton, C. (2002a). How to tutor students with reading problems. *Preventing School Failure, 47,* 42-44.

Parker, R., Hasbrouck, J. E., and Denton, C. (2002b). How to tutor students with comprehension problems. *Preventing School Failure, 47,* 45-47.

Parrott, C. A. (1986). Visual imagery training: Stimulating utilization of imaginal processes. *Journal of Mental Imagery, 10,* 47-64.

Paterno, J. (2001). *Secondary reading strategies.* Available online at www.angelfire.com/wa2/buildingcathedrals/SecondaryReadingStrategies.

Pearson, P. D., and Duke, N. K. (2002). Comprehension instruction in the primary grades. In C. C. Block and M. Pressley (Eds.), *Comprehension instruction: Research-based best practices.* New York: Guilford.

Peereman, R., Content, A., and Bonin, P. (1998). Is perception a two-way street: The case of feedback consistency in visual word recognition. *Journal of Memory and Language, 39,* 151-174.

Pennington, B. F. (1990). The genetics of dyslexia. *Journal of Child Psychology and Psychiatry, 31,* 193-201.

Pinker, S. (1994). *The language instinct: How the mind creates language.* New York: William Morrow.

Pinker, S. (1999). *Words and rules: The ingredients of language.* New York: Basic Books.

Pressley, M. (1998). *Reading instruction that works: The case for balanced teaching.* New York: Guilford.

Pressley, M., and Afflerbach, P. (1995). *Verbal protocols of reading: The nature of constructively responsive reading.* Hillsdale, NJ: Erlbaum.

Price, C., Moore, C., and Frackowiak, R. S. J. (1996). The effect of varying stimulus rates and duration of brain activity during reading. *Neuroimage, 3,* 40-52.

Rawson, M. B. (1995). *Dyslexia over the life span: A 55 year longitudinal study.* Cambridge, MA: Educator's Publishing Service.

Rayner, K., Foorman, B. R., Perfetti, C. A., Pesetsky, D., and Seidenberg, M. S. (2001, November). How psychological science informs the teaching of reading. *Psychological Science in the Public Interest, 2 ,* 31-74.

Reading Recovery Council (2002). *What evidence says about Reading Recovery.* Columbus, OH: Author.

Renvall, H., and Hari, R. (2002). Auditory cortical responses to speech-like stimuli in dyslexic adults. *Journal of Cognitive Neuroscience, 14,* 757-768.

Richards, T. (2001, Summer). Functional magnetic resonance imaging and spectroscopic imaging of the brain: Application of fMRI and fMRS to reading disabilities and education. *Learning Disability Quarterly, 24,* 189-204.

Rumsey, J., Horwitz, B., Donohue, B. C., Nace, K. L., Maisog, J. M., and Andreason, P. (1999). A functional lesion in developmental dyslexia: Left angular gyral flow predicts severity. *Brain and Language, 70,* 187-204.

Sams, G. (2003). *Dyslexia and exams.* Available online at http://www.dyslexia-parent.com.

Scientific Learning Corporation (SLC). (2000). *Fast ForWord reading: Why it works.* Oakland, CA: Author.

Share, D. L., and Stanovich, K. E. (1995). Cognitive processes in early reading development: Accommodating individual differences into a model of acquisition. *Issues in Education, 1,* 1-57.

Shaywitz, S. E. (2003). *Overcoming dyslexia: A new and complete science-based program for reading problems at any level.* New York: Knopf.

Shaywitz, S. E. (1996, November). Dyslexia. *Scientific American, 275,* 98-104.

Shaywitz, B., Shaywitz, S., Blachman, B., Pugh, K. R., Fulbright, R., Skudlarski, P., Mencl, E., Constable, T., Holahan, J., Marchione, K., Fletcher, J., Lyon, R., and Gore, J. (2003). *Development of left occipito-temporal systems for skilled reading following a phonologically-based intervention in children.* Paper presented at the conference of the Organization for Human Brain Mapping, June, 2003, New York.

Shaywitz, B. A., Shaywitz, S. E., and Gore, J. (1995). Sex differences in the functional organization of the brain for languages. *Nature, 373,* 607-609.

Simmons, D. C., and Kame'enui, E. J. (2003). *A consumer's guide to evaluating a core reading program grades K-3: A critical elements analysis.* Institute for the Development of Educational Achievement, University of Oregon. Available online at http://reading.uoregon.edu/appendices/con_guide_3.1.03.pdf.

Simos, P. G., Breier, J. I., Fletcher, J. M., Bergman, E., and Papanicolaou, A. C. (2000). Cerebral mechanisms involved in word reading in dyslexic children: A magnetic source imaging approach. *Cerebral Cortex, 10,* 809-816.

Singson, M., Mahony, D., and Mann, V. A. (2000). The relation between reading ability and morphological skills: Evidence from derivational suffixes. *Reading and Writing: An Interdisciplinary Journal, 12:3/4,* 219-252.

Sipe, L. R. (2001). Invention, convention, and intervention: Invented spelling and the teacher's role. *The Reading Teacher, 55,* 264-273.

Slater, W. H., and Horstman, F. R. (2002). Teaching reading and writing to struggling middle school and high school students: The case for reciprocal teaching. *Preventing School Failure, 46,* 163-166.

Slavin, R. E. (1995). *Cooperative learning: Theory, research and practice* (2nd ed.). Boston: Allyn & Bacon.

Slavin, R. E., and Cheung, A. (2003). *Effective programs for English language learners: A best-evidence synthesis.* Baltimore, MD: Johns Hopkins University, CRESPAR.

Smith, F., and Goodman, K. S. (1971). On the psycholinguistic method of teaching reading. *Elementary School Journal, 71,* 177-181.

Snow, C. E., Burns, M. S., and Griffin, P. (Eds.). (1998). *Preventing reading difficulties in young children.* Washington, DC: National Academy Press.

Solan, H. A., Shelley-Tremblay, J., Ficarra, A., Silverman, M., and Larson, S. (2003). Effect of attention therapy on reading comprehension. *Journal of Learning Disabilities, 36,* 556-563.

Sousa, D. A. (2001a). *How the brain learns.* Thousand Oaks, CA: Corwin Press.

Sousa, D. A. (2001b). *How the special needs brain learns.* Thousand Oaks, CA: Corwin Press.

Southwest Educational Development Laboratory (SEDL). (2001). *The cognitive foundations of learning to read.* Austin, TX: Author.

Speece, D. L., and Mills, C. (2003). Initial evidence that letter fluency tasks are valid indicators of early reading skill. *Journal of Special Education, 36,* 223-233.

Squire, L. R., & Kandel, E. R. (1999). *Memory: From mind to molecules.* New York: W. H. Freeman.

Stahl, S. A. (2000). *Promoting vocabulary development.* Austin, TX: Texas Education Agency.

Stinson, E. (2003). *Best practices in reading instruction.* Nashville, TN: NPT Educational Services.

Stone, G. O., Vanhoy, M., and Van Orden, G. C. (1997). Perception is a two-way street: Feedforward and feedback phonology in visual word recognition. *Journal of Memory and Language, 36,* 337-359.

Swaab, T. Y., Baynes, K., and Knight, R. T. (2002, September). Separable effects of priming and imageability on word processing: An ERP study. *Cognitive Brain Research, 15,* 99-103.

Swanborn, M. S. L., and de Glopper, K. (1999). Incidental word learning while reading: A meta-analysis. *Review of Educational Research, 69,* 261-285.

Tallal, P., Miller, S. L., Bedi, G., Byma, G., Wang, X., Nagarajan, S., Schreiner, C., Jenkins, W. M., and Merzenich, M. M. (1996, January). Fast-element enhanced speech improves language comprehension in language-learning impaired children. *Science, 271,* 81–84.

Tan, A., and Nicholson, T. (1997). Flashcards revisited: Training poor readers to read words faster improves their comprehension of text. *Journal of Educational Psychology, 89,* 276-288.

Taylor, B. M., Pearson, P. D., Clark, K. F., and Walpole, S. (2000). Effective schools and accomplished teachers: Lessons about primary reading instruction in low-income schools. *Elementary School Journal, 101,* 121-166.

Temple, E., Deutsch, G. K., Poldrack, R. A., Miller, S. L., Tallal, P., Merzenich, M. M., and Gabrieli, J. D. E. (2003, March). Neural deficits in children with dyslexia ameliorated by behavioral remediation: Evidence from functional MRI. *Proceedings of the National Academy of Sciences, 100,* 2860-2865.

Tiu, R. D., Jr., Thompson, L. A., and Lewis, B. A. (2003). The role of IQ in a component model of reading. *Journal of Learning Disabilities, 36,* 424-436.

Torgesen, J. K. (1999). Phonologically-based reading disabilities: Toward a coherent theory of one kind of learning disability. In R. Sternberg and L. Spear-Swerling (Eds.), *Perspectives on learning disabilities* (pp. 106-135). Boulder, CO: Westview Press.

Torgesen, J. K. (2001). Individual differences in response to early intervention in reading: The lingering problem of treatment resisters. *Learning Disabilities Research and Practice, 15,* 55-64.

Torgesen, J. K. (2002). The prevention of reading difficulties. *Journal of School Psychology, 40,* 7-26.

Torgesen, J. K. (2004). Lessons learned from research on interventions for students who have difficulty learning to read. In P. McCardle and V. Chhabra (Eds.), *The voice of evidence in reading research.* Baltimore, MD: Brookes.

Torgesen, J. K., Alexander, A. W., Wagner, R. K., Rashotte, C. A., Voller, K. K. S., and Conway, T. (2001). Intensive remedial instruction for children with severe reading disabilities. *Journal of Learning Disabilities, 34,* 33-58.

Treiman, R. A., and Cassar, M. (1997). Spelling acquisition in English. In C. A. Perfetti, L. Rieben, and M. Fayol (Eds.), *Learning to spell: Research, theory, and practice across languages* (pp. 61-80). Mahwah, NJ: Erlbaum.

Uhry, J. (1999). Invented spelling in kindergarten: The relationship with finger-point reading. *Reading and Writing, 11,* 441-464.

Vandervelden, M. C., and Siegel, L. S. (1997). Teaching phonological processing skills in early literacy: A developmental approach. *Learning Disability Quarterly, 20,* 63-81.

Van Petten, C., & Bloom, P. (1999, February). Speech boundaries, syntax, and the brain. *Nature Neuroscience, 2,* 103–104.

Vaughn, S., Linan-Thompson, S., and Hickman, P. (2003). Response to instruction as a means for identifying students with reading/learning disabilities. *Exceptional Children, 69,* 391-409.

Vaughn, S., Moody, S. W., and Schumm, J. S. (1998). Broken promises: Reading instruction in the resource room. *Exceptional Children, 64,* 211-225.

Vellutino, F., Scanlon, D., Sipay, E. R., Small, S. G., Pratt, A., Chen, R., and Denckla, M. B. (1996). Cognitive profiles of difficult-to-remediate and readily remediated poor readers: Early intervention as a vehicle for distinguishing between cognitive and experiential deficits as basic causes of specific reading disability. *Journal of Educational Psychology, 88,* 601-638.

Weiler, J. (1998). *Success for All: A summary of evaluations.* (ERIC/CUE Digest Number 139). New York: ERIC Clearinghouse on Urban Education.

West, C. K., Farmer, J. A., and Wolff, P. M. (1991). *Instructional design: Implications from cognitive science.* Englewood Cliffs, NJ: Prentice Hall.

Wilson, A. M., and Lesaux, N. K. (2001). Persistence of phonological processing deficits in college students with dyslexia who have age-appropriate reading skills. *Journal of Learning Disabilities, 34,* 394-400.

Wise, B. W., Ring, J., and Olson, R. K. (1999). Training phonological awareness with and without attention to articulation. *Journal of Experimental Child Psychology, 72,* 271-304.

Wright, B. A., Bowen, R. W., and Zecker, S. G. (2000). Nonlinguistic perceptual deficits associated with reading and language disorders. *Current Opinion in Neurobiology, 10,* 482-486.

Yatvin, J. (2003, April 30). I told you so! The misinterpretation of the National Reading Panel Report. *Education Week, 22,* 56, 44, 45.

Yopp, H. K., and Yopp, R. H. (2000). Supporting phonemic awareness development in the classroom. *The Reading Teacher, 54,* 130-143.

Zigmond, N., and Jenkins, J. (1995). Special education in restructured schools. *Phi Delta Kappan, 76,* 531-535.

Resources

~~~~~~

Note: All internet sites were active at time of publication.

Content Area Reading Online

Web site: www.content-reading.org

A subgroup of the International Reading Association, this site was formed to provide information on research and successful practices related to content area reading. The site offers valuable suggestions in several different subject areas.

The Council for Exceptional Children

1110 North Glebe Road

Suite 300

Arlington, VA 22201-5704

Tel.: 1-888-CEC-SPED

Web site: www.cec.sped.org

The Council's site has many suggestions for teachers and parents of children with learning disabilities as well as those who are gifted.

The Dyslexia Parents Resource

Web site: www.dyslexia-parent.com

Lots of hints and tips on how to deal with children who have been diagnosed with dyslexia.

The Dyslexia Teacher Online

Web site: www.dyslexia-teacher.com

This site offers plenty of information for teachers on research and practices related to working with dyslexic students.

Earobics Literacy Launch

Cognitive Concepts, Inc.

Web site: www.earobic.com

A research-based supplemental reading program for students in pre-kindergarten through grade 3. A combination of computer technology, multimedia tools, and print materials support components in phonological awareness, vocabulary, fluency, phonics, and reading comprehension.

Fast ForWord Reading Language Program

Scientific Learning Corporation

Web site: www.scientificlearning.com

A scientifically-based computer program that is designed for helping beginning readers develop phonemic awareness, letter-sound correspondences, fluent word recognition, vocabulary, and an appreciation of literature. Programs for older struggling readers are also available.

Florida Center for Reading Research

Web site: www.fcrr.org

This center was established by the state of Florida to analyze reading curricula and materials. The site offers assessment reports on various reading programs.

Graphic Organizers

Web site: www.graphic.org

This site has examples of different types of graphic organizers and suggestions on how to use them in lessons at all grade levels.

Inspiration Software, Inc.

Web site: http://inspiration.com

This company produces software that helps students construct all types of visual organizers for improving comprehension and building thinking skills. *Kidspiration* is designed for grades K through 5, and *Inspiration* is for grade 6 and higher. Demonstration versions can be downloaded from the site.

International Dyslexia Association

Chester Building, Suite 382

8600 LaSalle Road

Baltimore, MD 21286-2044

Tel.: 1-800-223-3123

Web site: www.interdys.org

International Reading Association

800 Barkdale Road

P.O. Box 8139

Newark, DE 19714-8139

Tel.: 1-800-336-READ

Web site: www.reading.org

The world's largest association devoted to reading maintains a rich source of information, including useful advice to parents and teachers who are helping children learn to read. This site also offers access to research articles and studies related to reading.

Kid's Health Web Site - Dyslexia:

Web site: www.kidshealth.org/parent/medical/learning/dyslexia.html

Information on the nature and treatment of dyslexia, written mainly for parents.

Lindamood Phonemic Sequencing Program (LiPS)

Lindamood Bell Learning Processes

Web site: www.lindamoodbell.com

The LiPS program is based on the interventions that researchers used to help struggling readers develop phonemic awareness and improve their reading achievement.

Literacy Connections

Web site: http://literacyvolunteer.homestead.com/index.html

The Literacy Connections Web site provides information on reading aloud, tutoring techniques, ESL literacy, and adult literacy. This site is a good resource for all reading teachers, literacy volunteers, and program directors.

Literacy and Technology

Web site: www.oswego.org/staff/cchamber/literacy/index.cfm

Developed by the Oswego City School District in New York, USA, this Web site includes links to resources that support the new literacies of the Internet as well as more traditional literacies.

Literature Circles Resource Center

Web site: http://fac-staff.seattleu.edu/kschlnoe/LitCircles/Overview/overview.html

Maintained by Seattle University's School of Education, this site offers educators many resources, suggestions, and sample lessons for using literature circles as part of a balanced literacy program.

National Association for the Education of Young Children
 1509 16th Street NW
 Washington, DC 20036
 Tel.: 1-800-4242460
 Web site: www.naeyc.org
 This long-standing organization supports efforts to improve professional practice and opportunities in the education of children from birth through third grade.

National Clearinghouse for English Language Acquisition and Language Instruction Educational Programs.
 Web site: www.ncela.gwu.edu/library/curriculum/index.htm#READING
 This site has information, articles, and Web resources for reading instruction and other important topics in the education of English language learners.

National Institute for Literacy
 1775 I Street, NW
 Suite 730
 Washington, DC 20006-2401
 Tel.: 202-233-2025
 Web site: www.nifl.gov
 An agency supported by the U.S. government that promotes activities to strengthen literacy for people of all ages. It has several reports available online that review scientific research studies in reading.

National Reading Panel (NRP).
 Web site: www.nationalreadingpanel.org
 Its report is available in its entirety or as an abbreviated 33-page summary from the panel's Web site.

National Reading Styles Institute
 P.O. Box 737
 Syosset, NY 11791
 Tel.:1-800-331-3117
 Web site: www.nrsi.com/nrsi.htm
 This site has information about reading styles and the research-based reading program developed by Marie Carbo.

Organization for Human Brain Mapping
 Web site: www.humanbrainmapping.org

An organization of scientists and clinicians involved in using brain imaging to understand more about the structures and functions of the brain. The site provides information about the organization as well as research abstracts from some of their seminars.

The Partnership for Reading

Web site: www.nifl.gov/partnershipforreading

This site has a database of the abstracts of over 450 research studies related to the teaching of reading in grades K to 3. The studies have met a high standard of research and are categorized by phonemic awareness, phonics, fluency, vocabulary, text comprehension, computer instruction, and teacher education.

READ 180

Scholastic, Inc.

Web site: http://teacher.scholastic.com/read180

This scientifically-researched computer program, designed for struggling readers in grades 4 and above, has shown considerable success in raising reading and overall achievement in urban school districts.

Reading Recovery Council of North America

1926 Kenny Road, Suite 100

Columbus, OH 43210-1069

Tel.: 614-292-7111

Web site: www.readingrecovery.org

This is the official site of the Reading Recovery program which has been used in numerous school districts for over a decade to help beginning struggling readers.

Road to Reading

Web site: http://208.183.128.8/read

The Road to Reading Web site offers elementary teachers information on valuable classroom strategies for reading and writing with students.

Students Achieving Independent Learning (SAIL)

Web site: www.sail2comprehension.com

SAIL is a text comprehension strategies instruction program that was originally designed to help low-achieving students in reading but has been found to be effective in enhacing reading comprehension in students at all ability levels.

Success for All Foundation

200 West Towsontown Boulevard

Baltimore, MD 21204-5200

Tel.: 1-800-584-4998

Web site: www.successforall.net

Here is all the information one needs to understand the history, components, implementation, and effectiveness of the Success for All program.

U.S. Department of Education

600 Maryland Avenue SW

Washington, DC 20202

Tel.: 1-800-USA-LEARN (872-5327)

Web site: www.ed.gov

This site includes access to the ERIC databases, explanations of the requirements of the No Child Left Behind legislation, and descriptions of all the other activities that are the responsibility of the Department of Education.

Index